Holding

Holding

A Memoir About Mothers,
Drugs, and Other Comforts

KARLEIGH FRISBIE BROGAN

STEERFORTH PRESS
LEBANON, NEW HAMPSHIRE

For information about permission to reproduce
selections from this book, write to:
Steerforth Press, 31 Hanover Street, Suite 1
Lebanon, New Hampshire 03766

Cataloging-in-Publication Data is available from the Library of Congress

ISBN 978-1-58642-412-1

Printed in the United States of America

EU RP (for authorities only): eucomply OÜ, Pärnu mnt. 139b-14, 11317,
Tallinn, Estonia, hello@eucompliancepartner.com, +33757690241

1 3 5 7 9 10 8 6 4 2

Contents

Author's Note — vii

Part One | Mothers

1. Eternal Substance — 3
2. Prediction Errors — 17
3. Angel Card — 26
4. Broke — 39
5. Gift (a triptych) — 57
6. Wite-Out — 71
7. Normal People — 81
8. Rudolph's Nose — 88
9. Looking Glass — 100
10. Goose Girl — 112
11. Admission — 119
12. Puppy, Piggy, Princess — 133
13. Celestial Bodies — 146
14. "The unending absence that follows . . ." — 159
15. The Snow Chapter — 173
16. Abandon — 181

Part Two | Mother Comforts

17. The Name of the Father — 193
18. Gimme Danger, Shelter, A Man
    After Midnight — 213

19. The Lie of the Bottom 223

20. The Bottom of the Lie 230

21. Merge 234

22. Final Rests 245

23. New Green Car 252

Part Three | Holding Out, Holding On, Holding Her

24. Regrowth: An Epilogue 263

Afterword 271

Selected Bibliography 275

Acknowledgments 281

Author's Note

The events in this book take place, in large part, between the years of 1997 and 2003. As is the nature of memoir, the book does not chronicle every incident that occurred during that six-year span and instead culls and curates distinct moments that serve the story and the larger message I am attempting to convey.

Though my memory is vivid and extensive (a friend calls me the steel trap), there is no way I have it all right. Memories are formed in the matrix of our own emotions and opinions – they are subjective and fallible, slightly reconstructed with every recollection. I rely, in part, on interviews with Glorianne and my mother, conversations with friends and family members, photographs, journal entries, and other ephemera I've saved or found. I use these sources to flesh out and reanimate the memories that have stayed with me all these years, the ones that have branded my gray matter and have shaped me in significant ways.

In an attempt to keep the dialogue as true as possible, I re-created it using the habitual language of each individual. Some names have been changed to protect these identities. There are no composite characters.

I had grown big, but my mother was bigger, and that would always be so.

— Jamaica Kincaid, *At the Bottom of the River*

We are all in the gutter, but some of us are looking at the stars.

— Oscar Wilde, *Lady Windermere's Fan*

Holding

Mothers

Eternal Substance

Holding an empty gas can, I scuffed across the service station's hot asphalt, approached every truck that tripped the dinger, every dusty windshield and sun-ruined hood. I had a story – one about my car going empty on the 101 as I was driving to see my mom, sick in a hospital in another county. I had my red plastic prop. Had pigtails that made me teen. Had puffy hands, finger-nails caked in dirt and glitter. My breath was bad, and my jeans rode pubic-bone low.

Men were easier. Especially when I tied bows in those pigs and rubbed a magazine on my wrists. They either dumped nickels and dimes from their ashtrays into my open palms or told me to fuck off. I spooked women, though. They scanned me out of the sides of their eyes and snapped their heads away when I neared, glimpsing invisible wristwatches. "I'm sorry," they'd say. They recognized the wrong of me. That unfurling re-rolled, pretend proper with a whiff of rot, Estée Lauder Pleasures notwithstanding.

The day before, I'd worked the Costco lot. Twenty bucks in two hours. But I liked more the shade of the Valero station, its turquoise canopy that reminded me of a swimming pool. Its relief from the staring white sun. The gas station had a grassy curb with a miniature palm tree that looked like a pineapple. It had passers-through who didn't recognize me from yesterday. Who only knew Santa Rosa as a ten-exit town with car dealer-ships and a couple of Denny's.

The view from the highway deceived. People who lived here

said it was heaven on earth with its ancient oak trees and mist-draped mornings and warm, fruit-bearing climate. They'd recite some ode, some Mark Twain quote. Others said it was an overpriced suburban shithole overrun with gang members and Section 8 housing and big-box stores. With drug addicts.

The heroin I did then, in 1997, in California, when I was twenty-one years old, was cooked in hidden kitchens, stirred in big pots with broom handles, cut with coffee, with shoe polish and dirt. It was formed into bricks, gleaming and oily and reeking of vinegar. I bought little chunks of it, taffy-wrapped in scraps of Safeway bag. That heroin is becoming extinct. It's now laced with fentanyl — strong, cheap, synthetic, and transmutable. It can't be spotted by helicopter like so many hectares of poppies. It doesn't require sun and water, nor the seasonal workers who scrape wounded pods with Jumex cans, collecting magic goo for mere pennies. Fentanyl is lab-born, its compounds can be scrambled, mix-and-matched, made into stronger analogs. A million flowers within a single grain of sand, more than a million deaths from the start of this book to its end.

It had been almost four hours since my last shot, and the heavy emptiness began to settle in my bones. Cussing under my breath, I forced smiles and muttered pleas to everyone who walked past where I sat on the curb. "Have a good day," I'd say to pairs of shoes.

The pain of withdrawal can't be described as stabbing or burning or aching or dull. It's not something you can clutch or cradle or put a bag of frozen peas on. It's an absence that feels like there's nothing left to feel, an inky sadness that smears the sunniest day. It's like in drowning dreams when you plunge into a body of water and can't find the surface in time. In that murky, light-swallowing green, panic gives way to resignation, to the reflex of breath that fills lungs with lake, with death. What feels like survival is, in fact, demise.

A Volvo pulled up to a pump. It was brown and boxy. Had dried flowers on the dash, beads dangling from the rearview mirror, and a faded bumper sticker that reminded tailgaters to practice random acts of kindness. A man, thirties, got out of the passenger side and scurried into the mini mart. I walked up to the car and tapped on the glass. I saw the woman's hair first – glossy and middle-parted, tucked behind an ear as she studied a road map.

"Hey sorry," I said, hands steepled.

Turning down the stereo, she looked at me with a face as open as a child's. She listened intently as I delivered my pitch, her brow pinching above the rim of her glasses. I told her about my stalled car, my hospitalized mama, my temporary unemployment. The lies felt like a pile of dead branches in my mouth. I yammered on, believing I could talk the story into truth.

The woman rummaged through her purse, extracted a couple of dollars from its depths, and handed them to me. "Swear I had more," she said, still digging. The man returned carrying a bag of ice over his shoulder, his flip-flops snapping, his gum, too.

"Hey, honey?" the woman asked, stepping out of the car, touching her glasses. "Got a few extra bucks? Her car went empty on the highway."

"How 'bout I just fill that thing up?" he asked, glancing at my gas can. He raised his eyebrows, catching my eye in our shared secret. "I'll drive you to your car, even." His gum chewing got excited.

"I'm good," I said.

He shook his head. "Yeah. That's kinda what I thought."

The woman said his name in a tone that both scolded and pled. "Zack!" Maybe it was "Luke!" or "Dick!"

"She's a junkie," Dick said.

"I'm not a junkie," I barked. "Asshole."

I was cleaved in two. The enraged half was also the hurt half, my default reaction to even the smallest suggestion of doubt. It vibrated red and hot, my brain switched to off. How dare this complete stranger challenge the image I kept of myself? How dare he know exactly who I was despite my best efforts to conceal it. Didn't I look honest in my petally blouse, a tiny Jesus cross around my neck? Didn't I speak politely enough? The other half was the hurt half too, but the hurt was a different kind. It was the hurt that came from hurting. It searched for eyes, made wordless apologies, tried to find ways back in to closed faces. I wanted to reassure the woman with the map and the glasses that our brief interaction wasn't a sham, that my dishonesty was honest in its desperation, its purpose. Her handout wasn't bankrolling my good time; it was keeping me alive. "Mama" was just a metaphor.

I had convinced myself that each exchange came with a tacit wink and nod. That every charitable dupe was savvier than they appeared, intentionally suspending disbelief, even if unconsciously. My story was no more than a mark of effort – the magician's flourish, the eight-hour shift, the expected work that made each dollar an earned dollar. But perhaps I was only fooling myself, fending off the shame that throbbed within me, the guilt that stung.

Unlike shame, guilt tends to be temporary. Circumstantial. Its concern is for others, and mine disappeared almost as quickly as my change-throwers' did. Shame's enterprise is the self. It comes from somewhere deep and ancient and female. It's repeated humiliation, disgrace, and self-disgust. It's embedded in my DNA, my inherited memories as old as Eve.* The gazes and appraisals, proscriptions and prescriptions from everybody else reinforce it, calcify it. My unseemly desperation didn't

*"For Adam was formed first, then Eve. And Adam was not the one deceived; it was the woman who was deceived and became a sinner. But women will be saved through childbearing – if they continue in faith, love, and holiness with propriety." – 1 Timothy 2:11-15.

dissolve it but merely deferred it, causing it to return as the self-hatred that occasioned the black tar I shot up. The very black tar that kept the shame temporarily tamped. That ultimately exacerbated it, perpetuated it. And so on and so forth.

Kneeling on the curb, I pulled crumpled bills and scummy coins from my pocket, lining them up on my thigh. I still needed six more dollars to buy a half gram. Twenty-four quarters. Sixty dimes. There was probably that much forgotten change only feet from where I sat — under floor mats or glued into cup holders sticky with spilled soda. I imagined descending the storm drains and collecting all the unwanted pennies. I counted slowly to six hundred. The tips of my fingers were sweating and I had to poop.

I heard my name. It emerged from the white noise of commuter traffic. I was surer of the voice than I was my own. I looked around and saw Mom's new SUV idling by the entrance of the gas station. Her dark hair was exact. Her eyes hidden behind lenses. I wanted to pretend I wasn't me. But she was surer of my person, of my kinetic three-dimensional form, than I was.

I faltered up to her car, not sure how to hold my face, looking not at her but all around, at nothing at all. When I had to finally look at her, I saw myself. Though we don't share many features — she's buttoned where I'm hooked, dimpled where I'm angled — we somehow look exactly the same. It's in the way our tiniest muscles carry worry across our faces, the arrangement of our eyes and noses, how our mouths silently form the words we listen to.

"What are you doing?" she asked from behind her dark sunglasses and easy listening. Her lips, outlined with a flaking shade of garnet, were so taut they quivered. "I thought you were in Oakland."

Air-conditioning escaped the window in icy swells. I peeked into the back. The booster seat was empty, just a sippy cup and a Barney plushie on the already crumb-covered upholstery.

"Do you have six dollars?" My face crumpled in premature defeat.

"What *is* that?" Mom scrunched her nose and touched the right side of her upper lip. "You have dirt or something."

I wiped the mirror image of her face. "Did I get it?"

She squinted and leaned.

"It's probably my mustache."

"Don't you Nair? You used to Nair."

"Do you have six dollars?" I asked again.

"For what? For drugs?"

"Five, then." I watched my fingers walk along the window's blue and tempered edge, which slowly rose above its steel housing, the vinyl lips that licked its surface. It was like putting my hand inside a dog's mouth. An act of trust or stupidity. Mom gave me an insulting five-inch crack. No, not insulting. Hurtful. "Please," I said.

I didn't want to see Mom's tongue reluctantly finding the roof of her mouth to deliver that one resolute syllable: *no.* I looked away.

"I haven't eaten since yesterday."

"There's the place up the street." She flicked her nails in the general direction.

"The soup kitchen?" The smudges my hands left on the glass – coin grime, old beer – came into sharp focus. Her face was a blur behind them.

"You told me you were clean."

"I am," I said, almost inaudibly, noncommittally. Her doubt, even when merited, hurt the most.

Mom never trusted me and my sibs. She didn't let us run the washing machine or punch our fists into pie dough. The whites would go pink, she'd say. The crust wouldn't flake. She hustled us all into our room with a pan of undercooked fish sticks when there was company, afraid we'd blurt something embarrassing into the perfumed cleavage of her guests.

If we told her we loved her, her face would worry. "What's wrong?" she'd ask. "Is something wrong?" And her concern would keep her from returning the words.

When I got older, my affection was met with suspicion. "What's this about?" she'd ask, stiffening inside the circumference of my embrace, sniffing for evidence of marijuana or cigarettes or sex. "What do you want? Money?"

She implied that the awards I received, though rare, must have been fluky or consolatory. She squinted her eyes at gold-starred certificates and asked how many others got one too. I needed, more than anything, for her to be proud of me. I needed to do something that would make her deliriously happy, that would gift her bragging rights. I fanaticized about being a Mary Lou Retton, my body airborne scissors slicing across the television screen. When I landed, arms in a vee and chin high, the camera would move to Mom, who'd be standing right in front, clapping. Crying. Over the years I showed her my cartwheels, my dance routines, my report cards, my flat stomach, the love letters shoved through my locker's vent, my perfectly tweezed brows and teased bangs. I wanted her to slip a medal around my neck. I wanted her to weep happy or weep sad for me like she did for Nikki Newman on *Young and the Restless* or that Wham! song with the sax.

Mom had passed half a dozen grapefruits through her hoo-ha – four with my dad, then two more with my step. By the time she was forty, she'd spent half her life with chapped nipples and morning sickness. She was addicted to babies – to their butter-scented heads and gassy coos, chonky legs going and going, one sock gone. But it seemed she didn't particularly like kids, especially once our milk teeth were replaced with big, crooked gum-shoots and our cowlicked hair whiffed of dirt and hormones. She often commented on our unsightly moltings and mutations as if they were atypical, unique to only her cursed children. In wistful sighs she'd praise the beauty of our long-limbed, smooth-haired friends. All the time it was "the Stuber girls are so pretty," or "the Petroni girls are so pretty," or "those girls from tap are just so fresh-faced!"

Mom romanticized the WASP-y blue-blood look from Ralph Lauren ads she'd see on the wide, aspirational pages of *Town & Country* magazine that no amount of crested cardigan or penny loafer could endow me. I couldn't change my muscle distribution, my facial symmetry, or my skin tone with a new wardrobe or riding lessons — not that we could've afforded a new wardrobe or riding lessons in the first place. From an early age, I assumed that the collective hideousness of me and the sibs had to do with our dad's non-whiteness.

Dad is Nicaraguan, but we just called him Spanish, since that was the language spoken by his mother, Grandma Coco, and the many aunts, blood and non-blood, who buzzed around the kitchen. The Spanish kids at my school were the ones who often lived in neighborhoods Mom was afraid to drive through. They got their clothes from the Goodwill. They were poor, and poor was bad. Poor let food sit out unrefrigerated all day and gave you the runs. Poor sparkled and shone with gold plating and cubic zirconia and crystal knickknacks from the Avon brochure. Poor smelled like too much cologne and purple household cleaner. Poor masked and gilded an ugly, stinking reality that caused Mom to hold her temples whenever we'd go see my paternal grandparents, bemoaning a migraine. She'd only eat pull-apart dinner rolls and the delicate chayote soup because she didn't trust the meat that had been stewing on the splattered range while adults shimmied and children galloped around to a disco-kissed Natalie Cole record. From an early age, I was very aware that I was constructed from something that made her physically ill.

I became preoccupied with finding a way to go from being

her ailment to her antidote. I loved her more than any person in the world. I remember hiding in the closet to cry when she told me I had to love God more than her. I knew God was watching me cry, knew He was reading my mind, thought I was a total puss. I asked Heavenly Father with my mind if it was okay that I loved Mom first, Him second. I took His failure to answer me as a yes.

Classically, anciently, spanning yet-unnamed seas and geographies both imagined and real, the mother-figure has been associated with the poppy. It was in the flower's fertility: her abundance of seeds, blue-black mineral-rich specks the wind shook from autumn's pods. It was in her form: the engorged body, round and crown-topped, the quartet of fragile petals that belied her robust constitution. It was in her soothing milk.

Nisaba, the Sumerian goddess of the harvest and mother of Gilgamesh, had been rendered on a stone vessel with six poppy heads popping out from behind her shoulders like epaulets. Demeter, Greek goddess of agriculture, maker of seasons, and bereaved mother of Persephone, was known as the poppy goddess and was frequently depicted holding a bouquet of them in one hand, a grain sheaf in the other. And Isis, Egyptian mother goddess, mourning widow, and protector of the New Kingdom, concocted medicine from poppies and honey for the sun god, Ra, to cure him of all sufferings. In bas-reliefs on temple walls, she holds kings in her lap, feeds them from her breasts.

To use heroin was to mother myself. To auto-nurse. Dope shrank my world, making it easy, predictable, and safe. It swaddled it in greasy bedsheets that smelled like me, steeped everything in an aura of oxytocin. Like a baby – who went under boob, over shoulder, into crib – my days were small and repetitive. Get money, get dope, get high, repeat.

I excelled at being a junkie and was, therefore, fulfilled.

Unlike every minimum-wage job, unlike clarinet or choir or community college, I didn't give up. It was the threat of dopesickness and the warmth of dopamine blasts that lit up my brain's Las Vegas that kept me going. It was the first thing ever to ding me like slots, to make the lights go and the coins drop. Every dollar I was handed, every car with tinted windows that slid up to the curb that I slipped into for a ride around the block, every vein I'd successfully entered, a flag of blood unfurling in the needle's chamber – all ding-ding-ding and not even yet the jackpot.

I had sucked at normal, young-adult life. Everything was always getting shut off, lapsing, getting sent to collections. Jobs were pointless, and college was not in my bloodline. The world was a hostile hostess and I was a reluctant guest, my irresponsibility born from ignorance and indignancy. I was too readily hopeless. *Help me!* I telepathically screamed out into the void, to God, my parents, the asshole just standing there, completely innocent and unaware of my suffering.

I was alone, my friends suddenly absent. They were playing house with boyfriends or moving into dorms afar. Some rented pricy makeshift bedrooms in San Francisco, the city down the freeway, through a tunnel, across a bridge. Some went overseas on work visas. Others were just busy doing the things they cared about.

But I didn't care about things. I wasn't into sociology or marine biology or Europe or backpacking or surfing or old-growth forests in danger of being clear-cut. Or about going to Peru with the church to build a school like my sister Aly had done. I didn't care deeply about anything because to care about stuff required a bravery I didn't possess. A way of thinking my brain didn't have the space to do. To care about stuff meant I'd have to get comfortable with failure, with vulnerability, with disappointing people

– myself mostly. It meant I'd have to stare into the face of death, the small, quotidian deaths and the big final alike.

Heroin made me feel like I cared about stuff. It made my chest feel light and hopeful and expansive. Like there was more room in my heart. It didn't impart the sweaty, tie-loosening confidence of coke I knew from movies. Nor did it impart the tweaky industriousness of meth or the goofy oblivion of weed. I still felt totally buried by life, but the burden lulled me like a weighted blanket. It held me down where I *wanted* to be, cradled precisely by the stark contrast it created – as the cuddle of opiates can really only be defined against the discomfort of everything else.

"Mother" is supreme comfort; she's primary pain. In Jungian analysis, the Great Mother archetype contains all: male and female, negative and positive, good and evil. She simultaneously delivers and devours. Induces fear and provides solace. She has the power to both give life and snatch it all back.

In Erich Neumann's *The Great Mother: An Analysis of the Archetype*, the mother – also known as the Great Round, the Great Container, the vessel – "tends to hold fast to everything that springs from it and to surround it like an eternal substance. Everything born of it belongs to it and remains subject to it." This is the *participation mystique*, a term adopted by Jung to refer to the eternal bond between mother and child, "the original situation of container and contained." It's when one cannot completely distinguish themselves from the other. When identities are tangled like so many jewelry-box chains.

I waded in that magic goo, that eternal substance, viscous and iridescent. It slowed my limbs and made me sleepy. Coaxed me back up inside, back to the whoosh of synced heartbeats, the amniotic float. With heroin, I felt, once again, safely contained.

———

Months before, I'd confessed to Mom. I had only been using for a few weeks, and my habit wasn't even yet a habit, but I couldn't wait. The admission felt at once indulgent, powerful, and terrifying, like firing a gun. "I'm addicted to heroin," I said, almost gleefully and without preamble. She was sitting on the edge of her bed, her wrist in a carpal-tunnel brace. "Heroin?" she repeated. "Is that with a needle?"

When I had arrived at the house earlier that day, it was chaos as usual. My sister Molly, high school dropout about to pop, watched a talk show with the volume up, wincing through the occasional Braxton Hicks. My brother Aaron and the neighbor boys took turns leaping from the roof onto the front lawn. There was a garden hose. A frozen pizza. A beeping oven. Doors that slammed and schwumped. My half brothers, Foster and Michael, darted through the kitchen dressed like Power Rangers, laughing and panting, after a cat.

No one looked up when I let myself in, dropped my purse on the floor, stared into the fridge, and helped myself to a foil-topped pudding cup that I ate while stomping down the hall to Mom's room.

"Oh, hi, sweetheart." Mom said, glancing up. She was folding a shirt. "Didn't know you were coming over."

I shrugged.

"Something going on?"

"No. Can't I just come over without a reason?"

"I don't understand why you always have to get this way with me."

"I'm not getting any way. I'm just asking a question."

"I have to start getting ready. We're going to symphony."

"Actually, there is something."

"Money?" she asked, her eyes on a sock snatched from the staticky pile of laundry.

"I'm a heroin addict."

I'd been hoping for a specific reaction. A dropped jaw. A blanching. Tears. Though she had turned her attention to me, she continued to glance at a sweater whose pilling she picked. I kept firing. *Yes, with a needle. These are my tracks. Look how I continue to ruin myself. Will you hold me? Will you hurt? Will you feel my hurt? Will you finally trust it?*

"Can I spend the night?" I asked, teary-eyed and on the verge of a tantrum.

Mom hemmed. "You're not going to do that stuff here in the house, are you?"

The hurt slowly filled my stomach and lungs and pushed against the back of my face. It moved into my fingertips, making them numb.

Lying in Molly's provisional living room bed, I watched *Judge Judy*. Mom's keys jingled near my head, and I could smell the minty leather of her purse. She said she'd be back in a few hours. Errands saved her from boredom, from confrontation and closeness. When she'd brought home my brother Aaron from the hospital, sixteen years earlier, I'd thought she had named him after them.

I told her I was hungry. *Starving* was the word I used. She asked if I wanted a chicken Caesar wrap from the place up by the video store. I said I was going to an NA meeting at six and, sure, I'd take the wrap, sauce on the side. She looked at me with a pleading face that said, *This is the best I can do.*

I drove to a meeting at the clubhouse in the park. There were several motorcycles. Work vans with cryptic bumper stickers: easy does it; friend of bill w. I sat in my car and watched as people filed in. Groups of three or four stood together in the parking lot, smoking and talking and drinking Starbucks. Their long shadows stretched across the asphalt. A woman with hair that blazed burgundy in the low sun, whose laugh was a cackle, greeted her friends with hugs that chimed as bracelets fell to her elbow. I'd wondered then if she'd do — not her specifically, though maybe — if she'd feel my hurt, if she'd know it. If she'd hold me, if not with her freckled arms against her big boobs, then with her undivided attention.

The thought had killed me. It was like killing Mom, which I realized I'd tried to do when I yanked up my sleeves and brandished my gruesome arms earlier that day.

The last people had stamped out cigs and trotted through the clubhouse doors. I looked at the clock on my dash: a minute till. I started the ignition and backed away. Didn't ever go inside. Didn't even go back to Mom's. I'd fled back to Oakland. Cried loud, indulgent tears the whole way. Screamed along to Hole's *Live Through This*. "There is no milk! There is no milk!" I didn't know sadness without anger. Didn't know hurt without blame. It was Mom's fault. The stupid world's fault. It was my fault. As soon as I got home, I got high. I couldn't get it in me fast enough.

There, at the gas station, pumps jiggled. Squeegees shrieked across windshields. Someone whacked a pack of cigarettes on the back of his hand. Under the swimming-pool canopy, I freaked out.

"I *am* clean!" I yelled, throwing my fists and kicking the pavement.

Mom made a grimace, rolled up the window, and inched forward.

"Don't leave!" I ran after her, banging my fist on the SUV's door. "Don't fucking leave!"

But she fled too. Pulled out into traffic and within seconds was lost in a sea of eastbound steel, all shades of champagne. Rear windshields reflected the fireball sunset that made the sky too pretty for this shit.

CHAPTER TWO

Prediction Errors

I made a few more bucks. Some guy had witnessed the whole spectacle with Mom, saw me punch one of those yellow concrete half poles and shove my hand into my mouth. He said I might've busted a knuckle and should at least slap some ice on it. Then he handed me a couple bucks. "It's something," he said. "It's nothing," he said.

My car, not in the breakdown lane of the 101, as the story went, was parked in the parking lot of a nearby mall. I threw the empty gas can in the trunk and returned to the squat where Dale and Tommy were packing the bed of a borrowed pickup. I pulled up behind its open tailgate. Tommy, startled, glared at my windshield. Dale, my boyfriend, flashed a thumbs-up, raising his eyebrows into a question.

"Almost twenty," I said, answering his brows, car door banging shut.

It was dusk on a residential street of identical boxes. They were peeling and lopsided, their windows and doors making faces. Grimacing, in-pain faces. Mutilated faces. Dead ones with plywood eyelids, beach towels or bedsheets instead of curtains. Grinding, dripping AC units. The street ended in shimmer. Dads whistled kids in for dinner. But there weren't a lot of dads. Moms and sons, mostly. Grandmas who stared out their apartment's weary eyes with weary eyes. A few boys huffed by on small bikes, their voices squeaking with prepubescence, loud over the whir of their tires. Somewhere down the street, the clack of skateboards.

Dale hefted a lumpy garbage bag into the truck. It leaked a thin, foul-smelling trail of last sips. "What's up with your hand?"

he asked. His pointy shoulder blades jutted and sank like pistons. "Banged it," I said. His black Ben Davis pants slid down his skinny frame. Visible through his yellowed undershirt was a stick-and-poke tattoo: fuck you cop, it said. He had a skull-and-crossbones inked with the sludge of cigarette ash and Jägermeister on his bicep.

Tommy knelt in the cool dim of the carport, sorting glass by brown, green, and clear. He had a lazy eye, a chin like a clenched fist. His jet-black hair was in a grown-out, undone mohawk that flopped to one side. He was shirtless and smelled of cumin and made my puss throb. A fake crush, I referred to it as. I told him I was dopesick, and he said his guy would be there in ten. Said, "You drive stick, right?" and asked if I'd take them to the recycle place past the big-box stores and the strip club, past the modular-home lots, with their waving flags and banners, past the last shabby farmhouses that refused to be torn down.

Back then, California recycling centers redeemed can and bottle deposits by weight instead of unit. We stomped pebbles into some of the cans but never all of them — that would've been pushing it. Today, I count bottles and cans as part of my grocery-store job. I stand under a pop-up canopy that keeps me out of the rain. I have a walkie-talkie in one hand and a tally counter in the other. Click, click, clicking all day, a constant line of people, many of whom arrive in packs, pool their money together. They wait to collect their fourteen dollars and forty cents — the maximum amount we're allowed to pay out per person. That's two dozen six-packs per. Cans must be uncrushed, free of dribbles and cigarette butts. I see their track marks and pinned pupils, know that some of them live in the tents that cluster in the median strips along the highways or in the RVs that line outskirt boulevards.

The scams are different now: They bring topless, not-yet-filled cans lifted from brewery backlots; cases of mini water bottles purchased with EBT, drained into the azalea behind me. Sometimes I turn a blind eye. Sometimes I say, "I know what you're up to, Jason. Last time," and make my lips flat. The vast majority of bottles and cans, however, are legitimately procured. Retrieved from dumpsters and garbage cans, loaded into strollers and bike trailers while the rest of us sleep. A graveyard shift of digging blindly through the rot, the stinky toxic sharp for a crappy buck-eighty an hour, at most.

"I'll drive you when I'm well," I told Tommy.

I was suspicious of Dale and Tommy's calm composures. Envious. I caught Dale's eye, whose ratio of iris to pupil was too great: a pinprick in so much acid-washed blue. "You fuckos got high without me."

"It was just some cottons," Dale said slackly. He looked like that R. Crumb poster everyone had in high school. stoned agin! His eyes drooped. His bones melted. His mouth collapsed like Grandpa Jim's after he'd snap out his dentures, a party gag for us grandkids before the cancer had spread everywhere.

Judging by his face, there was no way Dale had done only a wash of cottons — the bits of cosmetic puff we rolled between our fingers and dropped into our spoons. They act as filters, trapping black tar's particulates in their fibers when the dope's drawn up through the needle. We saved them in a cigar box. They were moldy, besooted from the bottoms of burnt spoons. They looked and felt like scabs. Mouse turds. When we were desperate, we'd rehydrate them and pound them out with an upside-down syringe, wring them with our fingers. They'd release a weak, filthy broth that contained, ideally, trace amounts of heroin we'd re-inject. They'd provide temporary relief, probably all placebo, as slamming cottons was essentially slamming finger grime and mildew and charcoal, infections like cotton fever,* flesh-eating bacteria, and sepsis.

*Paraphrasing the Wikipedia entry, cotton fever occurs when a particle of the cotton used to filter heroin gets into the bloodstream, causing fever,

"Liars," I said, letting myself into the house.

Tommy and his girlfriend, Annabelle, had been squatting in half of a vacant, bank-foreclosed duplex for almost a year. It had two stories, cheap wall-to-wall carpeting, and an en suite bathtub that never got used due to the water being off. Its lack of furniture made the whole place resemble one of those beige, double-decker cat condos. Or maybe it was the faint litter-box and wet-food odor despite no cat. It was probably more spacious than any house I'd ever lived in, though everyone huddled under the hiss of the propane lantern in the center of the living room.

A dealer came. His name was Toothy. He did business with Tommy in the kitchen. Tommy came back to the lamp and divvied as Annabelle watched over his shoulder.

"That's too much, Tommy!" she said as Tommy handed Dale our cut.

Annabelle wore a twisted jean skirt, its fly having traveled to her left hip, and a tank top with tiny rosettes all over it. Some of the rosettes had fallen off, leaving little boogers of glue behind. Her skinny limbs were yellow with old bruises. Her eye corners held the debris of yesterday's mascara. She ate cold french fries from her purse. To Tommy and Dale she baby-talked and whimpered, but with me she was a jerk. Albeit a caring jerk. "I remember you from high school," she'd said when I first started coming around. "You were hella lame. You wore tights under your shorts." Her laugh was husky and congested.

I wasn't sure if the tights-under-shorts situation was connected

---

chills, joint pain, kidney pain, nausea, and tremors. On the street, it was said that the fiber of cotton made its way through your veins and eventually attached itself to your heart. And that if you were an unlucky bastard, this could turn into endocarditis, a much more serious diagnosis that requires antibiotics or, in the case of one of my friends, heart surgery.

to my lameness or if she was just recalling two separate and unrelated facts. But I had laughed and agreed with her.

The room went silent as the four of us fixed. I pressed the pads of my fingers all over my arms, feeling for springy and plump, looking for the greenish-blue hint of vein just under the surface. My skin popped as I worked the dull needle into a thick artery that wormed down my forearm. When I pulled back the plunger, my bright blood curled into the chamber like smoke. Within seconds, I was experiencing something like health: My intestines stopped churning and my skin stopped crawling and my heart stopped racing.

The opiate nod exists in the gray space of in-between. In the neither/nor. It exists somewhere between asleep and awake – the perpetual state of newborn babies and house cats. Little dreamlets colored my consciousness, dazzled my eyelids with images I followed into fragmented narratives and literal trains of thought. (I often dreamed of a slow-moving steam engine with a red-and-gold caboose. Other times, a carousel of pastel horses with terrifying mouths.) The nod felt exactly like those moments after hitting the snooze button – the blissful awareness of slipping back into slumber.

The nod exists somewhere between alone and accompanied. My companions and I shared the same destination, a similar and simultaneous experience. We were together on an empathic level yet isolated within our internal explorations. It reminded me of summering at my family's lake cabin: Mom spending hot afternoons in the shade, thumbing fashion mags; Dad scraping the grill with a wad of aluminum foil or playing solitaire; my sisters, Aly and Molly, with their paint-with-water books; and my brother, Aaron, wiggling on a beach towel, surrounded by pillows so he wouldn't roll away. Me, I wrote "books" about living on a volcanic island where I had to travel by canoe over split-pea waters. I felt most connected to my family when we were all lost in our separateness. And so Dale and Tommy and Annabelle felt, in some ways, like family.

A friend with a preference for uppers once told me that "H seems like a real bummer party." It's true, the heroin scene wasn't energetic enough to be considered a proper party by most people's standards, but I found it to be more intensely social in the anthropological or maybe zoological sense of the word. Here were unlikely members coming together for what had become our basic survival. We pooled resources, planned scams, worked shifts. We helped one another out and, inevitably, ripped one another off. The people I've encountered over the years were, like me, usually tender-fleshed to the pain and commotion of life. Fittingly, our parties didn't pop off, but curled in. Our reveling was wrong-side up.

Perhaps most accurately, the nod exists somewhere between dead and alive. The breath shallows, the pulse thins, and the bodily systems lag. I'd watched friends tip too far, turn blue, and become unresponsive to slaps and shakes and mouth-to-mouth. I've read that near-death survivors often recount feeling euphoric when on that cusp, flooded with a warmth that is often described as being in the presence of God. Some see a light. Heroin artificially produces comparable sensations, verge-of-death unnecessary. It's a shortcut, a backward lifehack wherein ecstasy leads to death, not the other way around. I've often wondered if being high is what it feels like to be a ghost.

We're all born suffering. This is a fact. Maybe it's the sorrow of our mothers' labor transmitted through our pliant skulls, our last placental meal. To endure, we're equipped with a built-in protective scrim, a chemical drip of gentle illusion — dopamine, noradrenaline, GABA. Opiate use causes those natural chemicals to adjust to its presence, to cease or surge accordingly. New highways are paved in the brain. In heroin's absence, the infrastructure goes haywire. The brain's misfirings and dormant synapses make one feel sick, scared, in unimaginable despair. The enormous debt of on-demand pleasure.

Our brain's reward circuitry is stimulated not just when we get the reward but also when we *anticipate* one. There's the famous study where lab monkeys were stationed at consoles, a lever at their fingertips, a tube in their mouths, a lightbulb in their field of vision. The monkeys messed around with the levers and would occasionally do something that caused the light to turn on. Following the light, a blast of juice. The monkeys began to associate the light with the juice, and it was this light, not the juice itself, that made their neurons fire dopamine.

Sometimes the juice wouldn't come. Brain scientists call this *prediction error*, and it's from it that we develop goal-based behaviors. In other words, that initial blast of juice came as a surprise, and hence, the monkeys became hellbent on *figuring out* how to get more by looking for environmental cues (light). When the expected reward never came, dopamine levels plummeted below their regular stasis. For me this was the panic and tantrum when my guy no-showed, when the cigar box was perplexingly empty, when the dope was (as happened twice) fake.

This explains why the vinegar smell of spoon-cooked heroin aroused me the same way the sight of Tommy's shirtless bod did. But if I never received the molten tar or the hard cock of my fantasies and strategies, my obsession would only grow stronger.

Yet there's more than that. Addiction, I've learned firsthand, is extremely complex. It's as much emotional as it's physiological. The mere thought of giving up heroin made me mourn as if contemplating the death of a loved one. When I was dopesick, I was experiencing not only bodily symptoms but emotional anguish as well. The world suddenly felt cruel and pointless. The daylight taunted me, chafed against my skin, triggered fragments of memories that should have been warm and happy but instead traumatized me. Good memories were always worse than bad ones because they were, it seemed, all bullshit. They only served to remind me that I'd always been an outsider. That I didn't belong anywhere.

Having to go to the bathroom, I let myself out the squat's slider door and into the weedy backyard. There was a fly-swarmed bucket behind some oleander. A roll of toilet paper hung from a branch. As I squatted, my quads quivered and my pee shot sideways, warmly running down my leg and curling under the arch of my foot. The toilet paper was damp and wilted and flecked with bark mulch. I dabbed between my thighs, wiped my sprayed ankle, and tossed the wad atop the reeking sog.

Inside, Tommy tinkered with a VCR, and Annabelle dug through a cardboard box of clothes she'd found in front of the Salvation Army.

"What about this?" she asked, lifting up a dowdy polyester dress with long sleeves and a fussy collar.

"It's not really you," I said.

But I didn't really know who she was. A reliable liar, surly and brainy, raised up poor with a crank-head mom, a Harley dad. She was tough but also fragile, like a truck-stop waitress from a Hollywood movie. Rotgut, cream pie. Her sores bloomed gray through her ripened makeup, a wrong shade too pink, spackled on thick.

She went upstairs with Toothy, who had still been standing in the kitchen with a digital scale and an exploding beeper. Tommy was still all over the VCR, hoping to get it pawnable. Dale watched him work, and they talked about belts and wheels and then horror movies. Atop their conversation, suddenly, a measured moaning.

My skin prickled with fear that draped over my shoulders and the nape of my neck. A cape made of thumbtacks. I could hear Annabelle saying "oh fuck, oh god" over and over again through the ceiling. The ice cream truck playing "Home on the

Range" outside the front door only made the sex noises sadder. I was ashamed to be myself then. Ashamed to also have a vagina, a small wad of cash between my legs. A day's hustle. A bag of cans. I was afraid to be myself.

Annabelle cried out in phony bliss, and I tried not to hear it. It reminded me of being an always-worried kid. Of Mom, dewed with July and desire, in strappy heels that angered her feet, an anger she deliriously ignored as she packed frosty blue shadow onto her eyelids; of wrapping my head in my pillow to muffle the squeaks and sighs that made me cry out "Stop!" Of the denouement of restrained laughter, the sink running, a truck's engine growling hot in the driveway for the length of a long kiss before peeling into the night, away from our house, the cricket song resuming, and Mom in bed alone. I wanted then to crawl under the covers with her, have her hold me and tell me she was okay. But I was too afraid to see her seeing me scared of her afterglow, of her scent, of her knowing that I knew more than I should have known at age nine and a half. The next morning, neither of us mentioned my interrupting cry as she made special-occasion pancakes. The ones with chocolate chips, mouse-shaped.

When Annabelle came back downstairs, she plopped next to me on the couch. Not a shred of shame or suffering could I detect anywhere on her face. She opened a clamshell mirror and examined her chin. Dragged a greasy sponge around the rim of powder and blotted her T-zone. Smoked a leftover half-cigarette. Her body lotion emitted its sweetness in throbs. It was slick and alive, like tubbed buttercream sliding from the edges of a still-warm cake. But beneath its mask was another scent, a faint one. It was bitter and metallic. Pennies and ragweed. I wanted it to be the smell of her truth, a chemical betrayal that proved her to be just like me: a girl afraid.

CHAPTER THREE

Angel Card

Dale and I lived in a second-floor apartment in a shrimp-pink building that also smelled like shrimp. It was in Oakland, an hour's drive from Santa Rosa. Our neighborhood was tidy and vacant. It was scraggly palms and concrete yards and stucco houses painted like buttermints. When I'd go up the street for chocolate milk and cigarettes, my eyes darted around, keeping busy. Sometimes there'd be an old lady with a shopping trolley and plastic shoes. Or a car puttering by, not seeing the stop sign. But seeing me, I presumed. I thought that everyone saw me even though I couldn't really see anyone else. Not even my own boyfriend.

There was a brimming silence that summer that somehow made my ears full and ringing, like I was in a plane, above the troposphere. I wanted to prick the swollen air, let it gasp and collapse into itself. Only then would I be able to hear beyond my own mind, which was small and self-involved.

I didn't yet know how to get anywhere in that city, was intimidated by streets that pinballed me east or west before I could make up my mind which direction to go. I was constantly lost. Lonely. There was too much sky. I could look down faded streets for miles with no horizon of golden hillside or jagged purple to contain me. So I'd sit in our hot bedroom, slices of harsh sunlight coming in through bent blinds that made my pits drip under my T-shirt. I'd shoot up, have lazy, protracted sex with Dale, neither of us ever coming. I felt safe and contained in our room and ritual.

A couple times a week, at least, Dale and I hopped in my junker — a brownish-yellow Honda stick with a broken odometer — and drove up to Santa Rosa. We screeched and rattled over the low, western stretch of the Richmond Bridge, brackish air whistling through the car's old weather stripping. There'd be a gravelly tape in the tape deck, one speaker blown. Ash all over my left leg. It wasn't convenient to score at Tommy and Annabelle's, but it had become part of the addiction. They were reliable, predictable.

I've always been anxious. I was a serious, watchful child. The kid Mom or Grandma had to scoop up from slumber parties before the slumbering occurred. Who was afraid of PE and its accompanying balls. Afraid of the girls at the bus stop who wore Swatches and licked poles of sugarcane and threatened to beat me up for being a retard who stared hard. On family trips I watched red brake lights, read road signs out loud as the sibs slept or played slug bug. I'd shriek when we passed semis, when we approached slowed cars too aggressively, causing Mom to, once, swerve into a muddy shoulder, cursing that I had almost made a wreck.

In high school it was calories, sex, and substances I feared, the attendant expanding and opening of my body, the allowance of something other to enter me, hurt me, change me, have control over me. I nursed the same warm beer at keggers, never inhaled the piney smoke from blown-glass pipes. I subsisted on pickles, SnackWell's, and lunch meat. Refused to fall in love with people made of flesh and blood, reserving my lust for the greasy-haired subjects of glossy rock mags, whose pages I tacked to the ceiling above my top bunk.

I wanted to be like my best friend, Erica, to whom I clung fiercely. With her I was safe, loved, fulfilled. We'd share clothes, food, secrets. Her twin bed even on school nights, our legs entangled, my nose pressed against her freckled arm or in her permed red hair, breathing in her scent of violets, rainbreak, and dog. We bought each other gifts, anything that had to do with angels, faeries, butterflies, and other winged beings. She called me her mariposa. I called her my angel.

Unlike me, Erica swallowed gurgling bong rips and fucked reverse cowgirl and swung her strong legs into passenger seats, baring her gleaming teeth to the wind as if she were flying. She was college-bound, hell-bound — perfectly balanced. It was a mystery to me how she could receive or reject with such assurance and fearlessness. She knew exactly where her edges were, where she stopped and everything else began.

Jacques Lacan's *objet petit a* refers to the phantom limb, the vestige that appears when an infant perceives she is separated from her mother's body — from her breast, lap, and gaze — and thrust into the world as a socialized and symbolized individual with borders defined both by language and physical form. We only see this "object" the very moment it vanishes and unconsciously long for it with flawed nostalgia, idealizing it as a state of perpetual bliss when it never actually was. In fact, it was in this state that anxiety was born.

"Don't you know that it's not the longing for the maternal breast that provokes anxiety, but its imminence," Lacan states in *Anxiety: Seminar Book X*. He clarifies that "the security of presence is the possibility of absence."

In other words, it's the looming boob that teaches anxiety, not the absence of it. To wit: I think of myself now, mother of cat, a massive tuxie with Maine Coon blood, doglike and muscular. When I come home from work, name tag still on, boots still on, hands chapped and dirty, he plops into the curve of my body, his haunches rising and falling with breath, fur smelling of cinnamon. And these moments are so perfect and sweet, my body buzzes with the anxiety that he'll inevitably leave me. So I remain still and uncomfortable, so as not to disrupt our moment, knowing soon it will be over. And when he does leave my side, when he struts into the next room and scratches at his cardboard thing, I breathe a sigh of relief.

It seems I was so arrested in the original, infantile anxiety of Mom's doting proximity that, even after our figurative severance, I was constantly aware of her awareness of me, of her perception of me as either pride-and-joy or pain-in-neck. I was homesick for the latch, her arms, the time I thought we were one and the same, before I knew I was my own person. I found solace, completion, in the feverishly intimate friendships I forged with headstrong Rubenesque girls from whose insides I could imagine emerging.

Before I was ever dopesick, I was wombsick.

It makes sense that after high school I moved into a house of pretend orphans. A punk house. It was childhood redux – baby barrettes and maryjane shoes and secondhand Strawberry Short-cake sheets. In school we had been the freaks, the nerds, the gayrods. Now we ate food out of dumpsters. Drank 40s of King Cobra. Had scabies and head lice. Infected piercings. A bathtub stained with hair dye, a rainbow of molds. I didn't feel shitty about myself inside those grimy walls. I wasn't judged or shamed or ignored or pushed into becoming someone I was too afraid to be. There, I was a reenactor, reclaimer, rewriter of my child-hood. I was a poseur in intentionally ripped tights. I was extra-societal, exoskeletal – with a hardness that was as determined and make-believe as my innocence.

It was there I had become friends with Mercedes. Like Erica, like Mom, she had an arresting presence: tall with a maternal span of hips; a lived-in, preternatural beauty; and a subtle smirk of know-ing – or maybe it was of gracious amusement as she slummed with punk kids for the evening, taking swigs from my bottle of Boone's Strawberry Hill. All of it belied her mere nineteen years. She wore a big musty coat whose lining drooped from the bottom. Platform boots. Bangs so long they cloaked her eyes and scraped her cheeks. When she smiled at me, her irises glinted from behind dark hair. Her mouth was a perfect heart, like a valentine, a mole in nearby proximity. I wanted to kiss her, swallow her, know her, be her.

The acute intensity of our friendship lasted a few sultry months between June and September. She'd take me back to her house, where her mom was asleep down a hallway, behind an eternally closed door. She'd make me tortilla soup, and we'd watch anime or talk about sex: She'd had plenty of it, with rich boys and amoral men and explorative girls. She'd spread a photo album across our knees, tell me stories to accompany each photograph, so it felt as if I was reliving her past with her, the two of us side by side. At night we'd sleep together in her four-poster bed, its cotton sheets so worn that they had become silk. She'd fling an arm across my chest, mumble some bit of nonsensical dream. And I'd lie there, stirless, scintillating, listening to her breathing, my breathing, feeling both an airy serenity and the metallic zap of anxiety – the paradoxical qualities of desire, of euphoria. The awareness of full and the foreknowledge of lack. The body at odds with the mind.

Once, I accompanied her to the drugstore, where she bought Pee-Chee folders and binders and college-ruled notebooks for back-to-school. She bought little pots of eyeshadow in unnatural hues. Ponytail elastics. Sugar-free gum. Afterward we went and got wet burritos. Then we drove into the neighborhood by the fairgrounds. She parked the car near a cluster of stables, recently vacated as the horse races had just left town. She had me wait in the car as she went to go knock on a door somewhere down a row of shacks. When she returned, her glossy teeth winked at me.

When I asked where she went, she tossed her head back and laughed. Turned up the music – a glammy band from another era I'd never heard before.

We went back to the punk house, and she lured me into the bathroom. Looped her arm around mine and whispered in my ear. She sat on the edge of the bathtub, brandished a spoon she'd nabbed from the kitchen, and bent its handle dramatically. I watched as she plopped a sticky black chunk into its concavity and held it above a lighter. As she removed an orange-capped hypodermic needle from her purse and steadied it atop a cotton she had spun from the fluff of a Q-tip. Then, unbuttoning her fly and modestly baring a partial butt cheek to the blind wall behind us, she jabbed the needle into a thick pinch of ass fat. Or at least I think she did. I considered that maybe she'd actually just emptied the rig onto the filthy floor or into the dark fabric of her jeans. It was hard to believe that that woman, that *girl*, rather, who guided me and taught me and held me and fed me and saw me and heard me, would be so negligent with her own life. It had to have been a show to impress me. And it did impress me. The act put her in another camp, one I was unfamiliar with and intimidated by. After that night, our friendship faded.

It was around that time I'd first met Dale. He was in town for a party at the punk house. There were bands playing in the living room. Illegal fireworks. We had made out on a rotten back-yard couch. He was already living in Oakland, had fled Sonoma County months beforehand to go to Laney, Oakland's community college, then maybe someday Berkeley. He dreamed of studying numbers and stars, of traveling to Japan and shopping at Wild Oats, of learning how to play Go, how to sail in Lake Merritt then, maybe someday, the bay. He no longer wanted to act cool with a needle in his arm and plumbing chain around his neck, in those unwashed punk-band T-shirts. I didn't give two shits about his dreams. I thought they weren't his anyway, but society's. I had shown up at the shrimp-pink palace and fucked him on his birthday. Then never left.

Finding the cigar box in his closet, filled with the same orange-capped needles and bent spoons, had been a sort of permission. I begged him to get me high, threatened to find someone else who would if he continued to refuse. He finally agreed. "Just the tiniest babyshot," he said.

I had wanted to be someone else. To be bonked with amnesia

like the stars of Mom's soaps, turning into my antithesis. To forget the old chicken-shit me by ignoring her into oblivion. Earlier that summer, I had changed the spelling of my name, swapping my first initial with a *K*, a letter towering and resolute, substantial enough to hold on to all the superfluous consonants I tagged on to the end of my name. It looked, written out, how I wanted to be: brave and complex, containing multitudes and contradictions. Assertive yet silent, solid yet permeable. I wanted to be phase-changeable, to become as liquid as the black stuff that wed my blood and made its way, via heart, to my still-forming frontal cortex.

As if all my organs were made of tongue, I tasted that inaugural high in my entire body. It had the flavor of something organic — like soil, ferric and worm-turned. Like torn petals. A garden blooming on fast-forward. It was a flavor I'd come to associate with love. How I immediately loved the way the night drifted in through the window, smelling of car exhaust and fast-food chicken. And the song that played on the radio: not a lullaby but suddenly a lullaby! And Dale, such a perfect soul, like Gabriel in his glowing robes, barefoot and bringing lilies.

I teemed with love, felt its buoyancy in my heart, a certainty in myself and everything around me. A profound sense of safety. Though the drug made me drowsy, I had an unexpected energy — not a muscular one, but an emotional one. Like how a child feels past bedtime: sleepy but curious. And curiosity is love. Is bravery. Everything seemed full and bulbed, surrounded in gently quivering menisci. Raindrop world. Teardrop world. I couldn't tell if it was my heart expanding or if it was just everything else around me.

Thomas De Quincey, in *Confessions of an English Opium Eater*, compares the peaceful yet ever-shifting condition of his mind under opium's influence to the ocean:

> For it seemed to me as if then first I stood at a distance,
> and aloof from the uproar of life; as if the tumult, the
> fever, and the strife, were suspended . . . yet for all anxi-
> eties a halcyon calm; a tranquility that seemed no prod-
> uct of inertia, but as if resulting from mighty and equal
> antagonisms; infinite activities, infinite repose.

Comparisons between the womb and the sea have always been
made, a cliché at this point. The ocean is, after all, where all of
life theoretically began. Its saline waters are similar in composi-
tion to amniotic fluid, and both environments are known to be
isolated and self-sustaining, peaceful on the surface yet churning
with life just beneath – division and multiplication, ossification
and spark.

I took the ocean for granted. My whole life, it was near enough
to salt our air and bookend our days with woolly fog. Visible was
its subtle imprint of rust and warp on every shingle and chassis.
Even the towering eucalyptus that lined our back roads, standing sentinel and breaking Diablo winds while housing conspiracies of ravens in their shag, looked as sea-lashed as ship sails.
But for as close as the ocean was, it was far away. It loomed and
beckoned, its mightiness just out of sight, behind green rolling hills that dampened its crash. In high school I'd cut class to
go sit on its rough sands, finding a secluded cove that held the
charred remains of someone else's fire, a few empty bottles that
were the same translucent amber as the ropes of rotting kelp that
strewed the beach. In my mind, I'd pretend I lived there, in a cave
safe from high tide, under an anvil of earth. I thought then that
everyone had an ocean close by.

Dale and I left Oakland because there was an eviction notice on
the door. Or because our roommates kicked us out. Or maybe
we just left. I only remember that I felt the pull of home and

convinced Dale to go with me. To sell back the textbooks and give up with me. We packed our things in trash bags and returned.

We crossed over the bay and drove along the San Andreas Fault, up to the county that kept the sweet stink of cow shit and Gravenstein apples and Cabernet grapes. The tan hills looked like the burnished rumps of the sleepy horses that roamed them, mawing dry grass and twitching at flies. Oak trees captured silver and gold in their rustling leaves, tossed light and shadow across pasture and asphalt.

Sonoma County was my home. Not a house with four sides and a roof to return to, not even a single town to claim as my own, but an entire county whose hidden southernmost edge toed the bay's marshy shallows, making it part of the Bay Area on a technicality (though its membership was vociferously disputed and rejected by south bay and east bay and San Francisco residents, who thought it too far or too hick). Going home felt like drilling myself into the heartwood of those ancient silver-gold trees. Into the protected, resistant, insulated part. The nonliving part.

Dale and I showed up on his parents' front steps that evening. We promised we'd only stay a month, two tops. Our belongings spilled from the bags we piled in the entryway, and Glorianne, Dale's mother, sighed as she bent to pick up runaway balls of socks. She weaved between us like a cat. Duane, Dale's dad, remained on the couch, watching public broadcasting as he peeled an orange. His feet rested on the coffee table. Nearby, his tangy, worn-out shoes.

For the first few nights, we made a bed of couch cushions on the living room floor. We watched *Law and Order* and ate bowls of ice cream. Dale's childhood bedroom had become a de facto storage unit, its closet filled with heavy coats and formal attire. There were encyclopedias and boxes filled with Styrofoam inserts. Rolls of wallpaper. A door-sized poster of James Dean. A half-finished quilt. We unburied the old bed and cleared out space in the dresser. Everything intermingled. I knew not to throw anything away, no matter how worthless it appeared.

I'd been out there once before, to Dale's folks' house. They lived in a rural, unincorporated part of Sebastopol, the mist-softened small town I'd lived in till I was twelve. Theirs was the last house on a dead-end road whose sign was faded and hidden behind branches. They had a pond with a few pale koi; rows of barren, blighted apple trees; and a murky, rarely used swimming pool. Dale and I had gone out there together when we had first started dating. He and his brother, Ben, were assembling a prefab shed on the property. There were already a couple out there, padlocked and rusty. I paced all around that afternoon, bored and hungry.

That's the first time I met Glorianne. She was sitting criss-cross-applesauce on the flagstone walkway, her long silver hair enshrouding her plump body like an afghan. Piles of paper surrounded her. The sun and breeze caught the corners of the papers, the edges of her hair, making all of it lively and bright. Holding her reading glasses at the end of her nose, she examined a blue sheet from the top of a stack.

"This was a permission slip for Dale to go on a field trip," she said, reading it as she spoke to me, eyes scrolling. "He must have been in about the second grade. So darling." Then she lifted and waved it so I could take a look for myself. She lifted and waved it like she already knew me.

"What are you doing with all this stuff?" I asked.

"Sorting it," she said, looking up at me, finally, and beaming proudly. A strand of hair stuck to her lips.

Later that day, when Dale had grown antsy and tired, after his beer had transformed into the glisten on his chest and in the curls of his nape, he walked down to the heap of papers.

"What's with all *this*?" he asked, kicking some of it up with his boot. "Trash?"

I shrugged. "Your old homeworks."

He groaned as he dragged the trash can from the end of the drive and began hefting armfuls into it. Papers flapped, skittered in a gust as Glorianne came running down from the house barefoot, yelling for him to stop.

"What on earth are you doing?" she asked, out of breath and close to tears.

"I thought it was garbage," I said. "I'm sorry. It's my fault."

"There is no garbage. Do you understand that? Nothing is ever garbage."

How I learned. Save even the faded receipts whose numbers were lost to heat, the empty shoeboxes and expired coupons that clung to the fridge with a magnet with a witty saying in a typeface evocative of hieroglyph: denial is not a river in egypt.

One evening, before Duane was home from work, after our room was all set up, I stood at the entryway table, dragging my fingers through a basket of angel cards as I looked at myself in the mirror. I often looked for my reflection in mirrors and dark windows, secretly. To see if I could see myself as others did, to catch myself unawares. But all I ever saw was Mom's unsure mouth, her worried eyes, a body that moved guiltily, constrictedly — as if my clothes were too tight. I was afraid of spilling out.

"Aren't those fun?" Glorianne appeared from the kitchen, flicking a packet of Emergen-C. She wore a loose-fitting tunic and pants made from hemp. They were beet-dyed, potato-printed with spirals and wiggly shapes. Her gray hair was in a loose bun, fastened with a pencil.

"Go ahead and pick one," she said deliciously, her tongue clicking the word *pick*.

I plucked one from the bottom.

"courage," I read.

Glorianne clasped her hands together. "Peachy."

I liked her. She spilled out everywhere, unapologetically, granting me permission. She found wisdom and guidance in everything: in all the world's religions; in church pews and church basements alike; in colors and herbs and rocks and animals; in little cardstock strips printed with virtues.

I dropped the bent card back into its brass bowl, catching Dale's reflection in the mirror. His face was irked and sorry.

Glorianne twisted a ring on her finger. "I happen to know a lot about courage myself right now." She released a small laugh, had a look that said I didn't even know the half of it. "I was abandoned by my birth mother." Her eyes started to water, and her nose flared.

"My god. I'm so sorry." I was scared to put my hand on her shoulder but did. She grasped it, squeezed it, seemed hungry for it.

"Mom," Dale protested, "do you always have to bring up your shit?"

"Shush, Dale. I'm not talking to you." Glorianne resettled her eyes on me. They were moons. "Do you know what fear is?"

I nodded yes.

"*False evidence appearing real.* Have you heard that one?"

I shook no.

"It's good to hold on to that one." She tapped her temple before hugging me with all of her full body, pressing me against her breasts. She smelled like unscented bar soap.

Glorianne held on to many things. Not just the old permission slips, the 12-step slogans, the new-age refrigerator magnets. And never garbage or moldy food or dead animals like the people on reality TV. But beautiful things: credenzas made of swirly, glossy wood; chairs with brocade and brass filigree; and so much old glass — blistered and crimped, in hard-candy tinge, all of which rendered the dining room table useless. Everything was crammed and nested and flocked with dust that would no longer dust off. It was way too much pretty to even be pretty.

Glorianne searched through welfare shops and estate sales, kept her hauls in the back seat of her car for days or weeks or months before smuggling them inside to a bare patch of carpet, a corner. I soon learned that Glorianne was also searching for her birth mother. She was talking to someone, a lawyer maybe, an agent of some kind. Someone in another time zone that kept the lines tied up when Dale and I were trying to page our guy.

In 1944, Glorianne's mother was teenaged, her father a shadow. She was given up after five months of being dressed like a doll, held at the breast, cooed at by her child-aunties. It was that detail that pained her the most — how her mother could hand off her infant after all those bonds had been established. Glorianne was whisked from Oklahoma and brought to California with a barren mother and a military father. She grew up with swim lessons and citrus trees and cold furniture. Then there was a funeral, suitcases, another abandonment. A new mother married the uniformed widower, one that was ugly to Glorianne and sent her to a faraway school with hard beds and stiff skirts. Glorianne went, alone and brave, her hair so long it wrapped around her, shielded her from her father's tongue, which had once found its way into her mouth when he was sloshed with drink, his breath hot and ginny.

She twisted it all atop her head now, loosely clasping it so that it drooped to one side and framed her face with wisps. She looked like a frontier woman, sturdy and tired, her wagon packed and eyes searching for the horizon.

Mostly keeping to her bed, Glorianne watched the wall-mounted television, her big toe probing into her dog, Bree's, yellowed corkscrews. She sorted through piles of papers with her readers down on her nose tip: documents, certificates, photographs, clippings. She was homing in on her mom. Falling back into her orbit. Wading through the eternal substance.

CHAPTER FOUR

Broke

A month passed, then two, three. Dale and I were still there, at his folks' place, in and out of the house all day, keeping weird hours. I sensed Duane and Glorianne's growing suspicion. I knew they knew something was off about their son and his aimless girl-friend. It was in their subtle glances up from the newspaper, away from the TV. Their apprehensive yet unrelenting ques-tions. Dale and I fed them elaborate lies. We were out pound-ing the pavement, we'd say. Gathering applications and typing out résumés at the library. Duane had stopped us once when we quietly let ourselves in at some dark hour. He was watching the History Channel, not quite supine on the couch. "A little late to be getting home from a job interview," he said. We told him we'd met up with some friends afterward, did something extraordi-narily ordinary. Grabbed slices of pizza, threw a Frisbee around, had a couple beers. We assumed it would please him to hear that we were normal twenty-one-year-olds. "How are you affording this without jobs?" he asked. Which spawned another set of lies, and then another. We had promised Duane and Glorianne we'd find employment and, shortly thereafter, our own place — but we regularly abandoned all efforts and intentions upon the first shiver of dopesickness.

We couldn't conceivably maintain jobs and habits simulta-neously. First of all, our dealers didn't keep schedules, rarely honored the clock. We had to open our availability to them in a way that regular employment would preclude. Second, it was unlikely we could fix halfway through our shifts without anyone noticing. The time it took to cook up in a bathroom stall, to carefully set a full spoon on the back of the toilet and draw its contents without spilling them everywhere, to windmill arms and run them under hot faucets until veins bulged, to find and hit said veins, and, finally, to nod with chin to collarbone until the prisms that formed behind eyelids and the warmth that spread under skin had slightly faded, was too great. It was better for me to make my own hours. To be my own boss. I could earn enough to stay high by panhandling, flying signs that read hungry (technically not a lie) till I made fifty dollars. By lugging that gas can around.

When winter came, damp and mild, Dale and I had a roof over our heads. We had fresh air, privacy, and a safe cul-de-sac with apple trees and a well. There were sheep up the road, horses. The occasional doe with her spotted fawns sidling behind her. There were pink lilies that looked flirty against lopsided crossbuck fences. We had hot food. Hot showers. Cable TV. A change bowl to dig through. Wallets to snag from. Duane mildly rode our asses for a bit about our promise but soon gave up. It seemed he and Glorianne got used to having us around, maybe even wanted us there.

I grew up with safety nets galore. I took them for granted – their mesh permanently imprinting my hands and knees. The first house I remember living in had been my great-grandparents', Mom's paternal side. That was the house with Dad. We swooped in on it after my great-grandma, newly widowed, was killed in a head-on with a drunk. I was ten months old at the time, and Mom was already in her second trimester with Aly, who was named after said dead great-grandma. For a while, we all lived there in a dreamy bubble. It was warm with fireplace fire. Smelled like smoldering newspapers, chocolate chip cookies. Everything was harvest-colored, the palette of abundance. I didn't know yet that nothing in the house – not the goldenrod chairs or the nubby, pea-green couch, the half-finished needle-points or the plaster Mary in the backyard – belonged to us. That it had all come with the house. That we were essentially squatters. Cowbirds – Mom and Dad depositing their hatchlings into the well-built nests of other birds. The arrangement was that my parents would pay some easy, symbolic rent to my maternal grandparents, who were executors of the estate. As far as I know, they never paid a dime.

On their hands and knees, Mom and Dad collaged vision boards with glue sticks and pages from *Architectural Digest*: Jacuzzis, sports cars, mansions. Mom's eyes twinkled when Dad talked about his future fame and riches. She didn't work then because she was a stay-at-home mom, which was undoubtedly work, especially considering there were four of us kids by the time I was in kindergarten. But it didn't bring money. She sold Mary Kay for a while, which had her talking pink Cadillacs, had her on a plane to Dallas so she could attend the big seminar, which seemed like a megachurch, a beauty pageant, and night school rolled into one. "I got the Mary Kay enthusiasm down in my heart down in my heart down in my heart," she sang as she changed my brother Aaron's diaper. I knew the tune from vacation Bible school. "And if the devil doesn't like it he can sit on a tack sit on a tack," I responded enthusiastically.

Dad invested whatever money he had in a drafting table with a clip-on lamp and an assortment of shapely rulers. He drew comic strips and greeting cards and pictures of sailboats made from thousands of dots. He designed a sign for some guy at church, a guy he later called an asshole. Then Dad said he was going to be the next Mrs. Fields. He kept jars of raisins soaking in liquor. Bags of fancy nuts we weren't allowed to eat, not that we wanted to. He sold his cookies to his coworkers at the news station in San Francisco, KGO channel 7. When he was fired, he said his boss was an asshole too. Then he took the cookies and the greeting cards and the sailboats to the flea market on the weekends. He'd set up a card table with board games and warped pots and baby clothes. He'd speak to browsers in bad Spanish, words mispronounced and verbs ill conjugated. He had me accompany him because I was a good-luck charm. Said my pigtails and fudgy eyes lured bargain hunters into yanking out their wallets. Sometimes we made enough for me to buy a few bootleg cassette tapes – Billy Ocean or Hall and Oates – or a pile of jelly bracelets. Then it was acting. There was a casting call in the classifieds section of the newspaper. Dad showed up on set every morning for two whole months to be an extra in Francis Ford Coppola's _Peggy Sue Got Married_. Got paid a total of $163. Told everyone he'd get discovered, get his big break in due time, just you wait. He filled out the application for his SAG card, paid its dues before paying the electricity bill, carried it around in his wallet, showed it to Darlene and Eric and the others at Ross Dress for Less where he worked, in shoes. That was before he was fired. Before someone else became an asshole.

My grandparents threatened to kick us all out of our house and Dad called them choice names too. Mom covered my ears, threatened to leave Dad if he couldn't stay employed. Dad called her a money-grubbing whore, not to her face but to me, the eldest child, age nine at the time. He told me this matter-of-factly one evening after tucking me in. When I asked him if a _horror_ was a scary movie he said no, it was a woman who had sex with men for money, and I pictured Mom, who was supposedly out with the gals that night, on a steamy, blue-lit street corner lifting her skirt for passing cars. The information and the accompanying imagery made it impossible for me to sleep. I cried and prayed and hoped with all of my heart that Dad had been gravely mistaken.

I remember happening upon Mom crying in the kitchen. She sat on the toybox, the yellow phone receiver in her lap, its long cord making figure-eights across the linoleum. I thought Mom's crying maybe had something to do with what Dad had told me.

.I thought it was shame because, somehow, I already knew what shame looked like. It was the quality of her crying that struck me. It wasn't loud and passion-fueled, not something thrown at Dad's feet like I'd witnessed months before: "We need to feed our kids, you bum!" It wasn't the melty weep from a movie's happy ending, our pastor's sermon. It was full and silent. Brave yet afraid. It maintained composure while thoroughly dissolving her. It's what I'd come to understand much later in life as the cry of acceptance. Of resolve. Of an ending. Not a happy one with a song, the credits rolling, but not necessarily a sad one either. A real-life one.

"Mom!" I bleated, crying too. She didn't wipe her eyes or reassure me that everything was okay. She breathed through her nose as sheets of hot tears streamed down her cheeks, not a trace of makeup left on her face. The back of her head was against the brown floral wallpaper. I wanted to touch her but was too afraid. So I stood across from her, watching her, mirroring her.

Later, Mom told me she had been on the phone with her mom, Gramma.

"Why was Gramma mean to you?" I asked.

"She said I haven't been a very good mom."

"No!" I said, horrified. I told her over and over that she was the best mom in the whole wide world. I hugged her and she said, "Sweet girl." With her nose in my hair, I asked her if we were broke. I had overheard her saying the word a lot but I didn't know what it meant. I pictured something literally split into two parts. I even wondered if maybe it referred to divorce.*

---

*I watched the 1961 Hayley Mills version of *The Parent Trap* almost every Saturday morning. We had it on video – Betamax. Its stop-animation title sequence begins with foreboding lightning jags and a minor-key oboe. A framed cross-stitch that reads Bless Our Broken Home appears on the screen. The first time I saw the film, I imagined a huge storm was coming any minute to rip a literal house into halves. Though I learned, after that first

"Don't ever talk about that," Mom said, looking at me sternly. "Never tell anyone we don't have any money."

"Are we poor?"

"I hate that word," Mom said.

We weren't *poor* poor, even if on paper we were. We were middle-class imposters, appearing to have solid footing there, which isn't even possible, considering the middle class, by definition, is never stable; it shifts around just like the ground I was raised on – seismic plates sighing deep beneath me, unnoticed till the moment they crack the earth right down the middle, toppling bridges and highways, buildings.

It didn't matter that Mom had no money and Dad had no money, that neither of them had college educations nor any specialized training. The bail-outs and borrowed cash, the ingrained conventions and inherited markers, the family they had, friends they kept, and neighborhoods they lived in hid any financial destitution – socially if not statistically.

Maybe the word for them wasn't *poor* but *indebted* – not to bank lenders (Dad never had credit cards) but to society, their community, their families. It was a debt that came with some really high-interest shame, stress, resentment, et cetera. Had they been *poor* poor, without Gramma and Grampa financially shoring them, without their friends and neighbors and siblings to compare themselves to, without all the pretending and not-saying, maybe their obsessions with money, expressed uniquely by each of them, would have looked like need instead of greed.

––––

viewing, that the film was about divorce (which I was already familiar with due to friends who had two homes, two bedrooms, sometimes two dads), I still didn't understand metaphor. I thought perhaps maybe I missed the part where something had broken. For at least another year or two I associated the word *broke* (and all of its tenses) with inclement weather that had the ability to destroy both buildings and marriages.

Poverty is both subjective and relative, defined by an arbitrary line based on inaccurate, guessed expenditures and the socioeconomic status of those around you. Official metrics fail to consider how shitty your house is or how many unpaid ER bills you have because you don't have health insurance because you sit just above the fake line even though you're taking out payday loans just to afford your rip-off internet bill from a de facto monopoly so your kids can go to school and so you can look for a, hopefully, better job. Sociologist Matthew Desmond has pointed out that poverty is not just an income level but also "chronic pain, on top of tooth rot, on top of debt collector harassment, on top of the nauseating fear of eviction. It is the suffocation of your talents and your dreams." Dad defended those dreams. Mom depended on them.

Mom had been born and raised by money-fetishizing* bootstrappers who literally lined the walls of their mid-century ranch with the skimmed and unreported earnings from their mom-and-pop pharmacy.† She'd been born and raised in a world of postwar prosperity, unprecedented and singular, where the consumer choice was packaged for the masses as an act of democracy, of anti-communism. Where full-page, full-color ads sold not just products but dreams, guidelines. Where women were groomed to be auxiliary to men, without autonomy – financial or

---

*Desiring money not as a medium of exchange but as an object itself – a useless collection that grew exorbitantly over sixty-five years, much of it devalued after Grampa prematurely sold property that would come to be worth at least a thousand times what he received, or rendered worthless after the 2017 Tubbs wildfire melted and burned much of it.

†After Gramma died and Grampa went to a nursing home, Mom found 45k in hundreds stashed under the bathroom cabinetry, an Ace Hardware bag stuffed with Krugerrands under Grampa's socks, and a large cardboard box filled with bars of silver and gold in the cobwebbed crawl space under their house. She also found vats of moth-gotten rice, stashed unregistered firearms, and all manner of consumer goods (kitchen appliances, toys, clothing) still with tags or in their original packaging.

otherwise. Mom couldn't even have her own bank account until the year I was born. So there she was, a woman with childbearing hips, subconsciously aware of the godlike and ghostly money that had surrounded her her entire life, completely seduced by the messaging heard in the hum of a new fridge, woven into the warp and weft of a designer dress. It seems obsessions are sprung from the dank matrix of futile desire, where overexposure and inaccessibility collide.

Growing up, Dad had been seduced by the cowboy shows. The Cleavers. The white neighbors next door with the swimming pool. He'd rather have watched the black-and-white boob tube, or through the slats in the fence, than his own mother, otherwise so regal with her dictator's pompadour zagged in silver, tending to her corns with prematurely arthritic hands. She admonished her son to have pride, to refuse the secondhand handouts, to forget her first language, to keep a fresh hankie in his pocket, his shirt tucked in. And the words he heard were made urgent with the pow of a studio Smith & Wesson, the twinkle in John Wayne's eye, Jerry Mathers's smile. The splash of a cannonball over the fence. The pleasingly antiseptic smell of chlorine.

He grew prideful and entitled, as taught. It was a way to metabolize the shame. He butted heads with his teachers and then sergeants* and then bosses because he convinced himself he deserved their positions. He wouldn't be anyone's tool. It wasn't enough to get good grades or decorations or paychecks. He needed

---

*Dad had enlisted in the air force after high school. He bragged that he was mouthy and insubordinate to his superior officers, challenging their "idiotic" rules and traditions. He was discharged, honorarily, because he had supposedly threatened to go to the general court-martial after receiving an Article 15 (a non-judicial punishment) from his commander for his infraction of the Uniform Code of Military Justice. Dad, whose curl pattern is tightly coiled and kinky, refused to have his head closely clipped as was standard for white soldiers. But Dad wasn't white. He demanded to be extended the option given to Black soldiers and wear his hair picked out into an Afro.

to immediately capture the respect and envy of his cohort, his coworkers, his family, and society writ large. He wasn't going to be like his mother, a tiny immigrant woman who worked in a factory, whom people stepped in front of and spoke down to in loud, slow English, unaware that she came from wealth and status and intelligence in Nicaragua, unaware of where she came from, period – "no, not Mexico," she'd say over and over – whose father was a journalist for *La Prensa*, the anti-Somoza-regime newspaper that spearheaded a countrywide literacy campaign; who had grown up on acres of bananas, had maids that slapped masa with clean, wet hands, who soaked linens in lemon water and sunshine. Nor was Dad going to be like his father – the town fool. A self-described "jack of all trades and master of none" in a newspaper article – one of many that came out during his reign as the local gossip-column laughingstock. (It was a three-year span where Grandpa Jim went from entering look-alike contests on his vague resemblance to Clark Gable to running for state assemblyman on no platform whatsoever. He thought a platform was a plank of wood.) Grandpa Jim donned a dated suit with a Colonel Sanders bow and drove around a 1951 Daimler limousine on its last legs. He scribbled shaky autographs for old ladies at the bank or the bowling-alley diner. "You'll see me on the silver screen," he said, doing his best Rhett Butler. But he never made it into showbiz or politics or anything else he said he'd do. His constant disqualifications and misunderstandings, made public in a way he thought was evidence of stardom, was cheap, cruel entertainment for townsfolk who needed some heads to step on on their way up.

Dad always said that too: "You'll see me on the silver screen." He said it like revenge. And Mom, for a while anyway, wore his word like armor. These were ways they protected their rawest selves. External layers they projected outward, pushing against everyone else's projections.

Heroin encased my rawest self with its chemicals and its bad
rep and its permission to opt out of life. Was I the way I was
because of some dominant gene? Some parental example? Or
is it that we are all raw? That we all have our buffers and copes
whether it's wine or sex or church or shopping or mountain
biking or weight lifting or compulsively cleaning the house or
compulsively lying? It's all the same thing – the same bodily
response. The same yummy brain chemicals. The same preoccupation, sense of control, and comfy miniaturization of the
whole, big world.

When Mom asked me, at age nine, if I wanted her to divorce
Dad, I said yes. I felt my answer reverberate throughout my
whole body. It tingled. It felt like fear but also felt like calm. Like
floating atop a smooth blue expanse whose depths contained
hideous, fangy things, the drifting silhouettes of hammerheads
or giant squids. My belly, rising with air toward the sun, my
breath loud in my ears against the water's hum, I trusted myself
to stay put – half below, half above. Between worlds.

Dad was split too. He wasn't afraid of getting his hair mussed
or his shirt wrinkled. He'd drop on the floor, pretending to be
dead. "Dad, are you dead?" I'd ask him, joggling his thick torso,
waiting for him to blink. I'd tickle the bottom of his feet or dig
my fingers into his pits. Eventually he'd break, his wide smile
displaying every tooth in his head, silver and all. He'd fly me like
a plane, cover me in kisses. Sometimes we'd share drippy tins of
mustard sardines over the sink in the middle of the night. We'd
go to the dump together, hurl broken baby furniture and sacks
of diapers into a stinking hole in the earth. He'd tell me I was his
favorite. That was his sunny side.

Then there was the dark, cold, undersea part. The part that
gave me something to cry about. It was always a burnished
wooden spoon or a looped leather belt. "Move your hands!" he'd
yell. There was nothing I could do to avoid his rage, whose onset

was unforeseen and purposeless, mounting into a hasty, sloppy crescendo that left everything atremble: his hands, my mouth, a stack of plates in the cabinet. He always found a reason to call me an idiot. A *pendeja*. There was always something left on the floor, left in the rain, left in my classroom, left open, left on. His refrain: "Use your head for something besides a hat rack." He said it so often, and from such an early age, I'd only ever heard it as a single noise. A clump of disgust and disappointment. I had never taken apart the words or their individual meanings. I didn't realize the last noun was a hat rack because what even was a hat rack? All I knew was that it was bad and was spat from Dad's mouth. When he said it he hocked a loog. A hat rack was my stupid head. A hat rack was me with a belt on my ass, in front of everyone, *ha ha, what a dummy* they all must've been thinking. Hat rack was a nasty little girl who masturbated under the kitchen table so no one could see. Who learned early on that comfort and shame were inextricable.

After I decided that Mom and Dad would split, Dad moved back in with his parents, to their finished basement. Mom got the welfare checks and the food stamps. Grampa gave her an extended rental moratorium and some under-the-table insurance billing to do for his pharmacy, which she did at the kitchen table, me under it, sucking my thumb in private, messing my teeth up, feeling gross for liking the smell and feeling of flesh under my nose and in my mouth, not realizing it was like nursing. Gramma took us back-to-school shopping at the outlet mall, bought us loads of Spumoni sweatshirts covered in puffy kittens, bright ensembles by Esprit and Generra, which we couldn't wear to the DHS office with the stuck-together plastic chairs because we'd look not poor enough.

Mom eventually got a job bagging groceries and wrangling carts at Lucky so she could pay the after-school sitters who watched us while she bagged groceries and wrangled carts at

Lucky. I remember going with her to pick up her paycheck. We pulled up into the grocery store's parking lot, right beside a slim, silvery-blue car without a top.

"See that car?" Mom said. "That's a Mercedes-Benz. The next daddy you have is going to drive one."

I stared into it, at its empty bucket seats, and wondered what made it so special. Maybe it went faster? Or flew? Maybe it was made from the very sky it matched? Maybe it could take Mom more places than the Caprice ever could? Places she couldn't even imagine? Maybe it could make her no longer herself?

Before Dale, I knew the next guy I dated was going to have track marks and pinned pupils. A little kit he kept in a sunglasses case or a cigar box.

Mike, Mom's newest boyfriend, who appeared within a year of Mom and Dad's separation, drove a Mercedes-Benz. I hated him for it. I knew it meant they'd get married, a marriage I hoped to sabotage by glaring at him from across the dinner table. By reminding him that he was not my father. I fantasized about ruining his car. Taking a crayon to its silvery blue. He didn't try to win me over, didn't try to replace Dad either. He wasn't an asshole or a slimeball, like the red-faced man Mom had been seeing before the plan to divorce was finalized; the one who made me call out for her in the night when I heard them sinning. Mike was a quiet man who had cats and played piano. Erik Satie, Chopin études. A tall, thin mortgage broker with thinning adult-blond hair and tortoiseshell glasses. I'd never met a person so even-keeled. He seemed alien. One night, he tucked me in and made a face he called the frog face. It wasn't exaggerated and grotesque like Dad's faces. It was hardly even a face. He lightly puffed his cheeks and made a sound that was not quite a ribbit but a pop. I thought it was cute and funny and decided then that maybe I could love him.

All of us – me, Aly, Molly, baby Aaron, and Mom – moved immediately into his rented country cottage. He cleared out space for his huge trial family, moving things into an outbuilding to fit the bunkbeds. He sequestered off the added-on mudroom with a shower curtain, improvising a bedroom for Molly and me. I slept to the hum of the fridge, whose contours bulged through our curtain. Sometimes I read books by the light of its open door.

The house was situated on a commercial apple farm. Endless acres of trees, knuckled and fragrant, provided places to pretend. I built mysteries around abandoned machinery, wooden crates, the seasonal workers who carried ladders through orchard rows. Summer nights smelled sweet and vinegary. Like fruit rot and hot dirt. Like hot rollers and L'air du Temps and the microwave burritos we ate while Mom and Mike went to the symphony or to a fancy restaurant in Tiburon. Soon, my sisters and I, in heavy, handmade satin dresses, clutching nosegays of pink roses and baby's breath, walked step-together-step-together to a Beethoven piano concerto. Just like that, Dad Mike was my new daddy, as promised. His bachelor-cabin would no longer suffice for a family. *His* family.

Before my fifth-grade year at a new school with new friends even ended, we moved again, seven miles east to Santa Rosa, into a two-story, three-bedroom tract home I called a mansion. It had what I believed, or make-believed, to be the extravagant features of the homes I'd read about in *Sweet Valley High* books: a wet bar with pleather details, a living room with a semi-vaulted ceiling that could accommodate a Macy's Christmas tree, a half bath off the family room, and vacuum-cleaner-striped wall-to-wall carpeting whose cola-brown pile had been well trod by previous tenants. My new friends in the neighborhood lived in the exact same houses, only painted different colors – sandstone or slate. We rode our bikes around the subdivision, finding empty spaces to enact our imaginations. Construction sites and model homes replaced the apple orchards and gravel roads of our previous house.

Mom had another baby — Foster — and we moved again. This time to the prestigious zip code, the better school district. Our new house was smaller and moldy and smelled like the old woman who had lived there before us. Mom made everything dusty rose and calico and geese. Then, over slices of take-and-bake, she announced that she was pregnant yet again. This time with Michael. I earned a slap across the face when I asked her if she'd ever heard of the pill.

I was already pissed to have to share a room with two sisters, to hide clove cigarettes in a dresser I split with an eleven-year-old and wank to pictures of Axl Rose when the family was at Costco. I was frustrated that I didn't have what all my new classmates at my new school had: the hand-me-down cars, the new prom dresses, the allowances and freedoms and privacies. Each new sibling encroached on my personal space, cut into my portion of the household budget, and hijacked all of Mom's time and attention.

Our family was broke. As in broken-in-two-parts broke. One half consisted of Aly, Molly, Aaron, and me — the dregs of the regretted marriage. We felt like fosters, old furniture destined for the sidewalk, but also pack wolves. Our closeness was found in our shared circumstance, a visceral grief that was also our encoded joy, our wild laughter. We were in love with one another with such fierceness it struck others as inappropriate if not peculiar. There were rumors.

We were aware of our mutual otherness. We located it in our blood because that was the easiest, most obvious source. Once, Dad Mike joked that the Mexican gardeners he had hired to prune our yard were our cousins. He asked if we recognized them. It was meant to be harmless and funny. That's when we all learned how to communicate wordlessly, with only our eyes.

Sometimes I'd pass Aly in the hallway of our high school. She'd be pretending to rifle through her locker all lunch. I knew the move well. My eyes would meet hers, and we'd speak in silence before I'd shuffle off, following a pack of girls whose friendship with me was inconsistent.

The other half was the new family, the one whose surname became the vanity plates, the Christmas cards, the answering machine's outgoing message. It felt to us like Mom and Dad Mike were biding their time, just waiting for us older kids to hurry up and move out so they could get on with the life they really wanted — one that included passport vacations and ballroom lessons and a membership at the country club. Once the last one of us left, they moved into a big, airy house whose no-name street was christened, officially, eponymously.

I hurt too much then to be grateful for the brave man who took on four kids not his own. Who loved us and fed us and took us to Disneyland and Tahoe. Paid for our choir dresses and braces and countless retainers and casts and removals of tonsils and appendices and wisdom teeth. Who made the frog face as he tucked us in. The hurt was inevitable: A safety net has to assume a fall, but it never prevents one.

Aly, Molly, and I all moved out more or less around the same time. Aly went to live with her youth-pastor boyfriend at his grandmother's house. She was seventeen and wore a little gold cross around her neck. She fucked and prayed and, like me, binged and starved and stood on the scale naked, hoping to become as small and light and symbolic as the little gold cross. Molly, only fifteen, attended high school for a few weeks before dropping out, bored with its pointless lessons and social vapidities. She ran away periodically. Stayed with vegan punk kids, the cool girls who worked at the coffee shop, line cooks who spoke kitchen Spanish, and, eventually, me and Aly, who, at that point, shared a dark upstairs apartment we brightened

with gerbera daisies and Christmas lights. Before that, I had
rented the add-on bedroom at a distant relative's house. I was
eighteen years old. The relative was my ex-uncle-in-law's sister,
a horsey woman who played the piano at church and gave Foster
lessons. She had a pro-life sticker on her car. Framed Bible
verses everywhere. I didn't want to interact with her and her
husband, so I tiptoed in late with friends I hoped she thought
I was gay with. I kept all my food in my room. Moths got into
my laxative bran cereal. The seven-year-old daughter got into
my department-store makeup, leaving waxy chunks of broken
lipstick all over the bathmat. I blasted Black Sabbath the day I
moved out.

I had a job at Grampa's pharmacy. It started with clipping
coupons from mailers he'd redeem for monthly checks. I'd sign
stacks of insurance forms from the dot-matrix printer – *Daffy
Duck, Mickey Mouse* – before tearing off the edges and making
small accordions. I'd wipe counters with rubbing alcohol. Then
Grampa fudged some paperwork so I'd get a two-dollar raise and
a certificate to tape to the wall. He called it security for my future.
A safety net. I wore a white lab coat and answered phones and
scribbled six-digit prescription numbers on legal pads. I sent
faxes and signed TARs and slid tablets and capsules into lock-top
bottles. I was a pharmacy technician, just like the prematurely
balding surfer Grampa had hired a year before, whose name,
Dan, I wrote on my knee, in a heart, upside down.

Whenever Grampa eyed sales reps through the glass, young
and eager as Latter-Day Saints, approaching us with their brief-
cases and whitened teeth and clicking shoes, he'd grab his tuna
sandwich and hide in the back. "Tell them I died," he'd say.

They'd leave behind colorful pamphlets and blister packs
of samples. Piles of swag Grampa would have me throw in the
trash or keep, if I so desired. I had Vicodin pens and Purdue day
planners, a Percocet mug and Pepcid AC Post-its. I had, still have,

an Imitrex tote bag. There was even an MS Contin plushie – an anthropomorphized pill, a smiling, cuddly lentiform of legal heroin.

Opioid painkillers were no longer prescribed to only the terminally ill or the temporarily wounded. People with any kind of chronic pain were being treated with dope under the pretense of compassion. Grampa's pharmacy increasingly filled these prescriptions until pain management patients were the majority customer base. He didn't like this. For nearly forty years, his pharmacy had been a place his neighbors would come in for their low-dose aspirin and Lucky Strikes. Quinine sulfate for leg cramps and bubblegum-flavored antibiotics for their children's ear infections. Back then, women browsed the cosmetics counter, had my teenaged mom color-match them with a swatch of Cover Girl applied to the jawline. During the holidays, customers gifted him quick breads wrapped in red cellophane, bags of persimmons from backyard trees. Later, he received seasons-greetings cards autopenned by the Sacklers themselves.

Our regulars were on Medi-Cal, the state-funded medical assistance program. They smelled like chronic bronchitis and unwashed hair. I knew their names. Knew their excuses. Had to tell them we were still waiting on the doc, that I'd try again after two and they'd wait in their cars with Merits burning, dogs yipping. Their key chains were jangling piles of Bermuda, Betty Boop, and colorful NA fobs. Their children were faded in their wallets. Their substances were controlled precisely because they were out of control. They'd threaten and curse, kick the Leanin' Tree display over when their refills were denied.

I quit my job at the pharmacy because I knew I wasn't supposed to. I was supposed to stay forever. Marry up – a pharmacist maybe. A doctor, if I was lucky. Definitely not Dan. I was supposed to keep returning each day, scrub-faced and dispassionate, handing drugs across a sanitized counter to the people I knew I really was.

I sabotaged a stable job, called Grampa an asshole. I depended on bail-outs, loans, and cosigners, depended on my beauty and my sex. Mom was now the one who was resentfully scribbling IOUs into a little notebook, sighing. Adding to the growing list of figures under my name. I hated that book, its numbers that too quickly became insurmountable. It was evidence of my failings, a record of my irresponsibility, privilege, and entitlement. It got to a point where I no longer wanted any help because I couldn't stand the feelings of self-loathing that came with it. It got to the point where the help was cut off anyway. I had safety nets, yet I still managed to fall through them. I imagine those without any at all.

When I met Dale, I made him my safety net. On my cross-hatched knees, I begged him to save me. To provide something that would soften the impact.

CHAPTER FIVE

Gift (a triptych)

— one —

Glorianne, atop her bed, leaning against pillows that leaned against the headboard, licked her thumb and flipped a page. A Pottery Barn catalog on her thighs, knees easeled. Duane had long since given up sleeping beside her because of the junk mail. It spilled from the nightstand and onto their matrimonial bed, leaving only a sliver of space for her body.

I pushed coupon circulars out of the way and plopped down next to her.

"Can you pass me the Delia's?"

"The what's-it now?"

"The one with the girl."

"Ah. 'Tis the fashion she wants."

As I perused the pages, imagining myself in the various outfits, Glorianne talked about the clothes she used to wear in the 1960s, a style she called urbane and also bohemian. She had been living in San Francisco, after all, up in Diamond Heights where Dale had been born, cesarean because there were complications, something about a narrow birth canal.

"See anything that strikes your fancy?" she asked, eyeing me as I dogeared a corner.

"This is hella cute," I said, turning the page toward her. It was a T-shirt with a Union Jack, likely flammable.

She snagged the magazine from my hand and moved her glasses down. "Hand me my checkbook," she said, motioning toward her purse, a beige leather filing cabinet whose zipper no longer zipped.

"Thank you," I said so quietly it was nothing more than a peep. I avoided drawing attention to my words of gratitude because they'd only remind Glorianne of my endless take. But take I did. I felt I was owed something. Something intangible. I looked for it in the presents from Mom that arrived on schedule – Christmases, birthdays. The one-size-fits-all, even-Steven gifts we all got. Spatulas and slipper-socks. Even the things I begged for that ended up under the tree: the Led Zeppelin boxed set with the crop circles on the cover; the jean jacket with its statusy triangle; the Barbie kitchen that smelled like vanilla – I was always so full and then empty again.

One time, when I was about seven, Mom came home from her errands, put brown paper bags filled with cream of mushroom soup and two percent milk on the kitchen counter.

"Come here, girls," she said, reaching into her purse. She revealed three rubber balls, the kind I'd get from the machine at the grocery store where a quarter made a hen go *bock* and drop a plastic egg. Aly always got blue things because of her eyes – exotic in our family, a genetic improbability that was brought up at every family gathering. Recessive, Mom said. The mailman, Grandpa Jim accused. Molly typically got some variation of pink or purple because she was the least girly and Mom probably thought the shade offset her dirty knees and floppy hair that resisted ribbons. I got yellow because of Big Bird, my first true love. That day, however, Mom handed me a green ball. Green. Like bugs and boogers and the ugly-face stickers Mom stuck on all the poisons under the sink.

"I hate green!" I chucked the ball out the sliding glass door, where it was immediately lost.

Mom's knees popped as she squatted to my height. She looked at me with a sad face.

"I picked out green especially for you," she said.

"You did?"

She nodded. "When I look at green, I think of you. It's so pretty. Like trees." I thought she would cry.

I hugged her desperately around the neck. Lined my lips up to hers and kissed her. "I didn't know you thought of me," I cried, apologetically, "when you saw green."

From that day forward it was my favorite color. I told everyone I knew, to make it definite. I revised my activity books: *Favorite animal — bird, favorite food — pancakes, favorite color — ~~yellow~~ green*. I often thought about Mom thinking of me every time she saw a lawn or mint chip ice cream, the elm in our backyard. And the thought made my heart actually hurt, my throat go thick, my skin gooseflesh with immense, shivery love.

I wanted more rubber balls. Things that let me know Mom was paying attention to me. That I meant something, was someone enough to remind, reverberate, and be captured in an object or an experience. I wanted Mom to translate the invisible part of me.

Glorianne and I went through the rest of the catalog together.

"Oh heavens!" she cried at a pair of sailor-cut pants. "Those are so you!"

"You think?"

"Oh yes. They're classic. And classy. But still groovy." She gave me a nudge and a wink. "All the hip girls used to wear them. With the striped shirt. Very French. I'm jazzed to see them coming back."

I remembered that Glorianne had told me she wanted the Princess Diana Beanie Baby — a purple bear with a white rose embroidered on its breast that was supposedly worth hundreds, or even thousands, of dollars.

"My grandpa sells all the Beanies at one of his pharmacies," I said. "Pretty sure he has the Princess Di."

"My." Glorianne's eyes grew large. "Your grandfather has more than one pharmacy?"

"Well, he's a half owner."

"A partner?"

"Something like that." I shrugged. "We get a discount is what I'm saying."

"Oh? Of how much?"

"Like maybe half off?" I had no idea.

Glorianne considered this for a moment. "And this discount extends to me?"

I nodded. "Anyone I want it to."

As a kid, we'd drive out to Grampa's other pharmacy to go "Christmas shopping." Mom would hand us each twenty dollars, which most definitely came from Grampa anyway, and allowed us to pick out small gifts for one another. Unlike his pharmacy I'd worked at, the drugs seemed like an afterthought. The store was large and meandering. Glass display cases held Precious Moments figurines and Waterford crystal. Hanging from high were stained-glass suncatchers and bamboo wind chimes. There were board games and stuffed animals and mugs with cartoons and sayings on them, sampler boxes of cream-filleds and tins of flower-flavored suck-drops.

Glorianne and I drove out the next morning, after I'd gotten high and smoked half a cigarette. It was a fifteen-minute journey, past the fruit stands and the pie spot, in a one-horse with a bank, a liquor store, a hardware store, and a gas station. Also, a needle exchange in a parking lot one night a week, buccal-swab HIV testing out of a van.

Glorianne loosened a shopping cart from the corral and darted inside. Immediately we arrived at a cardboard display of colorful plushies with plastic eyeballs. Glorianne hurled one of each into her cart, hoping she'd eventually stumble upon the elusive purple bear.

I wandered aimlessly, putting a few things in my handbasket – chocolate, a porcelain bell with violets on it I thought I'd get Mom even though I hadn't a cent. My jeans slipped as I browsed the aisles, and I tugged them back up by a broken belt loop. I was approached by a woman I vaguely recognized. She asked if I needed help finding anything as she stared at my hands. They were puffy, scarred, swipes of blood and saliva on them, nails dirty. I told her I was good.

Glorianne called for me. Half of her hair had fallen out of its pencil, and she had lipstick on her teeth. "Would you be a lamb and go ask if they have any Princess Di's in the back?" She was out of breath, her face lightly dewed with perspiration.

I found the woman dusting greeting cards.

"Do you have any of those princess bears in back?" I asked.

"I'm sorry. What now?"

"It's a Beanie Baby? It's called the Princess Di bear? It's purple?"

"All the Beanie Babies are out on the sales floor," she said. "Oh, and please let your friend know we'd appreciate it if she puts back whatever she doesn't want."

"Oh, I think she wants them all!" I said jubilantly, hoping the woman would stop watching me once she knew we were there to spend real money. I felt like Julia Roberts in *Pretty Woman*.

Glorianne's cart was overflowing when she announced she was ready to check out. When we rolled up to the cash register, the woman set down her feather duster.

"You all set?" she asked.

"Yeah," I said. "Oh, and I get the family discount."

The woman's lips curled up into a smile. She was suddenly amused. "And why do you get the family discount?"

"Her grandfather is the owner," Glorianne interjected. I nodded.

"Your grandfather is Dave?"

"No. Joe. Joe Brazill."

"Well, he's not *thee* owner. He's just *an* owner. I'll have to speak to the pharmacist on duty and see if he can give me authorization to do that."

I couldn't stop hearing the word *just*. It was like a brick. I wanted to throw it. From behind the pharmacist's counter there was some murmuring, some craned necks. When she returned, she apologized she couldn't get ahold of my grandfather to verify who I claimed to be.

Glorianne's face worried. She started counting on her fingers, doing math in her head.

"Well, fudge," she said. "I guess I'll just take them all anyway."

The woman nodded dutifully and began ringing them up, all eighty or so of them, one at a time. An owl, a pony, a monkey, two puppies, a turkey, a cow, a tie-dyed snake.

"And you're sure no princess," Glorianne said, shakily smiling.

The woman shook her head as she punched numbers into the cash register.

"No, you're not sure, or no, there's none?" Glorianne laughed and the woman did not.

Glorianne's card was declined and the woman asked if she had another form of payment. Glorianne, flustered and gone pink, dug through her purse for her checkbook. When the woman called the bank to make sure the check was good, Glorianne swallowed her smile and looked at me with exhausted eyes. I knew the shame she was suffering and blamed myself for it. You try to do something nice and instead make them feel like shit. I was so angry I wanted to smash the stupid bell that I held in my handbasket. Why would Mom want some cheap-ass tchotchke anyway? Probably not even violets on it. Probably pansies, forget-me-nots. Mom used to plant violets in the shade along the front of our first house, delicate blue ones whose powdery scent disappeared the moment you noticed it.

I thought if I gave Mom the bell, Glorianne the bear, if I could just pin down the fleeting, render the ephemeral in porcelain, the rare in plush, my love, also, would be captured and crystallized, remaining true even when I confused it for hate, even when I was afraid to demonstrate it, to speak it into something that could be questioned or rejected.

Later that night, back at the house, I heard an argument. "This is madness," Duane said. "It has got to stop." He didn't yell, never did. He was from Ohio, after all. His words were even, short, and few, like the word *Ohio*. I caught a glimpse of Glorianne's sobbing face, red and wet, hiding behind her hands.

"I'll get rid of them," she said, pleading.

The next morning, I lifted the lid to the garbage can at the bottom of the drive. Eighty beanbags stared back at me. I knew how she felt when she put them there. That sick feeling of self-disgust was temporarily assuaged by the burning high of rage as she hurled them all into trash, amid the coffee grounds and empty containers, all the things leeched and gutted, substance and significance consumed. I tell myself now had the princess bear been in there I would have rescued it, hidden it in Glorianne's top drawer for only her to find. But the truth is I would have sold it. I reached in, grabbed stuffed animals by the handful.

— two —

The sibs and I spent most weekends at my paternal grandparents' house in Petaluma, a town twenty minutes away along back roads. We slept in the room that Dad had once shared with his brother. There was still a peace-sign sticker on the closet door. Grandma Coco had redecorated the room with pictures of Clark Gable she'd carefully torn from magazines and framed, rosaries slung over their corners. She covered both of the beds with repurposed tablecloths whose heavy, stiff white velvet trapped cigarette smoke and made me sneeze.

Everything at Grandma Coco's was a gift. There were boxes of truffles covered in red cellophane, rose-scented bicarbonate blocks in foiled paper that made my bathwater fancy, secret words veiled in the birdsong of Nica Spanish, whose meanings I tried to guess. Even our steaming dinner – pork and raisins and olives and potato wrapped in masa wrapped in *plátano* leaves wrapped in butcher paper – came tied up in a bow. We called them little presents.

Grandma Coco gave herself a present of fresh-cut flowers every week. She'd arrange them in a crystal vase with an aspirin at the bottom. She gifted herself long, perfumed baths to which she'd continually add hot water. She gifted herself regular manicures whose click was dignified.

She gave me permission to indulge. Passed the box of chocolates as we watched *Wheel of Fortune* and then *Evening Magazine* and then *Hunter*, far past bedtime. She poured me glasses of guava juice in jelly jars after I brushed my teeth. During commercial breaks she'd advise me to depilate with wax, to go to a girl with quick hands who'd make my legs satiny for me and me alone. To throw those worthless pink razors in the trash. She'd tell me she liked me blond, which was never blond but a pumpkiny shade of Sun In. "It's not too orange?" I'd ask. She'd wave her hand. "You look famous," she'd say, puckering her lips.

She indulged our shenanigans, and this was also a gift, one that made me wild with both fear and exhilaration. Once, on some April 1, right after the divorce when Dad was living in her downstairs, we brought with us a caged rat from Aly's classroom – a rat that was always out on loan to some student to teach the responsibility of pet-having. His name was Cookie, I think. Dad was aghast when he saw it, couldn't understand why people willingly welcomed plague-spreaders into their homes.

"It's not to come out of its cage," he said. "Your grandmother is terrified of rats. If that thing gets out, I'll knock you all to kingdom come. Understand?" And then he went off to sell his Electrolux vacuum cleaners door-to-door.

Grandma conspired with us to April Fools Dad. We'd hide Cookie in a milk carton. Seal it up good with layers of silver tape. Poke airholes. When Dad got home, he'd see the abandoned cage, see Grandma standing on the coffee table, shrieking, just like out of a *Tom and Jerry*.

Grandma uglied her face with sheer panic, screamed Dad's name over and over till he came storming up the stairs, eyes bugged and belt off. We were all laughing so hard our asses were anesthetized against the stinging leather.

"April Fools!" one of us yelled, smiling, flinching. And then we all yelled it, over which Grandma yelled, "Stop! Stop!" first in English and then in Spanish. Our tears were of joy just as evenly they were of fear and pain, neutralizing themselves, becoming nothing more than just wet. The whip came down quicker each time I laughed, and the laughter, like the sobbing, was two-faced: a response to the antics, the real-life sitcom, and to the nervousness brought on by Dad, likely bipolar, certainly narcissistic, a trait that would prevent him from ever getting a proper diagnosis much less gaining any self-awareness. He couldn't take a joke. Was even more enraged once he learned one was at his expense. No pizza for dinner, he said, referring to the grocery-store take-and-bake that had been in his freezer since the previous weekend. No Grandma after dinner (no game shows; no *Golden Girls* — Rose and Blanche and Dorothy and Sophia; no frostbitten Neapolitan ice cream from the giant tub; no soporific fumes from burning Chesterfield Kings and rose-scented candles that had me nodding off before the episode was even over); no dinner at all, actually; and no rat ever again, we're lucky he didn't kill the thing. Dad gave Grandma the silent treatment for the rest of the weekend and withheld us from her, which only made her want us more, and vice versa. "My babies!" she cried from the top of the stairs. Dad finally laughed a couple of days later, before Mom came to pick us up. "You guys really had me with that one," he said, his eyes watering as he reflected on the evening. "That was a good one." He nodded with an air of capitulation. "It's obvious you all inherited my humor."

I gifted myself with the thing that both exhilarated and scared me. Whose moments of transmutable ecstasy were worth the agony it burned off as. No, I did not toil at the thread mill like Grandma, becoming arthritic, watching my friend's hand get mauled in a machine, blood everywhere. Nor did I earn the right to hide or deny or neutralize or forgive or reward how tired and gnarled and poor I was with little sensual luxuries, all steamy and creamy, smelling of sacuanjoche blossoms – lemon, sex, and dusk. The tiniest metallic threads in her pantsuits even, twinkling like Christmas, which she kept in dry cleaner's plastic under the plaster bust of Jesus, doe-eyed and slender-nosed, keeping watch above her closet.

Gift giving is a way to build and bolster relationships. As both giver and receiver, in what we call self-care these days, I was, subconsciously, attempting to connect with myself. I didn't know who the fuck I was or where I belonged. Always edging along some narrow high-rise cornice, gusts on my back, toes slipping, I needed to be invited inside some open window. Or fall.

The gift to myself came wrapped in a ripped bit of plastic bag. A greasy nugget imprinted with the whorl of my dealer's thumb. I held it in my dirty palms because I didn't trust my pockets. I held it all the way from the Toys R Us parking lot, up the avenue where cars kissed at me and whistled, up a spiral ramp that smelled like evaporated piss. I held it over sagging chain-link that snagged my pants and ivy that grabbed my ankles. I held it as I followed a guy in a beanie down under the overpass, sidestepping, hearing only thick traffic and my heartbeat.

I had a crisp brown paper bag from the needle exchange. It had things in it I never used: a rubber tourniquet that looked like a noodle, alcohol wipes, a small bottle of bleach with illustrated instructions. A little way down, the guy got high. He wore a grimace as he shot into a hand vein. "Hurry up," he said to me through clenched teeth.

"Don't wait for me," I said. Because I couldn't be rushed. I wanted to luxuriate in my high on the side of the highway like Grandma did in her bath. There, hidden behind greenery and concrete, my butt on the moist and reeking earth, I gave myself what made it all worth it. What I put inside me: Chinese blood,* Afghan sweat,† white man's greed. Jazz music, said Harry Anslinger — fed, narc, racist — while cuffing Billie Holiday to

---

*The First Opium War (1839-1842) erupted after Chinese commissioner Lin Ze Xu ceased British ships trafficking opium into China and seized their cargo: three million pounds of opium that he later destroyed by dumping salt and limestone atop it before dumping it into the harbor. Seeing this as a humiliation to the Crown, the British navy mobilized. After months of threats and sanctions on both sides, the British opened fire. The Chinese were sorely defeated, giving the British control of the Pearl River estuary and possession of Hong Kong Island. The Second Opium War (1856-1860) was a result of the British pressing for renegotiation of the Nanking Treaty, which failed to deliver the trade policies it had promised — namely, the legalization of opium. France joined powers with Britain, and both American and Russian forces aided the effort by sending envoys. The war was marked by several bloody battles. Many of the casualties were civilians. After the sacking of Beijing, China ceded to British and French forces. The opium trade was legalized.

†As of 2021, Afghanistan produces more than 80 percent of the world's opium. Because of its arid climate and jagged terrain, it is not conducive to growing many crops other than poppies, which thrive in full sun and dry soil. Opium farms provide thousands of jobs to Afghan citizens, the majority of whom are impoverished, illiterate, and agrarian. Afghanistan has the highest infant mortality rate in the world, and the second highest maternal mortality rate.

her deathbed. I slammed the poet's muse, the druggist's faith. The stuff moled through El Chapo's tunnels, from Tijuana to San Diego, muled for forty hours inside desperate, nervous stomachs, expelled with the help of Ex-Lax. In my arm all the rain in Seattle. All the pain in Appalachia. The death of millions – rich and poor, young and old, somebodies, nobodies, bodies.

– three –

The non-gifts I held on to longest. Because unlike a thing that eventually becomes lost or grown out of, wilted or eaten or passed along, a void lasts forever. It sears into the amygdala, modifies the narratives we keep about ourselves, pops up again and again at the vaguest, most remote trigger, building strength and vividness, seeking and locating proof and validation of its messaging in all future circumstances, reinforcing and reinforcing. "I am unworthy," the void said. "I do not belong," it said. "I will never, ever make anyone proud."

December 1993, choral department winter concert, Santa Rosa High. I was a senior, a second soprano, freezing in the wings with the rest, in our velvet bodices or satin cummerbunds. We had rehearsed "Ave Maria" in Latin, a madrigal in Middle English, "Carol of the Bells." Under the hot lights, once the audience had shushed, our voices sparked from silence as if our conductor's finger were a struck match. Our voices grew and merged, became the bumps on my arms and the wet in my eyes. I belonged to this – this thing far greater than the sum of its four harmonizing parts. This thing that took yielding and trust, practice and commitment, an act of creation and communion. It had been my greatest achievement.

After, parents waited in the lobby with grocery-store bouquets – roses, of course, long-stemmed and blood red. They hugged and congratulated, discussed going for celebratory sundaes. I heard Dad Mike's distinct whistle. Followed its pitch and found my family standing by the doors, coats on, tired, eager to leave behind the chitchat and pleasantries, the teenaged squeals. Mom, distracted, asked, "Where did we park?" and then "Who was the, what do you call it? Soloist? Bigger gal?" No roses, no sundaes, no praise.

That night I couldn't stop shivering. I assumed it was a combination of my constricting gown and rain. I made a bed on the family room floor because the bedroom was too cold. I was not allowed to touch the thermostat. At some point, while everyone slept, I realized I was not well. My throat burned and muscles ached. The next morning, Mom left for errands. Dad Mike had a list of chores and asked me to help. "I'm sick," I said, but no one believed me.

Turned out to be strep. A week later I was still taking amoxicillin because I had to finish them all. It was the Sunday before Christmas and also my eighteenth birthday. Mom and Dad Mike were gone somewhere, with the little ones. I hoped they'd have a pink box when they returned, a cake in it, my name on it. Hopefully a wrapped gift too. Or a card with money. "Where'd they go?" I asked my siblings, and they shrugged. The hours ticked, and we watched Nickelodeon. Played Mario. A typical boring Sunday. Erica called even though she had celebrated with me a couple days before, had made me a collaged card and a pink box-mix cake. Dad didn't call, but he never did anyway. I had Honey Nut Cheerios for dinner. Then Aly left for youth group. Aaron went over to a friend's. It was dark out, late, and still no sign of Mom.

My TV show was interrupted by red lights streaking across the living room window. I looked out and saw an old fire truck dripping with teens. They sounded the horn, waved from their ladders. It was Aly's youth group. Dweebs who said things like "J-dawg's my homie" in reference to Jesus. They sang "Happy Birthday," the Beatles one, and then invited me to hop on for a slow cruise back to the church for some funky praise. I declined, feeling more morose than before.

When Mom, Dad Mike, and the kids got home there was no pink box. No present. No knowledge of even what day it was. Foster and Michael were told to go brush 'em, that it was past their bedtime. "Do you know what today is?" I asked Mom, who changed into her pajamas. "What's today?" she asked. When I told her it was my birthday, my eighteenth, legal adult, she sighed and said she'd forgotten. She wore the same sad face she'd had after I told her I hated green, squatting to my child height. She gave me an exhausted and somewhat defensive apology. Said she had a lot going on. Six kids. Christmastime and such.

I gave myself the non-gift of See's candy – three chocolates plucked from a soft-centers assortment – followed by a swig of ipecac I'd pilfered from Grampa's store. Hugging the toilet, I vomited till there was nothing left but the void. "I'm sick," I said, but no one believed me.

CHAPTER SIX

Wite-Out

In the lagging, overcast mornings or in the pale afternoons or in the nights that came suddenly, the orange sun slumping behind the trees, Glorianne and I would sit on her bed. A bare white leg, freed from the folds of her muumuu, would rest casually against my own as together we'd look at magazines or the TV that was forever mumbling away, the volume so low no words were discernible. It was a familiar comfort.

"What do you want to be?" Glorianne once asked.

"I don't know," I said. "Fashion designer?" I was immediately embarrassed. It sounded so big and unlikely. Pointless, even. Who did I think I was?

"Can you sew?"

"No. I can draw, though. Sort of."

Glorianne repositioned herself, rocking on her buttocks and becoming a smidge taller. She leaned in toward me, almost conspiratorially. I could smell her plain soap. Why fashion, she wanted to know. What about it drew me to it? Why did I like drawing? I wasn't used to this kind of interrogation. It was never important to know the reasons or motivations behind anything, as if to voice them could unravel any declaration. Besides, questions were time consuming, and nobody ever had time.

My interest in fashion must have originated from Mom's September issues, whose heft and scent were like something consecrated, holy. In the relief of our lake cabin's bedroom, the curtains pulled against the late-summer sun, the box fan set to a soothing whir, Mom and I, prone on the bed, elbows kissing, would study each page of *Vogue. Bazaar. Mademoiselle.* I was eight, nine, ten. Wore a sandy, half-dry swimsuit, a constellation of new freckles. Both of us barefoot, our ceiling-ward toes occasionally grazing, our hair rough from lake water, admiring slouchy gabardine and jewel-toned rayon, dolman sleeves and dropped waists. We rarely spoke, instead emitted enraptured *oohs!* in unison. We were not intimidated by the runway's absurd, exaggerated, or clashing fashion, for it was permissive. *Invent your own way!* it said. We knew to translate these looks into approachable, abbreviated things, to reduce them to synecdoches. A costume-y nautical getup became Mom's striped tee embroidered with a gold anchor found marked down at Marshalls. As a child, I loved the game of this, the creativity it inspired, the challenge it demanded – to work only with what I had available to me. I remember I wanted pedal-pushers like the girls in Bananarama, so I took to wearing my four-year-old sister Molly's jeans to school. I donned my galoshes even in summer because, if you squinted, they might pass for Janet Jackson's booties. "This time, I'm gonna do it my way," she said in her video for "Control." I worshipped her.

Mom, an enthusiastic consumer, took us to White Flower Day sales and Labor Day sales and Back-to-School sales and Dollar Days sales and Doorbuster sales and Last-Minute Shopper's Saturday sales. I'll never forget the evening she took us to Emporium Capwell for new school clothes. Not a soul was in the section I shopped, one that was neither for children nor for juniors but somewhere in between. It was confined to a quiet, softly lit corner in which every out-facing sleeve from the clearance rack was irresistible. I piled them all atop my arm and made my way to the dressing room, which, because of its vacancy, seemed like a secret world – a world of mirrors, a million me's. In my private room, I changed into the various outfits, aware they weren't entirely in style but knowing that if I were to pair this with that or that with this I could evoke Janet Jackson's white button-down or Madonna's off-the-shoulder sweater.

Mom was proud of my choices, smiled as I spun around so she could check the fits. Helped me wiggle out of a gray drop-waist dress with a big red bow I wore on the first day of school. I loved it for its shapelessness, its resemblance to a barrel, its almost-ugliness I could make hip with jelly shoes and globe earrings, lace gloves from the Halloween section at Sprouse-Reitz.

Fashion was the thread that tugged through me and Mom, connecting us, providing closeness.

Glorianne continued to ask questions that forced me deeper, to mine into myself to discover not simply answers but also the reasons for my answers. Her questions made me feel smarter about myself. Smarter in general.

"I saw in a magazine once this chick wearing a big, poufy skirt, a Cinderella-type deal, with, like, a wifebeater. It looked so cool, you know?"

"You like contrast. The unexpected." Her eyes narrowed, glinted. "What else?"

"Why do you care?" I asked, not meanly but sincerely.

When I was young, Mom and Dad chose the 1960 Joe Jones hit "You Talk Too Much" as my theme song. I hated it. It was a dumpy tune that made me hide and cry while they laughed over their meat loaf. "Toughen up," Dad would say. "We're just teasing you."

The song was dedicated to me because I'd often follow Mom into the bathroom, where she'd be wrestling hot rollers into her hair and gluing fake eyelashes atop her real ones. With a splayed issue of *Highlights*, I'd read aloud science facts and knock-knock jokes. Mom would groan and ask me to go play someplace else. But I'd keep babbling on and on, waiting for something from her. Maybe waiting for her to say *Interesting!* or *Who's there?*

I was emotionally needy and she was stretched thin, all of us tugging at her all the time, pulling her like taffy this way and that. She had to make breakfast, pack lunches, nurse, take some of us to school, pick some of us up. She had to Windex the toothpaste splatter off the mirror, defrost the pot roast. Run to the bank and then to the dime store. There were dentist appointments, booster shots, step class. She had to shave her legs and paint her nails. Watch her soap and read her experts. Give mini facials in tract-home living rooms: cleanse; tone; masque; moisturize. Pick up thumbprint cookies from the bakery, guest mints for the crystal dish, flowers from Safeway. Have the gals over because it was her turn to host. Load the dishwasher. Refill the ice trays. Insert the diaphragm, the spermicidal foam.

It's no wonder she couldn't give me the attention I required; it was already fragmented, scattered all over the place like so much broken glass. She, like everyone else to varying degrees, was preoccupied with maintaining the values of flash-ripened capitalism, the extrinsic markers of the middle class. Buy the things to beautify the body and the home, to reflect upward mobility, to keep up with the neighbors, to expand and then contract the mind without even leaving the couch, to gain acceptance, to pursue happiness. In the Reagan 1980s there was the diffuse anxiety to scramble to the top before those riding on amnesty or affirmative action could — the undocumented folks like Grandma Coco, who was deported back to Central America with Dad when he was a year old, before returning with paperwork in order, taking a thankless factory job and buying a small starter home whose mortgage she and Grandpa Jim defaulted on. Everyone, even Grandma, was a threat to the wealth many believed they were entitled to.

Mom suffered the cognitive dissonance of dragging around four young kids and collecting federal assistance while simultaneously denigrating the so-called welfare queens who shrank the wealth gap and diminished the status of what she was aiming to become. In other words, she was getting in her own way. Both a victim and an accomplice of the largely unchecked racist, classist, and misogynist rhetoric of the time. Atop this, a red button somewhere in Russia that could wipe it all away in an instant.

Nevertheless, Mom was by no means a negligent mother. She knew exactly where we kids were at all times. Constantly checked up on us to make sure we weren't climbing too high or putting things in our mouths we could choke on. There was plenty to worry about back then: white windowless vans, Halloween candy rigged with razor blades, Satanic child-sacrificing rituals. She knew all about it because she watched the nightly news avidly from the kitchen as she shook chicken legs in a Ziploc. Because she had seen the faces of missing children on the milk cartons. There was strangulation by superhero cape, asphyxiation by jawbreaker, so many drownings in backyard pools despite the warnings on novelty inner tubes. There was the I-5 Killer and the Freeway Killer and the Golden State Killer. The earthquake drills, the forest fires ("Only you"), and the sleeper waves that warned us away from the shoreline. Not to mention the Tot Finder stickers in bedroom windows, the Mr. Yuk ones under the sink. Everything was a threat in the 1980s — a nationwide overreaction to the second-wave feminist movement, which put mothers in the office and sent fathers hiking with divorce papers. It was an anxiety propagated by a hyperbolic and fearmongering media.

Mom had once cautioned me that a bunch of kids had died from sniffing Wite-Out and to stay away from the stuff. I recall later holding my breath as the girl one desk over dabbed it on her sixth-grade geography report. How I'd watch with a combination of fear, envy, and curiosity the classmates who removed bottles of it from their pencil boxes and painted over misspelled words. How casually they wielded death!

The first time I saw heroin was at a birthday party in 1996. I was twenty years old, naive, a fake-tough tagalong. I glimpsed it, inadvertently, through a flashbang gap in a bathroom door slammed shut with a quick foot and a curse word. In that sliver I saw a frothy pile of taffeta and tulle, pink and sky blue encrusted with jewels. I saw dirty, dimpled arms, greened by the slept-in bracelets of bicycle chain and rhinestone Petco cat collars. Those teenaged girls in vintage dresses, with greasy dyed-black hair and baby fat, held steady their needles, bit leather belts tight around soft biceps.

The sight of them through the crack in the door imprinted my brain the way a gruesome highway wreck does. I became obsessed – the instant memory both terrifying and exhilarating. It was something about the trespassing of flesh. The willingness to endure self-inflicted pain in order to experience pleasure.

Part of its impact was the context. The contrast. A birthday party at a plain, farmy house. School pictures of the birthday girl hanging in the hallway – cowlicks, freckles, missing teeth. A supermarket sheet cake with brightly dyed sugarfat. How innocent it all seemed. The mom and her friends were in the next room playing cards, classic rock, dumb.

I feared everyone's lack of fear there. So much so, I wanted it. It was a dizzying and disorienting feeling. I felt sickish. Swimmy. The sensation of sniffing Wite-Out, maybe.

When I finally tried heroin, it was not to get high. It was not for the reported bodily sensations or the altering of my environment. Its conscious aim was twofold: First, it was to erase the old me and become someone else. Someone who wasn't scared all the time, who wasn't constantly overwhelmed, who felt unable to bear the load of life. Who wasn't shy and uninteresting and adrift. I'd become Mercedes. Or one of the girls in the bathroom at the birthday party; the same kind of girl who had had Wite-Out in her pencil box and a jawbreaker bulging her cheek, staining her tongue blue. Second, it was to be heard. I was disheartened by my own voice. Embarrassed by its eager pitch, its limited pool of phrases. I learned at some point during puberty that my body spoke louder than the words I couldn't find. Doctors and dance instructors and relatives made asides about weight gain and cellulite and breast buds, respectively. Boys and old pervs gazed at my derrière and told me I was *fine*. I used track marks, half-mast eyes, and overall physical neglect the same way I had emaciation a couple of years before: to communicate nonverbally the pain I was in. The anger I carried. The defiant bravery I knew was somewhere inside of me. I wanted to reject everything and everyone with the same intense disinterest I'd believed everything and everyone held for me. To accept and confirm myself as the outsider I believed everyone already thought I was. To be able to impress, repulse, or trouble without ever even opening my mouth.

What I couldn't predict is that the chemicals heroin bestowed me, the physical sensations I had assumed would only be the inconsequential by-product of the preeminent *act* of getting high, were the exact ones my brain released when Mom held me, when she comforted and supported me. And that had been what I was really after.

How strange that a substance found in one specific flower is the same, structurally and functionally, as the peptides our bodies not only also produce but are able to receive and read as well. That this substance is compatible with the puzzle-piece receptor sites that teem our neurons, bespeckle our brain matter, smoothly locking into them as if it was always meant to be. And that the primary function of these chemicals, whether of inherent, botanical, or laboratorial origin, is to comfort. To mitigate pain, modulate emotions, and give a felt sensation to maternal affection.

In various studies over the past thirty years, mammals whose opiate-receptor sites had been either blocked with antagonists like Narcan or altered due to genetic mutations were unable to bond with their babies or mothers, respectively. It works the other way around too: In 2019, scientists in Japan found changes in the number of opiate receptors of baby mice who were separated from their mothers – pointing to a correlation between early life stress, maladaptive behaviors, and chronic physical pain in humans. The correlation between Mom holding me and me holding dope.

It was the drug itself, I soon realized, wrongly, that I needed – not the attention I'd get by doing it. It was the one thing that really liked me, loved me. Held me and comforted me and protected me from all the bad feelings. It was my terry-cloth mother,* my laboratory surrogate. It was the shameful thumb I sucked under the table while stroking the edge of my tattered baby blanket across my face.

Mom's protection of me was lopsided: too good at guarding my physical being from the dangers of the world but lacking when it came to conditioning and encouraging my psychological being. And without psychological strength, I couldn't calibrate the fears she'd instilled in me. They became outsized and irrepressible. Her fears were, ironically, what ended up crushing me – not the hot grill of a jackknifed semi or the cruel heart-shaped cavity in the chest of some dude I'd never even slept with. I moved through the world afraid because I couldn't trust anything: nothing internally (that is, myself) or externally.

In her essay "On Fear," Mary Ruefle describes a toddler whose facial expression rapidly alternates between joy and terror when she's met by a dog. "It struck me that her face would probably

---

*Referring to the mid-century experiments conducted on rhesus monkeys by psychologist Harry Harlow wherein infant primates were separated from their mothers and provided with two inanimate surrogates: one made from wire that held a bottle of food and the other made of soft terry cloth. The monkeys overwhelming chose the cuddly, comforting "mother" over the cold and stiff yet food-providing one.

continue to change, albeit at a slower rate, every time she was approached by a dog for the next couple of years, one day coming to rest on that expression that was likely to signify forever after how this human being felt about dogs." The young child had not yet learned, either by experience or instruction, what to choose – fear or joy.

I chose fear. Learned it through Mom's cautionary tales, through Dad's loose violence. I moved through the world stiff and breathless. Even after heroin anesthetized it, there was another fear that kept me going: that of dopesickness. Ruefle cited a passage about psy-ops in a CIA manual that stated that the fear of something is more motivating, more torturous than that actual something. In other words, what goes on psychologically when we anticipate something terrible is often more damaging than the actual physical pain we endure at the end of it. Recalling the aforementioned reward system, which produces more feelings of well-being when one's expecting a reward than when one receives said reward (remember: the monkeys, the light, the juice), it's clear we're driven by states of anticipation, both positive and negative, that utilize past events or accounts to determine future outcomes – that is to say we move only in the shadows and the foreglows. In the crepuscule between life and death.

Glorianne's protection was the fun-house mirror of Mom's: stretched where Mom's was pinched and vice versa. There, sprawled on her bed, she wasn't afraid to know me. To ask me my thoughts, to ask for a hug or receive one without questioning its motives. I'd go into her room with magazines and read her highlights from articles about the people and things I was obsessing on: Julia Butterfly Hill, Lauryn Hill, trepanning, Prada, orchids. "Interesting!"

Then I'd slink behind a hollow door, mere feet away, and cook my dope in a cereal spoon. I'd curse and yell when my blood coagulated in the needle's chamber before I could shoot it up, would curse and yell at Dale when I suspected he was holding out on me. I'd slam the front door at late hours, underdressed for the weather. Hop into strange cars going strange places; all that mattered was what was hidden behind the dash. I'd return wobbly and brash, banging around the kitchen for a midnight snack. About this, questions were hardly asked. At least not ones that went deep enough.

CHAPTER SEVEN

Normal People

Dale got a job as a line cook in the snack bar at the ice rink. Sous chef, he called it. Our friend Brandon oversaw the kitchen there and told Dale to drop off an application. We knew Brandon through Tommy and Annabelle, and also from his semi-defunct grunge band, which I'd seen open once or twice for other bands years before. On his first day, I met Dale for his shift meal. It was a bunch of junkies flipping burgers and making packet cocoa for ten-year-old figure skaters and their grandmas. All in a Swiss-chalet-style building. With Snoopy and Peppermint Patty everywhere. Dale and I split a turkey sandwich and a bag of Cooler Ranch Doritos.

Afterward we went over to Brandon's with a couple of the coworkers. Tommy and Annabelle were there. This chick I knew from high school with scoliosis and cheek dimples. Apparently, she sniffed crank. There were a couple people playing *Final Fantasy VII* on the PlayStation. There was a cold pizza. Scales and bongs and needles and stems and remote controls all over the coffee table.

"You should come get on the LAAM* with us," Brandon said to Dale, steadying his needle atop a bloated cotton. "Me and Steven are going tomorrow. Ass crack of dawn."

---

*OrLAAM, the trade name for levacetylmethadol, was a drug-replacement therapy option similar to methadone, only it was stronger and had a longer half-life, meaning it only needed to be taken every three days as opposed to daily. The reasons for its 2003 discontinuation are shrouded – some sites claim it was because it was too addictive; another pointed to potential cardiac complications; and one cited the rollout of Suboxone as a factor. As someone who was in that world from OrLAAM's inception to its discontinuation, I think it was largely because no one liked it.

Steven was older than us. Late thirties, possibly early forties. He had long, thick gray-blond hair, stained teeth, cracked hands. He drove a utility van. "They'll start you off on the methadone." He pronounced it *meth-a-don*. The methadon marathon.

I hated Brandon and Steven's announcement of impending recovery. It sucked the fun out of the room. What losers they were, I thought. Because what a loser they made me feel I was. I secretly hoped they'd sleep through their alarms or change their minds or relapse in a few days' time.

A couple of weeks later I got a job in the office of a hospice supplies warehouse. My old friend Jenn worked there and put in a good word for me. Every morning a heap of sales slips, invoices, and insurance billing appeared on my desk. I alphabetized it all by last name, shoving papers under their corresponding letters on a long vinyl strip, then placing them in their correct manila folders in their correct hanging files in their correct drawers. At lunch I'd drive down the street to a remote, industrial area and shoot up in my car. Then for the second half of my shift I'd nod off to Smash Mouth on the radio, Third Eye Blind. I'd make more coffee and then take a smoke break with the girl one cubicle over who wore a Raiders parka, had a square-tipped manicure, and drove a brand-new purple Camaro. I'd ask to leave early, again, and my boss would hand me a stack to fax before I could clock out.

It was fine at first, balancing a job with a heroin addiction, but soon it became impossible. This wasn't the first time. There had been the record store in Berkeley where I'd lasted only a month, the café in Santa Rosa I'd been fired from. I had to choose one or the other, and that time the job won. Being around other adults who had their own apartments, their own tiny patios with tiny grills, their own tabletop Christmas trees, flocked and pink, who had privacy and pride, made me want it all too. Moreover, I wanted to go a whole four hours without getting sick, whole days and weeks and months even. To forget the demand of dopesick-ness, its indescribable torture. I wanted to be like my coworkers, who could spontaneously go to the bar and grill after work and gossip, laugh, eat fried things, play pool, with no clue of heroin's pleasures and pains and urgencies at all.

"'Member how Brandon and Steven were talking about meth-adone?" I asked Dale. "I think we should do it."

As if he had been waiting for me to come around to the idea myself, he hugged me and emitted a sound, like a caught hiccup, that said he was overjoyed. He must've known if he'd broached the topic of us getting clean, I would have shot it down, thrown a tantrum, told him he was being stupid or selfish.

The methadone clinic was in an unmarked building behind a piano showroom. The parking lot fidgeted and swelled. Patients paced back and forth, chatted, smoked, got into fights. There were whispered transactions through rolled-down windows. A security guard who literally kicked rocks. Dale and I waited in line with people I judged for their waxen complexions and miss-ing limbs, missing teeth. *I don't belong here*, I thought. *I'm nothing like them.* I couldn't yet see that they were just like me, had felt overwhelmed by everything too. Had probably felt the sudden purpose and synthetic love from heroin too.

After three hours of paperwork and screenings and waiting, of lab tests that involved the time-consuming task of scraping blood from my pricked finger (since my arm veins were collapsed) and a chaperoned piss, I was finally given methadone. It was served in a paper cup, topped off with Kool-Aid to mask its bitter flavor. I flicked every last drop onto my tongue, desperate for it to kick in. The dosing nurse made me show her my empty mouth, my empty cup.

"Be back here tomorrow before nine," she said brusquely. "You're late, you're not dosed. Got it?" I was to return every morning for the following three weeks, during which my dosage would diminish by small degrees. The idea was that I'd glide painlessly into sobriety while skirting the worst symptoms of a cold-turkey withdrawal.

The methadone kicked in about an hour later. I was at my desk with my strip of alphabet when I suddenly realized I had been asleep, my cheek pressed onto a moist invoice. I stretched my eyes open with my fingers. Wiped my drool. Yawned over yawns. Slipped in and out of dreams. I felt dull and thick as mucosal buildup. As death rattle. I wanted the wheelchair, the oxygen tank, the suction pump. The hospice bed that moved up and down, whose billing code I could not locate on the sheet in front of me.

I drove home that evening dizzy and vaguely nauseous, though, improbably, not dopesick. I felt only the jag of melancholy when I remembered I wouldn't be doing a shot later. How bland my cigarettes and television shows would be without dope – the mark of accomplishment, the cherry on top, the reward. Without the comfy gratitude that fizzed through my body after some varied stretch in which I was stressed both physically and emotionally, my adrenal glands overtaxed. Without the alternating sick well, sick well.

I found Dale on our mattress reading a sci-fi paperback. He reported a similar feeling – a missingness, a doldrums. "I just want it to be tomorrow already," he said. "Or next year." We forwent dinner that night, skipped our Lennie Briscoe and DA Jack McCoy *Law and Order* fix. We didn't bother brushing our teeth and instead got under the covers before the sun was even down. With my head on his chest, he stroked my hair, breathed into it.

"Tomorrow we'll be able to see five of them," he murmured, raising his hand toward the ceiling and stretching his fingers apart, as if trying to catch something. "If we're lucky."

"Five what?" I asked.

"Planets. Mercury, though, might be tricky." He sat up, looked at me. "Make sure to come straight home after work so I can show you."

The next morning at the clinic, I got to skip the first window – where new patients went for their intake paperwork – and go directly around the corner to the second window. "Last name?" a woman asked. She handed me an index card with my birthday, identifying tattoos, and dosing schedule on it, which I then gave to the nurse at the third and final window. She read the card, adjusted a lever on a pump, watched me drink, and said, "Good girl."

When I turned around, the line had doubled. A woman with a clipboard paced up and down the length of it, keeping people in order. Those who were nodding off got a swat or a bark. "Eyes stay open or out you go," she said. She chastised one woman (who later became one of my closest friends) for her skirt. "I can almost see your cooch." She passed her a long coat from the donations pile and told her to make herself decent. The woman, Pamella, instead removed her sweater, a bulky fisherman's deal, and tied it around her waist. Whispered, "Cunt." Smiled conspiratorially at me.

The clinic had a water-stained drop ceiling and rough gray carpeting. Wobbly fluorescent lighting. Clogged toilets. There was a table covered in pamphlets for NA meetings and women's shelters, the Indian health clinic and TLC transitional housing. Surrounding a beam in the middle of the room was stuff dropped off by various ministries and nonprofits. There were packages of socks and grocery bags stuffed with used clothes, a random can of evaporated milk. Preemie diapers.

Either I had already acclimated to the methadone or my dosage had dropped significantly enough to negate the side effects, because I wasn't falling asleep that day. I plodded around work, from the fax machine to the filing cabinets, placidly smooth-brained. I ate lunch at my desk, a first that didn't go unnoticed.

"Hanging out with us today," the chick with the Camaro said. She ate slippery Jack in the Box tacos, sipped from a giant soda with a squawky straw. "Did you pick your Secret Santa?" She rolled her chair over to mine. "I got Helen," she whispered.

That evening, when I pulled onto our street, I saw Dale standing in the middle of the cul-de-sac, looking up at the sky. I got out and stood next to him. He pointed to a low star with a faint green hue, nearest the crescent moon. "Venus," he said. Up higher was Jupiter, a simple bright white dot whose ever-raging cyclone was invisible from where I stood. There was ringless Saturn. Pink Mars. They all seemed so close suddenly, those faraway planets with impossible atmospheres. I wrapped my arms around Dale, feeling closer to him too.

"And that's the Big Dipper," I said, proudly.

This is what happened over the next nineteen days: Dale and I went to my company's holiday party in the banquet room of a hotel. We dressed up — Dale in a metallic blue tie and me in a satiny black dress with spaghetti straps. We danced to "You Sexy Thing" and "Jungle Boogie." I drew Jenn's name for the Secret Santa and bought her a mug filled with Hershey's Kisses. My gift from Helen was a set of snowman cheese knives with the Ross sticker still on them and a crocheted pot holder I assumed she'd made. I attended a scrapbooking night at the office after hours, where we used special scissors to make fancy edges around the photographs we brought in. (I brought a picture of Mom sitting in a cane chair in front of the general store at the lake. She wears wedge-heeled sandals and green bell-bottoms, her hair in a Dorothy Hamill. She is holding me. I look like a stiff doll in a bonnet. The back says, in her distinct sinistral cursive: carly & mommy 6-12-76.) We glued our pictures askew onto shapes made from acid-free paper that guaranteed to keep our photos from fading. (We had the option to buy the acid-free paper, as well as the scissors, the punchers, and expensive albums afterward.) I went with Jenn to see *Titanic* on my birthday. I cried for the big, failed ship that slowly moaned its way to the bottom of the sea despite its promises of unsinkability. I cried for the fifteen hundred mostly steerage-class souls who didn't make it, who had danced jigs earlier that night, totally unaware they'd never see the Statue of Liberty. I accompanied Dale to *Snoopy on Ice: A Cool Christmas* and watched skaters leap from giant presents. We applauded when the rest of the audience applauded, gasped when the rest of the audience gasped. I felt like a normal person.

Until I didn't. Which happened suddenly too. The space between me and everything, everyone else expanding once again. I was far away. Somewhere cold. On Mars.

The day after our final, mostly-placebo, dose of methadone my bones began to ache and my legs began to thrash and my skin began to crawl. I had to leave work early due to the fear: a big, terrible doom that closed in around me until I was looking through a pinhole. The snowmen cheese knives, still on my desk, seemed demonic – cute garbage made by exploited children in some third-world factory to stuff into a landfill. A stupid song played: "I will do the dishes if you pay all the bills." The smell of old burnt coffee was triggering. So was the periodic glug from the watercooler. I ran out the front door in a panic, resisting the urge to key the purple car for no reason other than to release the pressure inside of me.

When I got home, I found Dale in the street again. He was not looking up at the sky. He was looking in the trash – digging, really – his whole upper body submerged. I went to help him. Here was a rolled-up maxi pad, and there was a gooey Styrofoam tray that had held last week's chicken thighs.

"Here's our rigs," I said, retrieving a bag from the depths.

Above us, an Ursid meteor shower reached its peak. But we didn't notice.

CHAPTER EIGHT

Rudolph's Nose

"Stand here," Glorianne said, handing me a wooden spoon. "Now keep stirring. You don't want to burn it. See how it's starting to fizz up like that? That's what you want. When it gets the color of honey, take it off."

It was Christmas Eve, and she was making her famous dessert, Chocolate Drizzle, whose recipe she'd contributed a decade earlier to a spiral-bound community-church cookbook. We referred to it as a cake, but it was more akin to candy, consisting of three distinct layers: a brownie base; a pale, pasty confection; and a hard, glassy laminate of dark chocolate. Glorianne left me in charge of the middle stuff, which turned out was nothing more than butter, sugar, and science.

I dragged the spoon through the shallow of melted butter and wondered what, exactly, was the color of honey. Was it a precise and unmistakable shade that would be obvious the moment I saw it? Every second that passed I assessed the hue of the pan's contents and believed it could be one or two seconds more honey-ish. But after three or four of those one or two seconds it turned abruptly too dark. The color of chaw spit, of cola whose ice had melted. It sizzled meanly and made bitter smoke.

"Shit fucking fuck," I hissed, lifting the pan from the burner.

"Are you all right?" Glorianne asked. "Did you burn yourself?"

"I ruined it. It happened so fast. I swear I was paying attention."

"Hey, hey," she said, patting my shoulder. "No biggie. Try it again." She handed me a new stick of butter.

The butter went from cold and hard to sliding all over the hot enamel in its own shine. From raw and bland to toasty to complex.

Chemically altered. Rearranged. Something other than what it
had been, and what it had been before that. I yanked it from the
burner a pulse before my instincts told me to, poured it into a
bowl because the instructions said to. Despite doing everything
I was supposed to do, it was contaminated with millions of dots.

"I give up," I said.

Glorianne glanced into the bowl. "What on earth are you
talking about? It's perfect."

"Look at all that burnt stuff, though. Maybe we can get it out
with a paper towel?"

"No! Those are the yummy bits! They're what make it what it
is."

I sought out error in everything I did, saw its dire glare even
when it wasn't there. The million dots of it a relief, a reason to
discontinue, a release of the pressure that closed in on me from
all angles, even amid the most inconsequential task. This was a
strain of perfectionism that wouldn't allow the tiniest error. It
was pre-defeated. Everything was much too precious to mar with
my own marred self.

Later, Dale and I headed over to Gramma and Grampa's. They
hosted every Christmas Eve — a celebration that included pink
cheeseballs paved in pecans and store-bought pies, a massive pile
of gifts under a fake, flamboyant tree, and hundred-dollar bills
tucked into slim cards. They lived in a black house. The only
black house I'd ever seen. It was a low, elongated ranch that looked
like a late-day shadow. When we arrived, cars were snaked along
the front yard, bumper-to-bumper, tires on grass. Or they were
squeezed up onto the driveway, trunks jutting out into the street,
no sidewalk to block. The familiar stick and squeak of the front
door gave way to the bowed linoleum of the dim entryway, where
purses and coats were heaped. When we walked in, everyone was
already eating — "kids" around the table off the kitchen, adults in

the wood-paneled dining room. I didn't know where I belonged. "Either one," Gramma said, but I couldn't decide where I wanted to be, where I made the most sense. Aly, Aaron, Foster, Michael, and my cousins Ben and Ashley sat at one table, making disgusting concoctions with the leftover food on their plates, which they then dared each other to eat. At the other table, the elders – the aunts and uncles and longtime family friends – leaned back in their creaking chairs with their arms crossed, top buttons surely undone, faces flushed with spirits. They grunted and sighed about things I almost understood, about people whose names I'd heard in conversations before.

By the looks of the depleted buffet, which queued along the kitchen counter, everyone was already on seconds. I took a plate and piled it with ravioli from a disposable aluminum pan, green Jell-O, green salad drowned in Newman's Own. I sailed into the dining room, loud and staticky, my right eye lazed outward. Dale trailed behind with hardly a thing on his plate, a cigarette tucked behind his ear. I scooched an empty chair between Mom and Molly, who nursed her baby at the table, her engorged breast streaked in dark stretch marks.

Gramma said to me: "You're worse than Brad!" because my uncle was notoriously late. She laughed then sucked on her front tooth, the fake one that was whiter than the rest. Mom fidgeted, shifted in her seat as I took mine, watched me with a look on her mouth. Stacey, Brad's girlfriend, rolled her eyes. She didn't hide the fact she couldn't stand me. She asked me how I was doing, baitingly, her eyes darting over to Mom, then Brad, who wore a poker face. I felt the familiar tug of hurt. It awakened my anger. I wanted to hurt back, to make everyone in the room feel sorry for me or be shocked and disgusted by me. I launched into a gratuitous story about having narrowly escaped rape a few days prior. It expelled from me like vomit. People cleared their throats and shot each other looks with raised brows. They stared uncomfortably at their scraped plates.

There was visible sweat on a few foreheads, mine included. Mom attempted to change the subject, but I steamrolled her.

"I was in the passenger seat," I said, loudly, almost proud. "I kicked him, hit him in the face. I just barely managed to open the door and he pushed me out of his car, drove off with all my money." My heart was racing. I was breathless. Telling the story reminded me of when I had confessed to Mom I was using. I continued to list off increasingly disturbing details, hoping for a reaction I never received.

No one wanted the conversation to be happening. The men got up, cleared dishes. Even Dale left the room, went out the sliding door to smoke.

"And so why were you in this person's car?" Mom asked, narrowing her eyes. It was her gotcha.

"He was a friend," I said, taking a bite of dinner roll. "Or that's what I thought, anyway."

"Well, how did he get your money? Why didn't you call the police?" A smug smile edged over her lips.

I felt trapped. Pushed my chin out and held back tears. Messed my fork through my Jell-O.

"Why are you bringing this up now, Karleigh? On Christmas Eve? At the dinner table? It's not appropriate."

Perhaps appropriateness was Mom's guiding concern. She made sure at all times to be seemly, comely, kindly, and tidy. In the company of others, she was one to listen and smile, rarely speak. And was mortified by women with volume and breeze and too many words. Cringed at their unkempt grays and racy disclosures, their table-slapping guffaws. She feared appearing low or coarse or loose or dumb by association, even if the association was nothing more than a body part.

It was worse if the crassness came from her own daughter. It was as if my behavior revealed some quashed truth about her. As Audre Lorde said in her biomythography, *Zami: A New Spelling of*

My Name: "I am a reflection of my mother's secret poetry as well as of her hidden angers."

To repress the earthy impulse and display only angelic decency was a holdover, a Victorian standard foisted upon white, bourgeoise mothers who were expected to uphold unattainable standards of virtuousness and providence in the face of a new industrial era. Psychologist Shari L. Thurer has written that the separation of work from home, and the resulting creation of binary spheres, was the leading reason for Mother's exaltation. Against the cold, cruel world of the factory, the bustling, filthy streets, was the warm, safe haven maintained by Mother. Domesticity was fetishized, and Mother was sanctified at the expense of being simplified. "Mother inspired outbursts of insipid rhapsody," wrote Thurer. "No longer mere flesh, but a glorified substance, a glow, she was idealized to the point of parody."

Despite Mom's overconcern for how others perceived her, she never hesitated to yank out a boob in public to feed us. In the 1970s and early '80s, this was either the hippie's political act or the hillbilly's lowbred way. Both indecent and threatening order. I don't know what made Mom more uncomfortable: to be seen as a bra-burning, second-wave feminist or as a dim-witted bumpkin. But it didn't matter, anyway. Her commitment to motherhood, to her children's good health, far outweighed the embarrassment of being scoffed at, stared at.

Mom wrote a letter to the editor of our local paper after a woman had shamed her for nursing in the mall. It was published on May 16, 1977. "I think He must be insulted," she wrote, appealing to Christian faith, "to see how some women have turned down the use of His perfect method of feeding a baby in favor of the bottle." Mom took the shame that hissed off the woman's lips and handed it back as guilt — those being our best weapons. Maybe our only weapons.

"Oh, I'm sorry, Mom," I said, caustic. "Is this an inconvenient time? Maybe I should've told him to wait to *rape* me until after the holidays so my mother could deal with it better."

"Don't be smart."

"Do you even care that I was almost a victim of *rape?*" I wanted to keep saying it: rape, rape, rape. I wanted the word to thrust inside her, leave her disgraced, empty, *guilty*.

The truth was, *I* didn't even care that I was almost a victim of rape. Or that I was, indeed, a victim of something. Had borne the jump-scare of a revealed penis, the velocity of heart rate, the vertigo of a surprise reality as I thrashed against flesh and plush in a parked car. It was par for the course, yet another transgression I'd shrugged off with the help of heroin. I was so disconnected from my body, it was as if it hadn't even happened to me at all. I believed the core of violence was contained in its retelling, not in its actual act. I used the violation as both armament and an appeal to pathos. They wanted a trainwreck, I'd give them a fucking trainwreck. I'd give them all the hot and twisted metal, the explosions and noxious smoke, a runaway cornfield meet between the old me and the present me — neither of them actually me.

The then-me had convinced herself she was only there to collect her free dinner and drug money, gifts to return or resell. The then-me didn't want to admit that the desires of the old me still existed, the part of her that wanted, as in olden days, happy golden days of yore. That wanted to repeat the sounding joy because tradition bolstered a sense of belonging. That wanted to snuggle up together like birds of a feather, to conspire by the fire, to strike the harp and join the chorus. But deeper still, and truer, was the acknowledgment that it had never been like those carols. That really, dinner tables aside, she never knew where she belonged.

When Mom and Dad were still married, holidays, particularly Christmases, were a source of stress and contention for them. Us

kids never really knew the extent of it – we were distracted by the
night sky, which we scrutinized from the back seat of the Caprice
on our way to San Francisco, searching among the stars for a
red aberration, an airplane or a tower light we had convinced
ourselves was Rudolph's nose. "This could be Little Grandma's
last year with us," Dad would say every year. "She's getting so
old." And Mom, known for her lead foot, would weave through
southbound holiday traffic, roll through crestal stop signs as we
cut through Pacific Heights.

Dad's maternal grandmother, the original Mercedes – who
came before Dad Mike's prophetic car and my influential friend
– was referred to by us as Little Grandma due to her eensy stat-
ure. She lived in a narrow apartment near Dolores Park, across
the street from a middle school. She'd followed her daughter,
Grandma Coco, not long after Grandma Coco returned to America
after having been deported. My great-grandfather Carlos stayed
behind in Managua. I never met him, but there are pictures, and
he looks like my brother Aaron, looks like me. Their youngest
son, Simón, lived in the apartment above Little Grandma's. He
was Dad's favorite uncle, used to take him to see Jefferson Airplane
or the Dead or Santana at the Winterland. Throughout the city,
under webs of crisscrossing electrical wires, up and down steep
hills of pastel-plastered houses, lived cousins and second cousins,
great-aunts and -uncles, new babies. They all had brown skin and
spoke Spanish. They'd be there, every Christmas Eve, all crammed
in Little Grandma's little living room, talking and talking, but I
couldn't understand them. I didn't know even half these relatives'
names, let alone how to pronounce them; didn't know what they
were to me. Overwhelmed, I'd seek refuge in Little Grandma's
bedroom, which had glow-in-the-dark Jesuses everywhere, glow-
in-the-dark hands on a mumbling bedside clock.

As soon as we were done eating, before even dessert, Mom
would put on her coat and tell us it was time to leave. Little

Grandma would insist we take leftovers, packing up margarine tubs and shoving them at us. And then we'd be in the car, Elvis's "Blue Christmas" on the radio, on our way to Gramma and Grampa's in time for pie and presents. And there, among the uncles who spun me around and put me on their shoulders, among the crass humor and practical jokes of Gramma and Aunt Diane, and the piles of torn and crumpled wrapping paper, which had moments before been neatly cornered, taped, ribboned, and bowed to a faceted Mattel box containing the exact Barbie I had wanted, had begged for, had circled in a catalog, I felt, momentarily, I belonged.

It wasn't till a few years later that I'd began to conflate seemingly harmless comments about Dad and his ethnicity with other, more disparaging ones about his personality. It sounded like this: *Your father is Hispanic. Your father is a bum, a dreamer, a liar, a manipulator, violent. You are Hispanic, what with that coarse, rebellious hair just like your father's. Therefore, you are a bum, a dreamer, a liar, a manipulator, violent. Therefore, all Hispanic people are. It's something inside of you that will never change.* I grew increasingly uncomfortable around my white family, believing they secretly judged me, were grossed out by me. I could feel acutely my otherness at family functions with Mom's side. The all-American second cousins with next-door faces, legs like hot dogs; the outdoorsy aunts with year-round suntans, ski racks on their all-wheel-drives; the good ol' boys with year-round sunburns, who fished and built decks and listened to new country. I was an imposter with my weak breaststroke, my fear of drowning, my preference for books over Sea-Doos. With my bristly pubic line and shapely hips, my coarse, rebellious hair. I did not fit. I was inappropriate.

I concluded that all my differences, my illness-at-ease, had something to do with my half-ness, which wasn't entirely accurate either, as I wasn't even half Nicaraguan, but a quarter. I said half because it was easier, was closer to the truth than the truth. Because Dad was Latino through and through – physically, culturally, experientially – I must have been half. To say I was only a quarter, an insignificant, unfelt, and unseen portion waved off with a dismissive hand, would be incorrect. What is Nicaraguan anyway but a mix of Indigenous American, Spaniard, English, Senegalese, and Ghanian (according to my specific DNA story), simmering over hundreds of years, migrating and morphing. The brain has no idea what the blood comprises, so it's probably best not to use scientific metrics – not halves, but *sides*. And in between a wide chasm.

The writer Malcolm Gladwell, who is half white and half West Indian, recalled the day a teammate, a West Indian man, asked him what he was.

> I remember blinking and stammering momentarily overwhelmed by that word *what*. I had always thought that my singular alienation was the result of who I was. But now it occurred to me that perhaps it was the result of something entirely external – the result of nuances of color and skin and lip and curl that put me just outside the world of people like [my teammate] and just outside the world of people I grew up with.

Opposite Gladwell, I had assumed that my "singular alienation" was a matter of *what* I was over *who* I was. That my queerness had something to do with my ethnic not-enough-ness. Not white enough, not brown enough. As if each side of me had been slightly contaminated by the other. I was impure. Freakish. A million dots. *A very shiny nose.*

Gladwell went on to say that he'd never felt whiter than when he was around West Indians, and never more West Indian than when he was around white people. It's this never-easing tension between imposter syndrome and identification that makes even something as low stakes as filling out forms a distressing experience. The choice between *Hispanic* or *white (non-Hispanic)* makes me anxious to the point of nausea. Neither option is true. To choose one would be to reject, betray, the other. It's easier to leave all boxes unticked. Easier still just to pick both, if I can, wondering if they will just cancel each other out.

I had these imposter/identification feelings with everything. I was both poorish and richish, as familiar with the supple leather interior of Dad Mike's luxury car as I was with the reeking, flood-damaged carpet of Dad's basement apartment, whose loose yarns I'd yank across the room, leaving runs that exposed the grid of jute below it. I'd received a pair of statusy Guess jeans from Mom and Dad Mike for Christmas the same year I got a box simply marked girl from Dad. Inside was a doll better suited for a first-grader (I was freshly eleven, already shaving with those pink razors, Dad rubbing his stinging deodorant on my various nicks to stop their bleeds). Molly's box said boy or girl and contained a jigsaw puzzle featuring a gender-neutral landscape. The volunteers seemed so happy when they dropped off the gifts. I feigned excitement for their sake. Weeks earlier Mom had me put all my old toys in a box. "These will be Christmas presents for needy kids," she'd said. I wondered if I'd reunite with my own castoff the following year.

Earlier that same year, I had started fifth grade at a new school in a different district. It was walking distance to Dad Mike's house and seemed more like a high school. It had lockers, cheerleaders, sports teams. Girls my own age already looked like teenagers with their trendy clothes and body-wave perms and periods. They took ballet lessons. Traveled to Paris. Lived in glass geometries on steep hillsides. Even those who lived in humble farmhouses were rich in a way I couldn't put my finger on. Rich in something other than money. I told them about the sprawling acreage I lived on, not fully understanding the difference between renting and owning. Not realizing there was an invisible fence between the apple farm's orchards and our backyard. I told them my house was Victorian because I thought Victorian meant *old*. I thought this was how one made friends at Twin Hills school. My home-room teacher was a woman named Ms. Ice-Robinson who wore big, triangle-shaped earrings and her hair in a sassy crop. She had us do yoga, meditate, build our own classroom tables (because individual desks hindered community), and learn the Javan art of batik. She had us make collages that represented ourselves: our goals, our beliefs, our families, our identities. Inspired by one of Mom's vision boards, I glued onto pages of cut poster board pictures of marble foyers, infinity pools, and fashion-ad families (think "dads" in yacht-club whites, their "daughters" wearing outsized taffeta bows in their hair). Ms. Ice-Robinson returned mine with an unsatisfactory mark and a *tsk-tsk*. Something about it lacking creativity, but I assume now it had more to do with the cringy display of materialism she associated with shallowness, un-enlightenment. I think she'd forgotten I was only a child.

Because my family's membership at church was spotty, I felt like a fraud at Sunday school too. I was a smirking skeptic who laughed out loud when our pastor said that God's eyes were everywhere, picturing pairs of eyeballs left in junk drawers, atop bookshelves, under couches. The children who kept regular attendance and memorized Bible verses watched me askance, swallowing their giggles.

I was a fraudulent clarinet player whose often silent instrument was hidden by the sounds of everyone else's. I faked the finger positions, made my eyes follow the sheet music I couldn't actually read. I am the fraudulent leftist who subscribes to the ideologies but not necessarily all the methods. The fraudulent writer who hasn't read the canon, doesn't grasp the allusions, my vocabulary lacking as it was not assembled naturally and osmotically since childhood but intentionally determined in middle age. I'm the fraudulent daughter.

I wonder if people ever really feel like they belong anywhere, or if they're all just pretending like me. Hiding their nervousness with glasses of Pinot Grigio, with beta-blockers, their incompetency with rehearsed phrases and practiced smiles, their betrayals in the pits of their stomachs, pits of their arms.

Mom looked at me pleadingly yet angrily. I had taken it too far. If I could've untold the story, unsaid that intrusive word, I would have. I spent the rest of the evening making up for it. Ladylike, I was, nodding and smiling, legs crossed, for Mom. Like Mom. Maybe they'd all forget. Maybe they'd all pretend. Maybe I was the furthest thing from their minds anyway. Mom watched me, her hands flattening and folding wrapping paper she plucked from the floor.

The next day, Christmas Day, Glorianne, Duane, Dale, his brother Ben, and I ate lamb chops and green beans around the dining room table, which had been cleared off and adorned with red and green table linens, the good silver. Classical music played on the CD player — Bach's Magnificat, maybe. We passed dishes around. Shared stories. Later, we sat around the tree with slices of Chocolate Drizzle. We passed presents around. Dale got a Leatherman pocketknife he kept flipping open to admire its blade. "Santa" brought me a pair of satin Charter Club pajamas. They were red with a black lace trim, matching the streaks of Manic Panic in my hair. I also received a votive holder made of wire and red glass beads, fashioned after an old-timey boudoir lamp, and a Yankee candle that purported to smell like cranberry. I never burned it because burning it would mean no longer having it. And I needed the proof of it. The evidence that I belonged somewhere.

CHAPTER NINE

Looking Glass

The new year brought news of probable water on the moon, a probable affair in the White House, probable rain, but days were mostly dry, socked in fog till the afternoon hours, the quietest hours in the house with Duane still at work and Glorianne napping, her dog asleep too, one ear perked.

I stood in the dining room, where dusty sunlight speared through a west-facing window, illuminating a city of glass — all pinks, greens, and yellows. There were plates and vases and sugar bowls. Whimsies shaped like hats, boots, and hens. I traced my finger along the ruffled rim of a candy dish, lifted it from its spot and wiped its dust with my shirt, then gently wrapped it in a dish towel and slipped it into my backpack.

I had been making justifications for days. There was a pitcher, teetering on a pile of linens, about to fall and smash into bits anyway. There was a slim, never-to-be-missed crystal platter slipped between a stack of miscellany, its gorgeous hand-cut starbursts wasted. I put a few more things in my bag, listening for steps down the hall.

I changed out of my pajamas and into a pair of pin-striped clearance-rack slacks Mom had bought me for a job interview some years before. "I'm just curious if these are worth anything," I said to the mirror, rehearsing. "They were my grandmother's." I made my eyes sorrowful.

I rolled up the right leg of my pants and silently coasted down the driveway on Duane's bike. It was a short ride down the highway to the antiques store with the windmill out front, the sign that declared they were open seven days. Bells on the door chimed when I opened it. An older man stood behind the counter inspecting a clock with a magnifying glass.

"What can I do you for?" he asked.

"Do you buy antiques?" A sign on the door said they did.

"Depends what you got." His voice was cowboy.

I unzipped my pack and unwrapped my goods, placing them gently on the counter. The man, who introduced himself as Bill, examined each one with a frown.

"Where'd you come across these, if you don't mind me asking?"

"They were my grandma's," I said.

He bent his brow at me.

"She passed, sadly."

"You oughta hang on to 'em. Keepsakes."

"I don't really need them," I said. "I more need the money so I can pay my bills. The gas. So they don't turn it off. Because I haven't been able to work. Taking care of my grandma and all. The one that died." I laughed uncomfortably and tried to read Bill's face. He was tilting the underside of a vase this way and that, squinting.

"But probably I'm gonna get a job at Safeway. Got an interview tomorrow."

"They're union," he said, flipping over a plate and reading the imprint. "Pay well." Then he stood back with his arms crossed, his mouth in a contemplative scowl.

I figured he'd give me nothing. Tell me it was a bunch of crap and toodle-oo.

"I can do fifty but no more than that," he said, flattening his lips. "There's a little chip on this one, and honestly I'm going to have a hard time getting rid of it."

He handed me actual cash from the till. Two twenties and a bunch of ones. I shoved it in my pocket and hustled to the door before he could change his mind.

"Your bag," he said, lifting it up and waving it.

"Oh, thanks," I said, breathless. I slid its straps back over my shoulders, so light it felt like potential.

"Good luck at that interview."

I had already forgotten what he was referring to.

I became obsessed with glass. I imagined an endless supply in shades of lollipop, each piece forcing Bill to open the till, to hand me fans of twenties I'd slip through window cracks for grams of black tar.

"What's in the sheds?" I asked Dale one afternoon.

He turned his entire body to face me. The glint in his aqua eyes was crystal-clear.

Early the next morning, in my pajamas and an oversized rain slicker I'd borrowed from the hall closet, I went and listened to a lock – for its whispered clicks, the subtle shifts in its tumblers' resistance. I wrote numbers on the back of my hand. Farther up the walkway, Dale stood on guard, ready to cough should Glori-anne appear. Finally, the shackle slackened under my hand: The first shed was open.

It was so jam-packed, I could hardly fit inside. From the top of the frontmost stack, I brought down a cardboard box. It was soft and bulging, its yellowed packing tape no longer taping. I put it on the damp ground outside and opened it. Inside were lumps of faded newsprint, mouse turds and dried spiders in every crevice and contour. I unwrapped the first lump: bone china I could see the stippled sunrise through. The next one had a bundle of tarnished silverware that clacked in my hand. There was mint-colored milk glass, gold-foiled barware, and Christmas ornaments as delicate as eggshells. I folded the pieces back into the newspaper and gently wedged everything into my empty backpack before putting the box back where I'd found it.

A two-hour drive up the coast from Sebastopol is a place known as Glass Beach, named so for its bedazzled shore. It's in the drizzly Mendocino County town of Fort Bragg, a former military base on an Indian reservation, both of which – the base and the reservation – were completely deserted by 1867. Pomo, Whilkut, Wappo, and Yuki tribes had been forced to relocate east to Bald Hill or Round Valley. Within two years, Fort Bragg had reestablished itself as a lumber town, erected mills on every creek bed.

In 1906, the same year the earthquake leveled everything from San Francisco to Santa Rosa to as far north as even Fort Bragg, an offshore dump was designated behind one of these lumber companies that, in the wake of the disaster, prospered as one of the primary suppliers of San Francisco's massive rebuilding effort. Everything from spent machinery parts to emptied bottles and vats – trash both domestic and industrial – was tossed into the water. As the dump site filled, it too relocated, a smidge up the coastline, and then once again, before being shut down by the state's Environmental Protection Agency in 1967.

Thirty years after the dump's closure, transformed waste began washing up on the shore. What appeared to be rare rocks had once been bottles of Nehi, of cough syrup or fatty local milk or machine oil, jars that had once held olives or pears, the shattered windowpanes of buildings that had toppled in seismic upset nearly a century before. The shards of so much multicolored glass had been tumbled smooth over the decades by the Pacific's ragged surf.

Though prohibited, tourists fill their pockets with the sugared glass stones. Some of it gets swept back out into the sea.

Sand is everywhere, ordinary and abundant. It's the beaches and deserts, the crumble of mantle and mountain. From it we make highways and iPhones, the colors for our canvases and walls, eyelids and fingernails. We make the very glass that has washed back upon it, the magnetic pull to its origin, the poetic return to the simplest element, the eternal substance.

Mixed with ash and lime and melted in the heat of two thousand miles deep, it's then cooled solid. Its invention is ancient, older than the Old Testament, its recipe preserved in cuneiform on a clay tablet from neo-Babylonian times. But earlier still is the volcano, nature's crucible, turning molten lava into obsidian.

Glass gave us the ability to see. Windows and mirrors. Lamps and lightbulbs. The stained fenestrae of cathedrals through which to observe God. Beakers and flasks. Medicine vials. The many lenses, concave and convex, to see planets and stars, cells dividing, words on a page. Crystal balls.

What did Glorianne see through all that old glass? Her ponytailed mother, thin in a homemade dress, holding her? The mother, she reminded me over and over and over again, who had abandoned her? The mother she was tirelessly looking for? Could Glorianne see the witch-broom trees scraping the weak sky? Could she hear the bullfrogs, the church bells, the wind? And what was it I saw in all that old glass?

February came and we watched Tara Lipinski and Michelle Kwan land triple-lutz-double-toe-loop combinations on the glassy ice in Nagano. Kwan was the probable winner, according to *Sports Illustrated*, but it was Lipinski who took the gold. I continued bringing things to Bill a few times a week, the sheds becoming lighter, the winds becoming stronger.

Bill preferred the Fenton, which Glorianne had plenty of: hobnail pitchers and coin dot candlesticks; carnival plates with dragons and peacocks; cane-handled macaroon jars and tasseled atomizers. Bill gave me short lessons about each item.

"Now, see this here?" he asked, holding up a vase I had brought. "See how it's got this sort of filmy look? That's stretch glass."

"Looks soft."

"That's right. A process called iridization gives it that effect. Doping, they call it. This piece here's from the late 1920s."

"How do you know for sure?"

He told me it was a matter of putting together clues. The brand marking on the bottom, or the omission of one. The specific color or pattern. "When you been doing this as long as I have, you recognize what's what pretty quick."

In 1906, same year as the earthquake and the dump opening, across the country, in Williamstown, West Virginia, a glassmaking factory was built. It was named Fenton after the two brothers who started it. Two brothers who, biblically, rivaled — one opening a competitor company across the river in Ohio that ultimately failed, as the story always goes.

Fenton got famous on carnival glass. Poor Man's Tiffany, people called it. Salts and metalloids were sprayed onto the glass, causing a reaction that altered the color and finish. The end product resembled a driveway puddle, a jewel bug's backside, the oil-filled stickers of my youth — ones I'd rub my fingers over to make swirls of violet, green, and gold. I thought this was why it was called carnival — because its dizzying, shifting colors were reminiscent of the oscillating lights of midway Tilt-A-Whirls. Really, it was because surplus pieces were given away as game-booth prizes at county fairs.

After the stock-market crash, American glassmakers began manufacturing what's now known as Depression glass — mass-produced, subpar tableware in translucent Easter hues. Sold in dime stores for pennies apiece. They came free in boxes of cereal or laundry detergent. Handed out at gas stations with a fill-up — promotional plates machine-embossed with the heads of presidents.

Fenton made an elevated, pricier line of Depression glass known as elegant glass. It was handmade and flawless, sold on the don't-touch floors of department stores. Those designs were textured with bumps and blisters and ridges, etched with floral patterns or candy-striped with milky bands. But it was the production of, specifically, mixing bowls and perfume bottles – commissioned by two different Chicago-based companies: Dormeyer, a kitchen appliance manufacturer, and Wrisley, a cosmetics company – that safeguarded Fenton from going under during the Depression and secured their future as one of the country's top glassmakers.

The most popular name in mid-century American glass built its legacy on the two versions, or perhaps two sides, of the mid-century American woman. She was either a nurturer or a seductress. Belonged in the kitchen or the bedroom. A generous, open bowl of nourishment or a slim, discreet flacon, filled with something exotic and ineffable, applied sparingly to the heartbeat.

The majority of Fenton's customer base were, naturally, women. They shopped for those pretty things that were both serviceable and ornamental, or somewhere between the two. Like themselves, they've been told. A "dish," Mom was called by boys who signed her yearbook. Either the thing that delivers or the thing that's devoured. In service of or served. As in on a platter. Cut crystal.

March was wet. I watched the red-carpet portion of the Oscars and then put daisies in my hair like Drew Barrymore, except mine were weeds. I plucked out my widow's peak while I was there, in front of the mirror. Painted a beauty mark on my face. Rode to Bill with a footstool strapped to my back, its scrolled mahogany legs cloudward.

Bill offered to come to me so I wouldn't have to do all this "back-and-forth nonsense." He gestured at the stool and waved his hand like a trout. I told him no dice. Gave him a bunch of lame excuses.

He gave me thirty bucks – less than I was expecting – because some of the upholstery tacks were missing. With the handful of change I'd swiped from Duane's car's ashtray, I was eight bucks shy of a gram. Later, when I leaned into our guy's window, he counted my bills and said, "You said a g." And I said, "I'm like a couple bucks short, Puppy," and begged with my eyes. And Puppy said, "Eight dollars. That's no little bit. I give you a half and that's it." And I cried, draped myself from his door with my arms, swayed from side to side. "I need a g or I'm gonna be sick in the morning. And hafting to make money in the morning on top of that. I promise I can pay you tomorrow." He said I said that last time and handed me a half. I yanked off my ring and showed him where it said 14k on the inside and said he could keep it if I could have another half and he said no, it was junk. I said it was my mom's and it was real even though I got it from Annabelle as a trade for my cottons. Puppy tapped the gas. "C'mon, man!" I said. "Don't do this to me." He drove away.

I dramatically threw myself onto the ground, hoping I'd crack my skull. I pressed my face into the dirt. Then I picked myself up, brushed myself off, walked up to and inside the house, straight down the hall to our room. The remainder of the evening was just like this. Violence followed by mildness. Quiet responding to loud.

Glorianne called me timidly from her room.

"What?" I yelled.

"I've been meaning to ask you about the carpet in your room."

"What about it?"

"Do you happen to know what the black marks all over it are?"

"How the fuck should I know?"

"It looks like soot or something."

"Okay, smartie. Sounds like you already got it all figured out. Why are you even going in our room anyway?"

"Well. It's not *your* room, technically. Or Dale's."

"Oh. I forgot. It's your *hoard's* room. Did you know that? That you're a hoarder? You want us to hurry up and get out so you can put all your piles of pointless shit in there."

"You're being very unkind right now," she said too kindly.

"I'm just being honest. The truth hurts."

"You are absolutely *not* being honest." She grinned. "There's a truth."

"Well, here's another: You're a fat bitch."

"Would you stop shouting at me?"

"No!" I slammed our bedroom door so hard it rattled the jamb.

The rage that was really hurt was really fear that had latched itself to Glorianne like a leech, providing me with some sort of false nourishment. It had started small, a few months back. Some tiny, ill-aimed abuse she took with a compliant gulp, a charitable read. The next one was a little crueler, a test to see how far she'd let me go. Made anxious and irrational by heroin's uncertain terms, I took everything out on Glorianne because she let me. Once I began stealing from her, I became meaner. Every sugar bowl, bud vase, and footstool I smuggled to Bill's made me livid. Every time she allowed my abuse, met it with compassion, turned it into an opportunity to save me, to deliver some new-age pep talk, my abuse became less empty and indiscriminate. It swelled with hate, resentment, and disrespect. Repulsion, even, aimed specifically at her. I saw her as weak, the proof of her weakness in all that glass. The proof of my weakness in all that dope.

I wanted her to be mean back. To have a backbone. To kick me out. But I also very much didn't want that at all. Just as complicated were my feelings toward her. I loved her tremendously. I knew that she *got* me, understood all the parts of me my own mother didn't. It felt as if our bodies were connected, invisibly fused along our edges, along the length of our arms that held down the same beast. Like Judith and her maidservant Abra in the painting *Judith Slaying Holofernes* by Artemisia Gentileschi. Inspired by a scene in the Apocrypha's Book of Judith, the painting depicts the two women murdering the Assyrian general

Holofernes. They stand above him, their bodies strong yet soft, their gazes strong yet soft. Blood streams from the fatal neck wound down layers of sumptuous white bedding.

The next day, Glorianne called to me. Her voice was small and concerned. She smoothed the edge of the comforter and motioned for me to sit.

"I'm sorry I made you upset yesterday." She took my hands in hers. "My mother gave me away," she reminded me. "Abandoned me." She sighed and looked upward, her eyes watering a little. Her top lip tucked in. "I'm doing a lot of work on myself right now and I know I'm not perfect."

From where I sat, I could see a tippy stack of bags shoved into a corner, there so long each one had settled into the one under it, their paper faded and dusty, their contents bulging. Outside her sliding glass door was the quartet of old chairs she'd purchased when we first moved in, their cushions already rain-ruined. On her television, the Home Shopping Network featured life-sized baby dolls with terrifying porcelain faces, offered at two FlexPays of only $59.37.

"Sorry if I was a bitch," I said.

"You didn't mean it," she said. "You're right here, after all." She patted my thigh. I leaned back on the extra pillow, and a few credit-card offers slipped to the floor. Glorianne lifted the remote and changed the channel.

"Have you been paying attention to all this madness?" she asked, turning up the TV. "What a circus." It was a replay of President Clinton's denial. He sat in a White House room, a colorful flower arrangement and the corner of a gilded frame behind him. "There was not a relationship," he said in his Arkansas drawl.

"Liar!" Glorianne shouted, pointing a finger.

A photograph of Monica Lewinsky slammed onto the screen. Like me, she had thick, dark hair and a gummy smile.

"What a dumb hoebag," I said, helping myself to a bite of

Glorianne's ice cream, curling against her arm. "Probably thinks he actually *loves* her." I scoffed.

Glorianne did it again: two gentle taps above my knee with the broad part of her hand. It was a patient *come now*, a consoling *there, there*, a knowing *wink wink*. It was shorthand for the words she didn't want to say out loud for fear of scaring me away from her. But she saw me — saw all of my damage, my doings and undoings. In that moment, there on her bed, she knew I called Lewinsky a name for the same reasons I called her, Glorianne, names: I had a hurt inside of me, a blind, spewing rage that ticked away, and that rage was at myself, at all the mirrors of me — the weaknesses I could spot in Lewinsky's blue dress, in Glorianne's blind eye, in Mom's quivering lips.

In heeled pleather boots, the pin-striped slacks, and Duane's coat, I rode to Bill's during a break in the storm. Bill was outside, dragging a chair back in.

"Well, look who it is," he said as I leaned my bike against the building. "Was wondering if you were gonna be by today."

"Got more of that cranberry you like."

"Let's have a look-see."

I followed him inside and plopped my beanie on the counter.

"Voilà," I said, removing a vase from my pack. It was pretty.

"Spiral optic," he said.

"I have the whole matching set. Look. A salad dressing thingie."

"A cruet. Beautiful. Your grandmother sure had some nice stuff. Big collector, I take it?"

"Yeah," I said. "I don't really want to talk about my grandma right now, if that's cool."

"My apologies," Bill said. "Losing a loved one's a mighty hurt."

My mind went to Glorianne, how she suffered the loss of the mother she never even had the chance to know. A pang of guilt stabbed me between the shoulder blades, and I shuddered.

"Cold one today," Bill said.

I nodded, giving myself a hug, swaying side-to-side. It was fine what I was doing, which was pretty much a service to Glorianne, anyway, right? All that useless glass was just a headache she'd have to eventually deal with in her old age. Or maybe Dale would have to. He'd have to hire one of those estate-sale companies to hock it, or haul it all to the dump – a dozen truckloads for sure. I was taking things Glorianne didn't even remember she had. The by-products of her brokenness. I was turning her grief into my gold. A win-win, as far as I was concerned. As long as she maintained her addiction, I could maintain mine.

CHAPTER TEN

Goose Girl

I missed Mom. I never didn't, even when I had still lived at home. I told her everything, mundane and all. That I cut bangs, for example. Or that I just loaded the dishwasher. Or had my oil changed. Or had a yeast infection. By reporting to her, I felt real. Like the proverbial falling tree of the forest observed. I needed to insert myself in her mind because only then did I fully exist.

I called her from the family room, house all to myself, told her as much. Said the couch was white and scratchy and folded out into a bed, that there was an ugly abstract painting that hung on the wall behind it.

"Where is everyone?" she asked.

"Duane and Glorianne are at some church thing."

"They go to that Unitarian one on the highway?"

"Past the Burger King."

What I really wanted was to share things that would bring us closer together. But closeness meant discomfort. It meant mutual pain. Hedgehog's dilemma, they call it. So whatever my phone calls lacked in substance was made up for with long-windedness and regularity. Maybe, I thought, by giving her a glut of information I was allowed to withhold tidbits. Like the fact that I was still using. Or that I felt that I had always disappointed her. That I disappointed everybody.

Mom withheld too. We never spoke of the husband before Dad, when she was eighteen or nineteen. Over the years, I had picked up clues by eavesdropping, interrogating. There were drugs and alcohol – on his end, not Mom's. There was verbal abuse. Maybe some physical abuse. There was jail time. I knew he had a sister because Mom had run into her at a drive-in once. We were all sitting in the back seat as they spoke in hushed tones outside the car. They hugged before Mom walked up to get our order. Frosty cones and foil-wrapped burgers. I also knew he used to work at Grampa's pharmacy in some capacity. A handyman or delivery boy. Maybe even a pharmacy technician, like Dan. There was a framed picture of their wedding day buried in one of Gramma's dresser drawers. In it, Mom wears a white gown, false hair, frosty blue eyeshadow up to her brow. Her expression is either too trusting or mistrustful, I can't tell. A frozen smile that doesn't match her eyes. I've seen the expression before on the pastel-clad tweens born into cults where they marry old men, become sisters with their mothers.

I wanted to know why Creedence Clearwater Revival made Mom immediately change the station. Why "Hang on Sloopy" made her cry or shout or run away and hide. I wanted to know about the time between the first husband and Dad, when she lived with a bunch of friends in a house in Santa Rosa, when a man had broken in, crawled through a bedroom window and assaulted one of her roommates. She had told me this in passing once, to remind me to lock my doors and windows. I wanted to know how she felt keeping secrets for Grampa, about his handsiness with his female employees, and keeping the promise to him to be a best friend to Gramma, even when that meant skipping school too often so she could accompany her to the Northgate Mall in Marin. I wanted to know why Dad. Why us, one after the other.

"I think I'm gonna go to school for fashion design," I said. "Probably Parsons. Or FIT. But I'll start at the JC. Maybe next semester. They have sewing classes. I'm gonna make a pencil dress out of metallic tweed. I'm thinking boatneck. Bracelet sleeves. *Urbane.*"

My conversations with her were essentially replays of me in her bathroom, age six, the *Highlights* magazine in my lap: dinosaurs,

Timbertoes, magnets. Eventually, I thought, I'd talk her into being interested in me. Proud of me. Or at least reassured by how normal I was.

"What about that time you said you wanted to be a lawyer? When you said you were going to get into Davis?"

"Oh yeah. I think I just picked law out of thin air. Maybe cuz I wouldn't have to take math classes. And cuz Brad took us to the campus. Remember that?"

Our uncle had been doing a PhD program there at the time. He invited me, Aly, and Molly for a tour when I was eighteen, right after I'd graduated high school. It was hot that day, the grounds mostly empty. What I enjoyed most about the tour was the food hall. And the gift shop. Brad bought me a crewneck Aggies sweatshirt and a bumper sticker. I came home and announced that I was going to apply because I thought it would make everyone happy. But it didn't, so I didn't.

"There's a lot of math in fashion, though, right?" Mom said.

"No? I mean, maybe? But it's different. Why do you always have to do that?"

"Do what?"

"Not like I could've gotten into Davis anyways!"

"You got A's."

"In yearbook. And choir. And physical science. Which was a bonehead class. Did you know that? For people too dumb for chemistry or physics. And guess what I did in that class? I cleaned wrestling mats."

"You what?"

"And loaded them into a van. The teacher was the wrestling coach. Anyways. I can't afford it."

"Can't you get scholarships? Tell them you're Hispanic."

There was a little stab beneath my ribs. The suggestion felt expedient — fraudulent even. It felt othering. Doubtful. Like a backdoor she believed I should trespass because it would be my only way in.

"I have a bunch of sketches. I showed them to Glorianne the other night. She really liked them. She thinks I'm good."

"Oh, you just reminded me. Know who I just ran into? Andrea Montague. On Fourth Street. You wouldn't believe how beautiful she is. Tall. Thin. Glowing! She's in school to be a scientist or something."

The stab grew. Spread upward, so I could feel it in my heart. I coughed.

"You're not still smoking, are you?"

"Barely."

"It's so bad for you, honey. It'll kill you. And it stinks. Do you want stinky breath?"

I broke off a piece of tar and put it into a spoon.

"I just worry about you."

I held a lighter under the spoon, the phone's receiver under my jaw.

I interpreted her good-faith questions as doubt, her caution as disappointment, her professed worry as a stand-in for confessed love. I heard her fond appraisal of other people's daughters as hints at my inadequacies by comparison. I couldn't even take a compliment from her without hearing qualifiers, ulterior motives, or ignorance. Because I believed my existence was only validated by her perception of me, my sense of self was unstable, uncertain, and weak. As I approached new roads in life, and their various forks, I asked myself what she would think of my choices. And with every one, whether it be to do drugs or to go off to college, I'd see her heartbroken.

In the Brothers Grimm fairy tale "The Goose Girl," the titular character, a princess, stuffs a handkerchief dappled with her mother's blood into her bosom. Her mother insists it will protect her daughter during her travels. Accompanying the princess on her journey is her handmaid, who, once on the road, is defiant and refuses to be of service to the princess. The princess, meek and diffident, doesn't balk or argue, and stoops to her handmaid's orders. The handkerchief, appalled, speaks: "If your mother knew, her heart would break."

It isn't until the hankie is lost, slipped from the princess's bodice and into the river, that the handmaid is able to completely dominate the princess, demanding that they swap horses, clothing, duties, titles – lives. Put another way, only once the princess is able to ignore her guilty conscience, the echoes of her mother's desires for her, and her own need for her mother's approval, is she able to become someone else. Someone wholly separate from her mother.

But even as someone else, a lowly gooseherd in a faraway place, her persistent mother-guilt resumes, this time through the severed head of her beloved horse: "Alas, Young Queen, how ill you fare!" the equine mount, hanging on an archway wall, says. "If your tender mother knew, her heart would surely break in two."

From the moment I could see her seeing me, making me smile with her smiles, I wanted to give her the gift of being proud of me. Of clapping her hands together and saying *Yay!* every time I did something. It was a gift that made her beam like sunshine – and that sunshine expanded inside of me and warmed me. This is when her happiness became my own. When I started to care more about how she thought about me than how *I* thought about me. When I started to conflate guilt with love, for when I didn't gladden her I felt that stab in the proximity of my heart.

Mom's feelings and opinions about things I did or did not do were often determined by other people's feelings and opinions about what I did or did not do. Even complete strangers. For example, when I graduated with my MFA many years later, in 2019, one of my professors – a brilliant and distinguished author whose latest book Mom had read about in *People* or *O Magazine* or *Elle* – told Mom that I was a very good writer. Mom looked surprised. "She is?" she asked. "You really think that?" My professor, both confused and amused, said, "You should be proud." And only then was she. Not that she had to be convinced. Mom doesn't suffer from a lack of feelings or opinions, she's just learned not to trust anything that springs from her own mind or body. I'm the exact same way.

Sometimes, I imagine her dead – maybe a year or two after her passing, when the grieving is no longer acute. Though painful, I close my eyes and try to feel how I'd feel. I enter this thought experiment with the expectation that I'll have a sense of freedom – free to be the junkie loser I am; free to be the success I've never believed I could be. But I fool myself each time. What I feel instead is the loss of her – stark and vast. And with that loss there's no longer any difference between loser and success, between peasant and princess, between free and bound. There's nothing left at all.

And if I imagine this hypothetical, feel the attendant pall of meaninglessness cast broadly, so must Mom. We've learned by mirroring each other, after all. All six of us, without instructions, needy in every sense of the word, screaming for her attention before we were even completely separate, seconds old, umbilical cords intact. And all Mom's work, not seen as work at all but as an unpaid and undervalued expectation, became her identity. To lose just one of us, her sense of self is compromised. All meaning she has made vanishes.

There's a poem by Adrienne Rich that references "The Goose Girl" in its middle stanza – specifically the refrain as uttered by the horse head as it hangs in the archway. It's a poem about doorways, passageways, gateways – the structures that mark a passing, that separate one place from another, one stage from another. It is a poem about poetry. It is, by my read, also a poem about women, about the mothers and/or daughters we are. A poem about how the things that define and stabilize are also the things that inspirit pain, that at once articulate it and absorb it. "The Fact of a Doorframe / means there is something to hold / onto with both hands / while slowly thrusting my forehead against the wood / and taking it away / one of the oldest motions of suffering."

Mom was my doorframe. Or if not her, flesh and blood, then the symbol of her. The yearning she imprinted on me, the gesture of holding on tightly in order to be held. Like standing, as I have, in the doorway during a 7.3 on the Richter, grasping the jamb as everything crashed around me.

The goose girl does not end up a goose girl. She reclaims her royal station, marries her prince, makes sure the handmaid suffers a violent death for her chicanery. The story ends without any more mother-guilt, without any mention of Mother at all.

As I slid the needle out from the top of my foot, I told Mom about the strip steak Dale had grilled over a hibachi the night before. As I lay down on my back, lifting that foot to the ceiling so the dope would hurry and rush down to my brain, I told her my rag had started. As I shifted, slipping, a part of me sleeping, I told her about a song I liked – Sarah McLachlan's "Angel." I hummed, sang a phrase, asked if she'd heard it on the radio. Soon she sighed and gave the long "Welllll . . ." that always came before "I should probably let you go." But I never wanted her to let me go. I kept her on as long as I could, postponing the inevitable click, the severed line between us. "Just one more thing," I said. "I'll make it quick!"

CHAPTER ELEVEN

Admission

I woke one morning to the swirling song of a thrush on an apple branch and decided that I wanted, truly wanted, to be clean. Maybe it was the green tips that poked though the earth that made me hopeful, the first glimpse of petal peeking from their sepals, ruffly and neon. Maybe it was the ground beneath my feet, the chaos of bulbs stirring and roots stretching, that inspired me. I wanted to be more like those tulips and irises, those trees that smelled like jizz. They were all so determined, with their embarrassing scents and doomed blooms, pushing through pavement anyway.

I called Mom and admitted everything. The methadone detox didn't stick. My attempts at cold turkey were too excruciating. I needed longer care, better guidance, tools. Mom said, "I just can't trust you anymore. Clean. Not clean. Clean. Not clean. Which is it?"

"I *was* clean."

"Exactly. So what's going to stop you from relapsing again if we help you out?"

"Rehab will be different," I said.

"How can we be sure of that?"

"Please just trust me," I said.

She took the problem to Dad Mike and they discussed it for a couple of days. Moved it around in their mouths like a lozenge till it became sharp and brittle. When they called me back I went outside to the koi pond bridge, squatted on its curvature, watched a snail.

"Hi, Karleigh Anne. Dad here. Got you on speaker. Your mother's here too."

"Hi, sweetie," she said.

"So here's the deal. We talked it over and decided that you need to put in some effort, as a show of your commitment. If you sell all your remaining assets — your car, your guitar, your stereo, your records maybe — and use that toward the cost of rehab, we'll loan you the rest of the money you'll need. And then, further down the line, we can discuss repayment. Set up some kind of payment plan. How does that sound?"

It sounded like shit to me. It seemed unfair to have to symbolically prove my seriousness by sacrificing the few janky but beloved things I still owned (an old Honda with close to three hundred thousand miles; a China-made budget-line Squier guitar; an all-in-one Aiwa stereo I bought through an Amway-adjacent catalog; milk crates of Pixies and Stooges and Guided by Voices, stuffy-nosed punk bands I'd seen play in filthy living rooms and after-hours post-office lobbies, girls from Olympia that warbled and barked, every Stones record). I started sniffling, weeping silently. Covering the mouthpiece so they wouldn't know.

I was always timorously reaching for something, an object or an experience or a skill, all of which required financial and emotional support. Between me and these things I passively grasped were *no*'s. Were impossible tasks or payment plans or embedded life lessons. Shadows of doubt. Subtextual messages that said I wasn't worth the investment or the time or the attention, that I wasn't able or mature or driven enough. This started with the cookie batter Mom spooned onto cookie sheets. "Can I help?" I'd ask. The violets she planted in the shade along the front of the house. "Can I do it?" This was cheerleading camp and choir competitions, uniforms and senior pictures. This was homework. College. Rehab. I learned to make a show of trying hard for the thing, but if I finally got it, I stopped trying *at* the thing. Kicked-off-the-squad cheerleader. Totaler of car. Community-college dropout, never even having cracked my copy of *Beloved*.

The thing is, it was never about the thing. It was about whether Mom believed in me. I suppose I needed her to prove her commitment too.

Every time I gave up, I gave Mom and Dad Mike more reason to doubt my future undertakings, more reason to deny support for them. The burden of proof endlessly moved from Mom's shoulders and back to mine and so on. It was a big, heavy thing.

I accused them of not loving me enough, of not caring whether I lived or died.

"If you were really so concerned about dying," Dad Mike said, "you would sell your things. It's just stuff, after all."

"I agree with Dad, honey," Mom said. "You can always get another car. Another guitar."

"I don't care about my car! Or my stupid guitar! It's not even about that!"

We were at a deadlock in a game of *on principle*.

At the same time, Dale had confessed to Duane and Glorianne. Once the initial relief of having some kind of explanation for our odd behavior passed, they both became gravely concerned. Glorianne was emotive, Duane pragmatic.

I was not their daughter. Hadn't even been their son's girlfriend for a full year. Yet. Putting me in rehab was never a question for them. They had to move some money around to afford it. To hold off on plans to spruce up the bathroom with raffia wallpaper.

They found a place nearby into which we'd be admitted the following day. I imagined soft beds, strong pills, maybe an IV drip. A quiet, beige room with round-the-clock nurses. I pictured myself sitting on a rock, contemplating, wildflowers surrounding me. Or running the shoreline with a dog. I had seen images like these in pamphlets at the methadone clinic and on TV commercials for places with names like Serenity Village. New Horizons.

The rehab was up a twisting, narrow road, hidden in wild, haphazard green. It had been a private hunting lodge shared by five families, built by a famed San Francisco Arts and Crafts movement architect in 1906. Inside was all burnished wood, carved beams and mezzanines, crisscrossing stairs. I remember a hearth, the smell of pancakes and antibacterial soap. There was a bare and sterile intake room, where I was handed a clipboard and a pen. A woman in stretch-waist slacks explained why the facility was hesitant to admit couples. "If he fails, chances are, you'll fail. And vice-a-versa."

The first three days I cried till there were no tears left in me, my face glazed in snot. I hated the sunlight, the fresh spring air coming in through the open doors. It was all so aggressive. Dishonest. I had flashbacks of Sundays. Of church and chores. Birdsong and blossoms. Mom in a dress that buttoned in the back, making a triangle that exposed the deep groove of her spine. It hurt my eyes. I wanted to be back in the dark humus of dope. Squiggling with the worms in the earthy rot.

I spent an hour on the toilet, crying still, as an enormous, rock-hard shit tore its way out of my asshole. Because constipation was a side effect of opiates, I'd typically go days on end without a number two. When I was dopesick, the urge to go would present itself suddenly and uncontrollably. Doing a shot would forestall the bowel movement, whose pain, time commitment, and potential embarrassment had it let loose in my pants I feared. I kept shit inside me as long as I could, knowing it was only getting bigger and more dangerous.

Atop the toilet seat, I contorted my body in all manner of positions: I leaned forward so my breasts rested on my thighs; I spread my legs and lifted my knees up as if I were in labor; I flexed one butt cheek, twisting in a way that created an instant hemorrhoid. I was sweating from places I didn't know could sweat. Maybe it wasn't sweat. Maybe it was full-body tears.

A girl I knew from the methadone clinic had advised me to stick a couple fingers up my puss and push against the "shared wall" to manually off-load some of the bear down. I tried her suggestion, feeling a sharp edge that must've been a very large, dry poop. I pressed back and down, the blood vessels in my eyeballs popping. It came, finally, barreling down my bowels without brakes, bloodying the toilet bowl as I bit down on my sleeve. Afterward, momentarily, I felt higher than I did from the buprenorphine sublingual I received under the tongue twice a day as I sat atop a papered table, my arm in a blood-pressure cuff.

Supposedly the buprenorphine dulled the edges of my physical symptoms – though that may have been the clonidine patch. Or the dim lighting of my room. It didn't do a thing for my emotional state, the hardest part of withdrawal. I floated from meals to meetings to checkups in clammy despair. I'd wake throughout the night, hair wet and legs violent, my hands between them, rode raw. Even in sleep, my brain scraped dopamine wherever it could. Somnambulant masturbation, it's called. Once, I went and sat in the intake office with the night nurse, a guy named Manny with a thick, black ponytail. He showed me pictures of his family as I winced through pangs of diffuse discomfort, jags of acute depression that struck like bolts of lightning. I tried to concentrate on the old photographs with unbalanced yellows, on his slow, soothing voice. Maybe he was putting together a family album, piecing together his history. Maybe he, like me, was trying to capture something he both missed and never experienced.

On the third night, some of the other residents and I stood around a picnic table under a bug-swarmed light. We smoked cigarettes. There was a girl everyone called Opie whose story involved a year in China and an opium den. There was the woman who lived in a gated community with a golf course and a man-made lake, who used her daughter's college fund to tweak. There was the blond dental hygienist who swallowed crank in parachutes of Kleenex. The Hollywood cliché who railed lines and tossed back shots of vodka, whose name I'd spot in end credits for years thereafter. There was the girl I shared a room with, a fellow heroin addict who stole my cigarettes and one of my shirts, escaping two days later. There was even a guy in there for pot.

There, amid a crew of addicts, people with whom I had so much in common, I chose to see only what made me stand apart. I thought I deserved an award for having it worst – the worst drug of choice, the worst habit, the worst kick, the worst misery, the worst history. A medal around my neck even Mom would acknowledge.

One night a week, we were allowed to make a ten-minute phone call from a little, private alcove off the main room. I used the first half of my call on Mom, invited her to family day. She said the piano guy was coming. And that Foster had soccer afterward, sorry. I hung up quick, without a good-bye, hoping to pass the hurt back to her. I called Mercedes, to whom I hadn't spoken in months. Sometimes she'd still get ahold of me, ask if I was holding, if I knew where to score. Her need for me in those rare moments made me euphoric. Now I needed her. I pictured myself running to her rumbling car under the cover of night, the sudden stare of a motion-sensor light, the two of us whooping as we peeled off into the darkness, night nurses shaking fists in our dust. I told Mercedes I could take her somewhere fun, could get her fucked up. She apologized. Told me it was probably better if I stayed there, got clean. I sucked my teeth and hung up, fighting off the tingling that heralded tears.

Maryanne, the tweaker from Lake County, tapped on the door's window with her press-ons because it was her turn. She wanted to call her daughter, she said. "Your daughter," I repeated, opening the door. My mouth jerked down and wobbled. My eyes broke. I walked through the main room with my hands over my face.

Glorianne came on family day. She brought cartons of cigarettes and Nutter Butter crème patties. Hippie soap and vitamins. Worry dolls in a painted oval box to stash under my pillow. Velvet Chinese slippers wrapped in dusty butcher paper. She hugged me, rocking back and forth, swaying on the balls of her feet. She told me I was strong, beautiful, brave. None of it was consoling. All it did was make me doubt her judgment, her emotional stability – who was she kidding? The supporting evidence was in the things she loved: a plush bear said to represent a dead princess; a glass cup, same age as the mother she never knew, which she kept hidden in a toolshed; a husband with whom sex was a distant memory seldom recalled, no longer even a bed or a meal or an idea to share; a son who called her crazy, who sided with his father even when his father called him a faggot for wearing eyeliner; someone else's daughter, a liar, a junkie, and a thief, self-centered and cruel, who increasingly denied return affection because that would feel too much like loving herself.

Day five, I took a verboten bath with Dale. I went in first, and a few minutes later he slipped through the door. As the tub filled, I looked at myself in the mirror. My reflection was ever-so-slightly off. Uncanny. Like I was a wax statue of myself, or a taxidermy with glass eyes, no light behind them. I wondered if this was the real me, unfiltered and unretouched. I wondered if I traipsed through life clueless of how I truly appeared.

We sat in tepid water, Dale's legs wrapped around my waist, my head against his chest.

"I want to leave," Dale said.

"Me too," I said.

"This place just makes me want to use more."

"Same. I can't relate to anyone here. None of them have a clue of how bad it really is."

"Here's the thing: We don't even need to be here anymore. We've kicked. The hard shit's over with. Staying could actually be detrimental."

I nodded gravely.

"Let's leave tomorrow," he said. "After the first meeting. During the free hour."

"I'll pack my stuff now."

"And Karleigh?" Dale looked at me with raised eyebrows. "We're not relapsing."

"No fucking way." I offered him my hooked pinkie, to which he latched his own. "We're not relapsing."

The next morning Dale and I were called into the office by an administrator whose name I forget. I'll call her Sandi. She said the staff was aware of our tandem bath. That it was a violation of their code of conduct and grounds for expulsion. How fortunate, I thought. But then Sandi said she was *not* going to expel us. That she was only going to give us a warning.

"Your lucky day," Sandi said.

"But I want to go," Dale said.

Sandi smiled. "That's precisely why you should stay."

As we got up to leave the office, Sandi had me wait.

"This is why we we're leery about admitting couples. Your entire recovery is now at risk. You can do whatever you want to do, but I truly hope you stay the course, no matter what Dale ultimately decides for himself. Your recovery is your own."

"I'll stay," I said. I didn't mean it. I halfway meant it. I didn't know what I wanted right then.

I went back downstairs as Dale stayed to talk to Sandi separately. I drank my orange-flavored sludge of psyllium husks and tried to read the book I'd packed. *She's Come Undone.* Or maybe it was *Eve's Apple.* Some book about myself, written by a man. I read the same sentence over and over again, unable to move forward, to turn the page. The pothead plucked at a toss-around beach guitar with sad nylon strings. The Hollywood guy's magazine was loud. Laughter drifted in from outside on curls of cigarette smoke. I heard a rumble from above. Dale was wheeling his suitcase across the mezzanine.

"Ope!" Hollywood said, looking up from his *Rolling Stone.* "Dead man walking."

I called up to Dale. "What are you doing?"

"Leaving. Remember?"

"Hold on!" I said, leaping, forgetting my book.

"Don't leave, little sister," Hollywood said. "Let him go."

"Hell. She'll go if she wants to go," a woman said, shooing with her hand. She leaned against the propped-open door, a bent leg making a triangle with the doorjamb. She was haloed in late-morning sun. "She'll be ready when she's ready."

I kept hearing these. All of these sayings like sandwiches with nothing in the middle. Not even technically sandwiches. Not even technically sayings because what exactly were they saying? nothing changes if nothing changes, a poster on the wall declared dumbly. first things first. Both ends of these platitudes stared across the void at their own reflections. What I didn't see then was the inherent metaphor: that my interpretation of anything at all can only go as far as myself. Foolish hears foolish. Deep sees deep. Petty finds petty and open is endless. The lessons are not in the tautologies themselves, nor are they in my understanding of them. The lessons are in my understanding of how I understand. Why I see the way I see.

Dale and I scurried through the crowd of inpatients who cackled and flapped under the redwoods, sunlight fracturing their sweatshirts, their waking faces. They yelled out to us: begged us to stay, told us to leave. Said we'd be back, if not there, then somewhere else. That it was all the same thing anyway. We kept our heads down and our feet moving.

An old woman driving up Green Hill Road saw our extended thumbs and suitcases and pulled over. She took us to Dale's parents' front door. *What an idiot*, I thought.

No one was home. The air in the house felt new. The rooms looked somehow hopeful, expectant. There were daffodils in a vase and wiped countertops and groceries that had not yet been put away.

"I just remembered it's my mom's birthday," Dale said.

"Cool. Maybe they went somewhere."

Dale looked at me, and then at the floor, and then back at me. I knew what it meant.

"What are you thinking?" I asked, knowing already the answer.

"What do you mean?"

"What do you mean 'what do you mean'?"

"What are *you* thinking?"

"I don't know. I asked you."

"Are you thinking . . . ?" Dale arched an eyebrow.

"Maybe. Are you?"

"Maybe?"

"We didn't really get an official last time."

"I'll call him," one of us said.

The high felt new and hopeful too. Overwhelming. Oceanic. It expanded inside of me, tickling the edges of my body, reminding me where I stopped and the rest of creation began, where the precise brink of my life was. I teared up with sudden, severe emotion that both energized and exhausted me. I plopped onto the couch, the last light of day moving down my face, making glowing red orbs on my closed eyelids. Dale stepped outside and outside drifted inside — the whiff of clover, of soil and mustard flowers; that spiraling thrush-song and the somber call of the collared dove. It reminded me of Sundays. Of church and chores. Of Mom in that pretty dress. Her toned back. This time, I loved it all. I missed it. Needed it.

When Duane and Glorianne came through the front door, I was surprised because I'd forgotten where I was, where I was supposed to be. They were surprised for the same reason.

"Surprise!" I said.

"Happy birthday, Mom," Dale said, high as a kite.

Glorianne wore a crisp dress. Lipstick. A big, smooth barrette in her hair. She held a small gift bag with a fan of tissue paper poking from the top. Her face went pale and coarse.

"What on earth?" she cried. "What are you doing here?"

"We're clean, Mom. Done-zo."

"No no no no no no no," she said, gasping. "This is not right." She woozed around the room, scanning seat cushions and table-tops for the cordless phone receiver.

"Unbelievable," Duane said. "You know we're taking you back right this second."

"Yes, hello? This is Glorianne Carter."

"Go. Get in the car, you two." His mouth was tight.

"Yes, that's right. My son and his girlfriend."

"They can't make us stay, Dad. We're adults."

"Glorianne, you look so beautiful today! Like a fern," I said, touching her dress.

"I'll hold."

"What a goddamn stunt."

"Your dress is my favorite color."

"This is unreal, you know that, Dale? Unreal."

"Oh, dread. Sure, sure. Yes. I understand. Is there someone else I might speak to?"

"Would you just look at that sky right now? Rainbow sherbet!"

The next morning, Dale and I did the rest of the dope because it would have been unholy to waste it. I called Mom, and her voice was groggy, breathy, a faint thread of glimmering panic laced through it. She asked if I was okay. I announced I was clean, home from rehab. Home early because twenty-eight days was a scam. She pointed out how early it was, dark still. That I'd woken her. I heard Dad Mike, through the muffle of bedsheets, ask, "Karleigh?"

"I want to see you," I said. "Can we celebrate?"

Mom sighed.

A couple of hours later she stood on the porch. Shiny bob and bright veneers. Capri pants and status purse. Glorianne answered the door in her muumuu. Her long hair entwining her like fog.

"Hang on, Mom!" I said, careening past both of them, out the door, trying to light a cigarette butt with a breezy match.

"I wish you had quit smoking, too," Mom said.

"I think she has bigger things to worry about right now," Glorianne said, putting a hand on Mom's shoulder.

"First things first," I said, rocking on the heels of my boots.

"You're going to stink up the car."

"I know this isn't my business," Glorianne said to Mom, "but maybe you should ease up on her a little bit."

I couldn't see Mom's face, but I knew exactly what it looked like. At once offended, smug, and polite. A tight smile, a pinched brow, eyes hiding behind sunglasses. "Honey, I'll meet you down at the car. We should get going."

I tossed my cigarette butt into Glorianne's petunias. Stomped it out, mightily, crushing velvety petals with the toe of my boot.

"Do you like her?" Mom asked once we were in her SUV.

"Glorianne? I guess." I shrugged.

"I don't know if I like her." Mom looked in her rearview, as if to make sure Glorianne wasn't sitting behind us. "She's a bit of a weirdo."

I had Mom take me to a diner housed in a gingerbread Victorian in Occidental — a nineteenth-century railroad-stop-*cum*-Italian-settlement-*cum*-artist-enclave nine miles up the road through redwoods and greenage. The restaurant had a juice bar and a wheat-grass press and baked goods made from spelt. Farm eggs. Local art.

On the table was a sugar shaker filled with turbinado and broken saltines. I swirled its brown crystals into my coffee, asked for more half-n-half. When the server came back with another full creamer, Mom and I ordered. Both of us huevos rancheros.

"Well," Mom said. "Tell me about rehab."

I said the first few days were hard. Very hard. But I did it. I triumphed. By day four I realized that sticking around would be a risk to my sobriety. A den of thieves, I called it.

"I wish you would have stayed the course," she said, breaking her yolk.

"That's interesting."

"What's interesting?"

"That you wish I would've stayed. You and Dad Mike didn't even want me to go to rehab."

"That's not true."

"The weirdo paid for it. The weirdo came to family day."

"I'm sure she's not happy you left early."

"She brought me worry dolls."

"I hope they got reimbursed."

"What difference does it make if the end result is the same? I'm clean now. Mission accomplished." I took a bite of goopy torti-lla. "You're not even proud of me. 'I wish you would've quit smok-ing.'" I said this mockingly, an octave higher.

Mom shifted in her seat. Looked up at the ceiling. Looked back at me. "Honey, I'm very proud of you. If you're telling me the truth, I'm very proud of you."

I went hot. "'If I'm telling you the truth'? The fuck is that supposed to mean?"

"Karleigh Anne, please. Let's not do this."

"Why would I not be telling you the truth?" I couldn't say the word *lying* because it was too true.

"Look. We both know you've told me many times before you were clean when you weren't."

"This time's different."

"I hope so."

"Don't hope. Just know. Just trust me for once."

Mom's eyes teared up and she mumbled something I couldn't hear.

"I can't understand you, Mom."

"I said," she said, her mouth in a resolute slit, "your eye is doing that thing."

When I was high, my right eye lazed outward to one side. Exotropia it's called. It gave me double vision that I could correct by closing one eye. I could align my eyes by standing in front of a mirror and slowly moving my face toward it. Only when my nose was nearly touching the glass would my eyes cooperate, pulling in toward each other like binary stars. That morning, Mom had two faces.

Mom didn't want to have to deal the coup de grâce. To point out the tell she'd willingly ignored for more than an hour, more than a year, for my sake. I looked at her, so solemnly saddened, and pictured her squatting down to my size, handing me a green rubber ball. I wanted to put my arms around her. I wanted to slap her. And then soothe her and tell her how sorry I was. I wanted to protect her. To punish her. To do to her the things I wanted to do to myself.

"Glorianne is more my mom than you are," I said. I was not telling the truth.

Puppy, Piggy, Princess

The hopefulness of spring was a distant memory. Temperatures shot into the triple digits. Apples fell. The petunias shriveled. Dale and I got high and scooped bugs out of the pool with the pool skimmer, then got into its frigid, untreated water, the bottom slimy under our toes. Rehab had receded into the back of our minds, Duane's and Glorianne's too, it seemed, as they never brought it up again.

We asked Glorianne for a ride into Santa Rosa because: (a) no gas, and (b) it substantiated the half-truth that we were looking for work. There were probably more psychological reasons as well, like the fact we were giving Glorianne an opportunity to feel needed and helpful as she unwittingly shuttled us around to drug dealers. This wasn't the first time we had her drive us into town. Dale would tuck in a button-down shirt, which would billow from his frame like a sail. I'd be in the pin-striped stovepipes whose cheap fabric made my crotch sweat. We'd tell her Home Depot or Target or JCPenney – some big store to become unfindable in. We'd watch her drive away before crossing the avenue, fast-walking to the feed store or the beeper store or the car stereo place to meet a guy with a fake name and spinner rims.

She dropped us now at the edge of an industrial pocket, Quonset huts with roller doors and corrugated aluminum walls. Hot, cracked blacktop. When we could no longer see her car, we ducked into the neighborhood just west of it, past an auto body shop, a lottery retailer. We threw rocks at an upstairs window, through which I could see a Bulls jersey tacked to the wall, slantwise.

Puppy came down. There was a freestanding ironing board in the kitchen. A woman who had the plump cheeks of youth, naked eyelids, no brows. Her hair was pulled tightly off her glowing face in a damp, heavy hank that emitted a faint peach scent. She held a baby with enormous eyes and an enormous bow around her head, chubby earlobes that grasped tiny diamonds. It was the first time I'd seen Puppy's house, his wife and daughter. Off the kitchen, in the family room, an old woman watched TV.

Puppy called Dale *Babyface* and Babyface asked for a g of chiva. They went upstairs to the room with the jersey. The room, I'd learn, also had a safe, a scale. I stayed standing in the kitchen the whole time, my thumbs looped through my backpack straps, smiling at the baby. Puppy's wife stood in the same place too. Smiled at the baby, then at me smiling at the baby. My smile began to hurt. I could tell hers did too. I looked up at the ceiling when I heard footfalls above me, to indicate to Puppy's wife that soon we'd be out of her hair. Dale shuffled downstairs, snapped, pointed to the door, and we were gone.

Of course, Puppy's wife had to know what her husband was selling, but she looked so pure and virtuous I couldn't square it. Not that purity or virtue was ascertainable by eye. Maybe the merchandise didn't matter to her, or to Puppy, because in the end, it's all dirty. Aside from the illegal status of Puppy's wares – a classification we could argue has more to do with controlling and incarcerating poor and marginalized individuals than with public health concerns or moral scruples – they weren't much different from the goods and services offered by ethically questionable corporations and industries. The ones with exploitative or harmful business practices or the ones that destroy the environment and communities or the ones that perpetuate hate and bigotry. What, then, if her husband got arrested? Or shot? Killed? What would happen to her and their baby, the grandma who watched Telemundo on a brand-new thirty-four-inch Panasonic – the one he'd been shopping for the time I met him in Sears, second floor, electronics? He had had pink onesies from layette tucked under his arm. Had me hand him my cash casually, out in the open, because it was more inconspicuous to be conspicuous.

Maybe that made him a shitty dealer. Not cut out for the life. Maybe it made him a shitty dealer that he told me I was a nice girl – too nice to be putting poison in my arms. Too nice to be so hideously desperate.

My desperation was fed by his desperation, which was fed by my desperation, and on and on and on. A chain that linked back onto itself. It starts with the farmers who live in the mountains of Mexico, in Guerrero or Sinaloa, in remote regions forgotten by the government, by time. With no jobs, resources, or public institutions to depend on, they're forced by the passive threats of starvation and destitution, the active threats of .50-caliber rifles and firebombs to supply cartels. Fearing death, displacement, and discomfort, they seed their craggy parcels with illegal poppies whose soothing latex is bled out and transported to manufacturing facilities. Unless, that is, the military files in with their machetes and bonfires. Then the enslaved farmer will have to start over, a season's worth of income lost.

Then there are the cooks, the young men who desire more than to pick fruit or stock groceries at a store that's owned by the cartel anyway. They need to support their spouses and young children. They want the respect of their families and peers. They cook in hollowed-out, abandoned homes, in open fields, hidden amid grazing livestock, stirring big pots over open flames. These days, they position themselves so the wind hits the backs of their heads because to inhale the fentanyl-laced gruel is to die.

Then there are the mules. Some convey dope in secret compartments in their cars or hide it among or inside the merchandise of a cargo truck. Some walk for miles through dark, underground tunnels. Others, known as body-packers, transport the goods in their stomachs, removed via bowel movement – a life-threatening secret should the drug-filled condom leak.

Then there are the dealers, the runners. Some are small-time, bottom-rung guys you went to high school with whose product has been passed through many hands, cut with more dirt and more sugar each pass. Some are little brothers with baby teeth who will meet you at the apartment complex playground. Some are people like Puppy who spend entire days driving all over the county, the state, beyond the border, gun in glove compartment. They return their pages hours later, exhausted, stressed out, saying, "Twenty minutes," before hanging up. They marry their girlfriends, baptize their daughters, throw all-day cook-outs for the entire extended family. They buy razor scooters for all the nieces and nephews, hundred-pound TVs for their grandmothers-in-law. They tell girls like me that we're too nice for drugs. That we should quit. Because they might see the soft center beneath the rough surface. Maybe they see their wives and daughters and mothers and grandmothers. We tell them they should quit the life too. That they too are too human.

And then, at last, there's us, so many of us, the addicts who are ruled by withdrawal. Who are desperate for the phone to ring or the headlights to flash, the familiar face of our savior behind the windshield. We are desperate for dope in hand, dope in pocket, dope in spoon, dope in vein, dope in brain. We are desperate for all the mean noise in our heads to quiet, for the lightness of chest – of heart and breath. For the safety and coziness opiates provide. For their sure shortcut to feelings of love and acceptance, human necessities, human beings unnecessary.

The cartel drug lords – greedy, power hungry, and vengeful – use human desperation to build their empires and stuff their coffers. It's desperation they're intimately familiar with, the very desperation that had galvanized them to rise ranks in the first place. Desperation they've learned to manipulate through a life of having it. All of us are played, from the farmer to the junkie, the dealer with her stack of cash, or the cook with his useless bandanna tied around his face — toxic fumes a tolerated threat, nothing compared with a bullet to the head, a remote grave.

When Dale and I left Puppy's, we walked along the railroad tracks to a coffee shop known for its live acoustic jams and lesbo staff. It had terracotta sponge-painted walls adorned with giant wooden mermaids that had once figureheaded the bows of old ships or possibly carnival rides. They had watched over me my eighteenth year as I wrote in my journal, some Ani DiFranco wannabe clipping a pickup mic to her guitar. They had watched me, often sitting alone, desperate to connect with somebody but too shy to ever say a word. Instead, I spied longingly out the window at the punk kids, the weirdos and queers, who sat along the tracks, the sun setting behind their disheveled silhouettes. What fun they looked to be having. How loved they must have felt in that orange-pink warmth of late August.

Dale and I went inside. The woman behind the counter was one of the owners (she and her wife co-owned it). She had a thick ponytail, wore overalls and a ROYGBIV of brushed aluminum rings around her neck. I'd interacted with her hundreds of times, even if just to tell her the half-n-half was empty. Her familiarity was a comfort, and I thought I might like to work there. To learn how to use the big red roaster in the middle of the café or make collaged signs for new blends. To hand warm, empty mugs to quiet, burgeoning freaks who'd sit at a window seat for hours, pen ink all over their fingers.

I asked her for an application, a glass of water, and the bathroom key, which was attached to a spatula. In the bathroom, I shrugged off my backpack, unzipped it, and gently slipped the application between the pages of my sketchbook so it would stay crisp and unbent. Then I removed my half of the dope we had just scored from Puppy. Cooked up a shot. Tried a hand vein but missed. Tried a foot vein and ditto. I went to the mirror and puffed my cheeks. Tried the jugular. The needle felt especially cold and invasive there, its slim steel against the heartbound roar of dark skull blood. Before I'd even finished emptying the rig, my skin took on a subtle pallor and I thought for a moment I had killed myself. When I came out of the bathroom, I felt my body being grabbed, thrown into the blinding sunlight. I believed, at first, it was God handling me. I stumbled and slammed into the doorjamb, falling on the concrete just outside the door. Above me was a pair of big hands that were attached to strong arms that were attached to a body in overalls. I saw her face. I knew then she must have been saving me, would put her mouth to mine and pass me some of her life.

"Get out of here," she said. Her ponytail looked angry. "I have no tolerance for that shit in my café."

I grogged my head around, confused, scrunching my eyes against the bright outside, against her scowl. "I was taking a dump," I said.

"My ass." She took my forearm and helped me up. "Step foot in here again, I'm calling the cops."

"But I wasn't doing drugs! Please! I wasn't doing anything!"

She walked inside, shutting the open door behind her. I banged it with a fist. "Stupid bitch," I called into the glass. In the door's reflection, I saw only my face.

The Beanie Babies were in a trash bag in our closet, awaiting their day, which had arrived, fortuitously, the day after Dale and I, upon leaving a pawnshop where we'd brought Duane's rarely used and not-to-be-missed leaf blower, saw a flyer taped to the window of a toy store that advertised a Beanie Baby convention. It was to be held in a conference room at the Red Lion Inn, mere blocks from the coffee shop from which I'd been recently 86'd.

It said free admission and collectibles show and door prizes and, most important, buy sell trade.

After nearly a year in the closet, I could no longer detect the faint whiff of banana peel on them. We tossed them into the trunk of my car and headed into Santa Rosa. Picture two scumbags, twitching and limping and arguing as they jaywalk the boulevard, taking turns dragging a trash bag across the street. Picture them presumptuously marching into the lobby of a chain hotel. It's cool and carpeted and smells faintly of chlorine and coffee. They follow signs to a large room where about a dozen people are setting up folding tables and arranging plush animals atop them, snapping plastic protectors over heart-shaped tags. A few people watch the couple but most continue heaping bears. Penguins, robins, ostriches, ducks – complete aviaries. Cryptozoos of dragons and unicorns. The princess in her acrylic case, sitting high above the rest of the menagerie. A man asks the couple if they are tabling, but they don't understand his question so they pretend not to hear him. They walk into the middle of the mostly empty room, a sad affair it's so far proving to be, and dump the contents of the shredded bag onto the floor. Eighty Beanies. "A dollar each," they say. "One dollar per, no bulk discounts." The collectors, or vendors, whatever they are – middle-aged, largely women – drop their displays and scramble toward the polychrome pile. They act quickly, nervously, as if they know the flash sale isn't legitimate. There are hands reaching over hands. Grabbing, blocking. Off to the side, bargaining and bidding. Trading horses for cows. Digging for bills. A woman asks politely, "Ma'am? Would you accept a local check?"

The whole scene lasted under fifteen minutes. Dale and I walked out of the hotel about eighty dollars richer. I kept the owl whose tag said hoot and put him on my dash for luck. We bought two grams and a pack of GPC cigarettes.

Everything after that was tinged with kaleidoscopic absurdity, as if I'd taken the mythical tab of acid that had me *permafried*. The abrupt shift in my perspective was due, chiefly, to the abrupt shift in power. People who would've otherwise given me sideways looks were now giving me some semblance of respect – no matter it was rushed, breaths held. As if we had swapped roles, Freaky Fridayed, these ostensibly normal people with ostensibly normal lives, over-the-hill toy enthusiasts with pictures of new grandchildren in their wallets, became as uncouthly desperate as I had been. The hasty, heart-racing experience both equalized and alienated. On the one (bloated, blood-smeared) hand, I saw that we were all the same thing: little stupid suffering animals who told ourselves we were special, gazing up blindly from our trash heaps for something to save us. And though this realization passed a warm shudder of compassion and camaraderie through my body, it also, on the other (grabbing, glomming) hand, dehumanized, making it possible for me to take advantage of people without the repercussion of guilt, of good conscience, as if dipping my toe into the black pool of sociopathy.

Afterward, sitting on the curb outside Longs Drugs, Dale and I shared a kiwi-strawberry Snapple. A coin-operated merry-go-round rotated behind us, a small kid alternating between joy and terror as the thing slowly spun, "Pop Goes the Weasel." His mother was clapping, *"Eres muy valiente, mijo!"* It was over a hundred degrees out – a heat that added to the surreality of the day. The vast parking lot glimmered with mirage. Across the avenue, lawns had gone tan and patchy.

Two women exited the store. One was visibly upset. She deplored the store's one-hour photofinishing department. Said it had been almost two hours and still her pictures were not ready and she was pissed. Was going to write a letter. Had gotten the name of the bitch employee in her little vest. Was going to get her fired, going to make her wish she'd never come to work that day.

I felt the onset of a panic attack – the chilly surge that's followed by terrifying depersonalization. I took a swig of the Snapple to make sure I was actual. Felt its damp, papered glass under my fingertips, its icy-cold sweetness moving down my esophagus and into my stomach, wrapping around my rib cage, and settling behind my eyes like a nascent migraine. More so than usual, in a way that was acute and estranging and collapsing of both logic and language, I failed to understand the woman's anger. I had wished my own woes were only so luxuriously petty. It seemed, suddenly, we existed in completely different worlds that played out alongside each other simultaneously. Some of us were like stagehands, shadows moving through a setting, privy to the illusion. We were largely invisible, though became hypervisible when we threatened to disrupt the assumed, taken-for-granted, and collectively supported reality. That's the day I began to think of normal people, the maintainers of the normal world, as actors. And because I thought of them as different (yet the same – all of us doomed morons slithering around in the gutters), it became easier to use them as instruments for my survival.

What I felt at the time as awful enlightenment, a peeking past the curtains, was really a malfunctioning of my imagination. I had reduced, in this example, a woman to a cipher who had no life or problems other than what I had observed in a parking lot for thirty seconds – her life only existing in my eye. I cast assumptions and formed generalizations about every member of society, a group I felt I was no longer part of. A group I believed I'd been exiled from.

Perhaps this perceived cleave in existence, in humankind, and my subsequent withdrawal from society necessitated my contin-uation as a heroin user. By separating, I was effectually othering the people I violated, the unwitting benefactors of my addiction; I was calloused against the glares and the stares, the names and accusations flung at me; I had a reason to keep using – or, more precisely, no reason to stop. I also suspect the split was simply a result of no longer identifying or having anything functionally in common with most of the operating world. Though we were all goal-driven, our goals were too disparate to reconcile. I had to increasingly abandon my morals, dissolve my boundaries. I had to harden up to death, brave sketchy situations I would have otherwise fled from. I think of soldiers who return from combat feeling displaced and alone. I think of that scene in *The Hurt Locker*, the absurdity of the cereal aisle, grossly vast and redundant, colorful boxes seeming to vibrate under the pallor of artificial lighting, against the bland, subliminal murmur of Muzak. The realization the viewer has then, that Kathryn Bigelow captures so poignantly, is that normal life *is* absurd. The third theory is this: As a person who had already felt like an outsider for most of her life, like someone who belonged nowhere, I was poised for such a sundering. One could say it was a self-fulfilling prophecy made manifest the moment I asked Dale to put a needle in my arm. Or that it was the amplified conclusion to, the accumulation of, all the ways in which *I* felt othered. And because I had always felt, been, othered, I could only see in terms of that.

My stuff — the high-mileage Honda, the knockoff guitar, the riot grrrl records — all became pointless since life itself was pointless. Over the next couple of months I sold my car for a hundred bucks to a friend of a friend — never even bothering to transfer the title. I traded my guitar for a quarter gram, barely enough to get me well. I took pennies for each LP — sold in bulk to a rip-off record store whose owner, feeling justified to lowball me after seeing my tracks, marked them up two hundred times, displayed them on the wall. Even my clothes: the low-slung jeans and camis emblazoned with kanji or aliens or sparkly Rolling Stones mouths; the 1950s housedresses with metal zippers and hidden snaps I'd worn ironically with combat boots; even the Union Jack tee from Glorianne was too soon on the racks of a resale store. It

was freeing to rid myself of the unnecessary. To let go of my attachment to things. To decide for others their attachments to things.

I'd visit Mom just so I could sneak upstairs with a fork, work
its tines into the slot of Foster's piggybank, pluck ten- and
twenty-dollar bills. I told myself I'd repay him someday, even if
someday was years later. I borrowed Aaron's bass guitar, his mini
amp, took them to the pawnshop. Even paid the interest for a few
months, kept the ticket in my wallet. I filched a blue-and-white
Wedgwood jar from the back of Glorianne's curio cabinet, a blue-
and-white Gibson Girl plate from the kitchen's garden window,
shuffling the others to obscure the vacant spot it had left behind.

At Bill's, an older woman who looked like Gramma and whose
name started with an *M*, Marge or Maude or something, watched
from the corner of her eye as I sold the plate. She followed me
outside and, as I was mounting Duane's bike, asked if I had more.
She wanted the Gibson Girls. All of them. No matter what. Whatever Bill was paying, she'd pay double. Hideously desperate.

I told her I had three or four more and she scribbled her address
and phone number on the back of an old receipt. I'd figure out a
way to explain the plates' disappearance later. Though it would
be messy and implausible under the pressure of Glorianne's gaze,
at least it'd be fluid, devoid of consciousness, conscientiousness
— like the utterances of tongues-speakers, handling serpents to
convince themselves if not the congregation.

Dale and I went that night to the woman's apartment. It was
neat and lonely. Had a vague soup smell. I cased it quickly and saw
nothing. A worthless TV with bunny ears. A Hummel figurine.
A framed picture of an elderly man I had assumed was her late
husband. I sensed immediately that she regretted making plans
with us. The flicker of hesitation in her movements, the subtle
tremble of hand and mouth. The watchful eyes. We handed her
the plates and she looked them over. Stained crazing, an unfortunate nick, a duplicate. She'd just take one, if that was all right.

"No," I said. "It's not all right. You said you'd buy all of them. Pay us twice as much even."

She looked at me, and then Dale, hoping, maybe, for our faces to soften. "I did say that, didn't I?"

"You did."

She counted bills and grimaced. "What if I write you a post-dated check?"

"We really need the money today."

"How about I give you most of it in cash now and pay the rest in three days?"

I looked at Dale. His face shrugged. "Fine. We'll be back here in three days."

She emptied her wallet, counted dollars made from loose change she had poured from a jar. Stacks of dimes and nickels.

Three days later, Dale pounded on her door in vain. I peeked through the windows at a dim and empty room. A cup on the table. A *TV Guide* on an armchair. I pictured her upstairs, hiding in a bedroom I imagined smelling of fake roses, the phone receiver to her head, her finger hovering over the 9, *if you'd like to make a call please hang up and try again.*

We spotted her weeks later in Safeway, putting a package of Pepperidge Farm cookies in her cart. We startled her. Started friendly with her. Warmly. Then begged her. Bullied her. Besieged her. Directed her to the ATM at the front of the supermarket. I followed her so closely I could smell her fear. She shielded the pin pad with a cupped hand. Handed over the balance as agreed upon ("I did say that, didn't I?"). I shoved the money in my pocket and told her, sincerely, to enjoy her Mint Milanos.

Sometimes these women parade across my memory. There's Puppy's wife, still gently smiling like a painting of a saint. And her daughter, an adult now, her eyes ever enormous. Maybe Puppy's left the life. Maybe Puppy's wife left him. I hope she's somewhere far away from that West Ninth Street apartment. In a place uninterrupted by desperate strangers. I think about the owner of the coffee shop,* who's since sold it, its mermaids gone. I feel her hands tossing me. Then see them reaching for me. Then I see her hands in the dirt – there's a kneeling pad and a trowel. I see them with earth under their nails, with soap, wringing a kitchen towel. I picture Maude or Marge. She's no longer in the dim apartment, no longer alone. She's surrounded by nieces and grand-nieces and it's Christmas. She's smiling. Her husband's photo is on her dresser. So's the Hummel figurine, pink cheeks and knees, a headkerchief. Not the Gibson Girl plates, though. She's forgotten those, mercifully. As she's forgotten me. Not because of her old age but because of my profound insignificance in her long, full life. And I take comfort in knowing that it's not just her who's forgotten, but everyone, I hope. I should be the only one to hold the pain of these memories. The beauty too – as they've all helped me find my way back.

*The sudden vertigo I felt after having written this chapter, when, while half researching and half snooping, I stumbled across an archive of a 1999 article about how the owners of the coffee shop had "clamped down on the crush of people hanging around outside their doors in the evening." It was newsworthy at the time, locally anyway, because the café was known for its vibrant night scene. The owner who had 86'd me said to the reporter: "The last straw came from people who asked for a glass of water, grabbed a spoon, and headed for the bathroom." I knew immediately she must have been referring to me and Dale. Feeling nauseous over this discovery, I googled the woman's name and found a contact number for her, but no email. I was tempted to text her. To not only apologize but also thank her for providing me with a boundary. A consequence. Remorse. My actions were a single straw among many, and quite possibly the one that facilitated an unfortunate change in the café's policies. But her actions were a single straw among many that had amounted to, much later, a decision to get clean. I wanted to tell how grateful I was for that. I talked myself out of it because a text message is too intimate, too creepy and stalker-y. I can only hope she's well.

CHAPTER THIRTEEN

Celestial Bodies

I spent most of the time waiting. Walking up the road and back down again, over and over. In pajama pants and a mink-collared vintage coat. My hair looped in a frayed elastic.

"Twenty minutes," they'd always say before the click.

Twenty minutes meant two hours. Three, or maybe eight. Sometimes never. The meeting spot was anywhere on the road up to the house – a steep and wavy mile, like a state-fair slide, lined with fences and horse trailers, spans of small ranches. American flags. The top of the road came to a T, to a tree whose ropy lap of roots I'd sit in, watching ant riots and bully-crows and the dusky creepings of opossums and raccoons. My heart paused every time I saw headlights. I'd stare right through the darkened windshields of the sparsely passing cars, just in case it was him. Him being any number of guys we scored through.

On this road, bare trees looked like smoke against the sky. There was actual smoke, too, rising from lonely chimneys or open burns. It smelled woodsy, musky, almost human. Fog softened edges, settled on my skin like flu. It dewed TV-blued windows and shit-spattered windshields. I walked with an empty brain, counting my steps, my eyes swallowing familiar information without appraisal: Pothole. Flagpole. Woodpile. Cat. Then, as the sky went dark, everything disappeared.

As time passed, I'd disappear too. No longer able to see where the darkness ended and my body began. I had no streetlights or sidewalks to guide me, just memory, intuition, and dilated pupils. My eardrums would become so sensitive they'd ache, detect even the slightest variation in pitch: a car still miles away

I'd not so much hear but feel as a vibration floating somewhere above the crown of my head. Freezing like prey, I'd will the sound to get louder, closer.

I'd become increasingly sick. My skin tremoring and muscles clenching. I'd imagine burying my body in the heavy muck along the side of road – its weight conforming to my contours, spilling into the ruts of my ribs and hips, holding me down like a great hand.

Dopesickness felt like a scattering of my parts – so riddled with something so much worse than pain I had to ditch them and keep walking without legs, breathing without lungs. "Me" became a burning point outside of, or perhaps deeply inside of, myself.

Sometimes, I was the opossum whose silhouette I watched hobble through dew-point, across the quiet field on its nightly commute. I transplanted my soul inside its hoary coat, saw through its beady night-vision eyes, felt its pointy teeth jam-pack my jaw, pretended to be dead. Other times, a clutch of cold wind turned me into the star-packed night itself. I'd look for Dale's planets, for Cassiopeia, Andromeda's queen mother, known for her beauty. Or for Orion's belt. Dad's belt. The belt held taut between my teeth.

This night, with a new, sharp chill that presaged fall, that para-doxical scent of dense moisture and dry leaves, I had already walked for seven hours. Twice, Dale had come looking for me on the bike, holding the out-of-range cordless phone receiver in case our guy called, bringing me a toaster waffle wrapped in a paper towel, a sweatshirt. He shared a smoke with me before heading back.

It seemed like hallucination when Puppy glided up to the tree where I sat, saving me like a life raft in a black ocean. I was cold and confused. My nose numb and running. Puppy's car was ground-hovering and softly booming. It emitted a purple dash-board glow and the flat cologne smell of a paper tree that hung from the mirror.

Our exchange was quick. I kept my hands balled in the sleeves of my sweatshirt and jogged in place to stay warm. My voice was fog. He counted the money in front of me before reaching into the glove box and retrieving a gram. He told me I was pretty then asked about Babyface, a tagged-on question that both qualified the preceding compliment and loaded it. As if he wanted to leave an image in my mind and take it away at the same time, *objet petit a*. It was his strategy, a performance of man-to-man respect that was simultaneously a convenient way out of a wrong idea — should I have found the idea wrong. He glided away the same way he approached me — though now he reminded me of a stingray. Stealthy. Smooth. Bottom-feeding.

I was not in love with Dale. Had never been. I loved him but wouldn't realize how much for many years. Because heroin was the basis for and bedrock of my relationship with him, it was never about him as an individual. I regarded him not as a whole, separate human, but only in relation to myself, an ancillary appendage. He was my shelter, my protector. My business part-ner and security blanket. We looked after each other, kept an eye out for blue lips and shallow breath. For cops and scammers. For Glorianne moving quickly down the hall. Together, we weren't alone. We shared aims and anxieties, feelings of alienation. We were each other's misery and self-loathing, but also each other's comfort and relief.

I watched him hunched over a bent spoon and a Bic flame, his once-animated face now slackened into a perpetual grimace and his eyes gone dull. All that math and science and clever humor that used to zip through his brain and out his mouth had slowed to a trickle, obstructed by heroin's sediment. It was easier that way. He murmured something I couldn't understand, a joke to himself, and smiled dopily. I was turned on. Felt it in my pussy the way Tommy, shirtless and flirting, used to make me feel. I imagined Dale's dick entering me, but his dick was a needle and his cum was dope. Or maybe it was the other way around. The wires had become crossed. They still are sometimes, almost a quarter century later. I can think about heroin when my husband is going down on me and be moved to orgasm, a sick secret I've just confessed. A damage I've tried to reverse with eye-movement therapy and guided meditation and prayer.

"I'm going to fuck Puppy," I announced to Dale.

He took a deep breath like he'd been expecting the conversation for some time but hoped it would never transpire. Because how do you react when you simultaneously want something and don't? When you know it's wrong to support your girlfriend in not necessarily her desire to hook but her resolve to, even though you know it will make your life much easier in many ways, or at least you think it will?

"Is that really what you want to do?" he asked too casually for my taste.

Rapid boiling of blood, sudden blindness.

"Fuck you, dude. I hate you."

Dale pinched his bottom lip into a taco.

"What I 'really want to do'? Are you an idiot? Of course it's not what I really want to do. But I have no fucking choice. Unless you have a better idea."

"Let me think. Just cool down a sec."

"If only Puppy was into dudes."

"What did you just say?" Dale's teeth clenched. "What the hell's that supposed to mean?"

"This shit always falls on me and it's not fair."

"What do you mean 'this shit'?"

"Like, I'm the one who sells to Bill. I'm the one who goes digging around your mom's stuff. I'm the thief."

"You insist on doing it!"

"Cuz I know you won't! You won't even try. You'd let us go sick. Or you'd go down there in your raggedy-ass clothes, eyes all pinned, and Bill would kick you out. Call the cops on you. Game over."

"Wow. You're really making assumptions."

"I'm the one who waits in the cold every night for hours. I'm the one who gets her boobs stared at and her hair touched. Now I have to be the one that sucks and fucks, know why? Because I'M THE WOMAN." The room buzzed in the absence of my yelling.

"Karleigh," Dale said as he slowly and cautiously placed his hand on my shoulder. I wanted to bite it. "I really don't want you to do this."

"Too fucking bad."

Later that day, before nightfall, Dale stood outside of the garage with his Leatherman knife up his sleeve and a half-smoked cigarette behind his ear. I was inside the garage with Puppy, naked from the waist down on a folding cot with rusted springs and musty ticking. Puppy's paunch swayed over my stiff body, sweat dripping from his forehead onto my face. He smelled like ketchup. I stared at a fly in the window, struggling inside a clot of dusty web, its buzz muffled and sporadic.

Puppy climbed off me, cursing his gone-limp dick, rawing it in his frantic hands. I waited, frozen, refusing to offer up my hand or my mouth.

"I'm ready," he said, rolling back atop me. Our bodies, awkwardly syncopated, were a boat's bow thudding against a choppy wake. I was wave-pummeled, resisting. Dry inside. He pulled out and spewed onto my belly with tired surrender. The fly in the window had not given up.

I remembered when Dad had told me that Mom was a whore and how I had confused the word with *horror*, a word I knew from the video store. And how scared I was when he explained what it meant, in the literal sense, his lack of clarification intentional to ensure I'd be disgusted with her. Or terrified of her. And terrified

I was, not of her but *for* her, who must've felt she had no other option than to pretend to make babies with complete strangers for money to buy us English muffins and Trapper Keepers. How I believed for a while that the man before Dad Mike, the butcher with the truck, was just a horny customer. That Dad Mike himself was too. Lured by Mom's privates just as Mom was lured by his luxury car. And how even after I realized my misunderstanding, this other, salacious version of what roles they all played was still true too. How I came to believe that there was really no such thing as intimacy, that everything, at the end of the day, was transactional. And when I heard Annabelle fucking Toothy in the squat that one time, only a year before but it felt like ages, I was afraid because I knew I'd eventually do it too. That in some ways, I had already been doing it.

Just like people became nonentities to me (myself included), prostitution became a nonissue. Though I hadn't thought of it as an act of moral bankruptcy or biblical sin since I was much younger, I was still troubled by the shame of it — how eye-rollingly predictable of women, how embarrassingly desperate. But the shame of it seemed to cancel itself out: having sex for money (or drugs or rent or Amazon cards) was at once shame denying and shame saturating. Rejection and acceptance in concert. Our lot.

Shame has a built-in dichotomy. Or maybe, shame *is* a dichotomy. The more I tried to discount it or shrug it off or flip it over into something to be proud of, the more I was actually aware of its presence, threatening in the corner of my sky like a storm. I went on pretending that sex work was no big whoop — even convinced myself of it. But my body, the very sold commodity, registered every traumatizing bit — *kept the score*, as they say. It stored it somewhere under my skin, perhaps in the mackerel sky of my fat-puckered thighs that those just-barely-men grabbed onto and slapped from behind, or maybe it was in the bile of some pointless organ, bubbling up out of my throat burning and nasty – insults flung, lies spat.

Women were fucked from the jump, formed from a man's vertebral bone, tempted temptresses, redeemed only through baby making – made painful to boot by God Himself. They were impossible: gave birth with intact hymen; gave birth as nonagenarian. If she was headstrong or cunning or outspoken or smart, she was a harlot. Diminished and disempowered. Disappeared from history.

Women only account for somewhere between 5 to 8 percent of the Bible's population, depending on what version you read. And of those women, many have been reduced to trickster wielders of their sex – humanity and individuality vanished. Mary Magdalene, Jesus's companion and devout disciple, is interpreted as a whore. Is possibly not even a whole woman but an economical composite of several. She was a sinner, a "woman of the city" with her tears and her ointment, with those exorcised "seven demons" – which Christians read as a euphemism for prostitution. There's Tamar, who was made ineligible for remarriage by her father-in-law after she failed to give him grandchildren with two of his sons, both of whom were killed off by God for their wickedness, Tamar blamed. Determined to add to the family lineage, she disguised herself as a whore and solicited herself to her father-in-law. Only after proving she was with child, his child, was her life spared, as her act of harlotry carried a death sentence otherwise. There's Rahab, the Jericho innkeeper (another euphemism) whose virtuosity and activism were eclipsed by her alleged whoredom. And, of course, there's Delilah, betrayer of the amply tressed Samson, whose name would come to signify, to quote the *Encyclopedia Britannica*, "a voluptuous, treacherous woman." Her name and likeness would appear in Broadway plays, pop songs, and paperbacks centuries into the future. She is the original femme fatale, the exaggerated embodiment of weaponized sexuality.

A woman was her body and her body could fell even the most honorable man. Yet it was her body that created life, that created citizens and good countrymen. This conundrum was resolved with the Enlightenment, when the language of science could isolate a woman's anatomy from her personhood. In the eighteenth and nineteenth centuries, there was a shift away from the apprenticed folk medicine of female midwives to formally trained male practitioners. According to Nora Doyle in her book *Maternal Bodies*, a Western preoccupation with decency compelled doctors to remove the mother herself from the act of childbearing and focus solely on the disembodied and therefore sexless organs and systems within her body. "Childbearing came to seem less a result of women's labor and more the outcome of a tense relationship between the uterus and the man-midwife." Mothers were erased from medical literature. In life, their bodies betrayed no evidence of motherhood – they were to be restrained: slim and frail. To be curvaceous and strong was to be savage, undisciplined, non-white, unholy. Mothers disappeared, and their disappearance perpetuated the age-old false binary that sees women as either vulgar or virtuous. As saints or whores.

Actual sex workers, though known as public women, are in an industry kept invisible so as to maintain civic decorum and protect men's privacy. Its sites are forced into districts over tracks and on the edges, veiled by the shadows of night, kept inside unregulated houses and businesses that appear to be something they are not. Lingerie stores. Tanning salons. Massage parlors. Because the work is made invisible, so are the workers, making them vulnerable to exploitation, trafficking, abuse, and disease without any legal or medical recourse.

My dealers gave me work. I gave blow jobs to second-cousin birthday boys, fucked their random friends for dusty crumbles of tar. I was shortchanged, ripped off, called names. I lay there, but it wasn't actually me. I erased myself, becoming a sill-fly. I'd stare out of compound eyes, seeing colors I couldn't imagine. I released myself from the burden of being a woman. But I was not a man either. I was the hammer on the garage's workbench – all leaden head with no thought at all, sitting there, untouched, for twenty years. "I'm not me, I'm not me," my lips silently formed, sometimes mistaken for small kisses or orgiastic trembles by those pitifully naive and porn-schooled young men who wore cologne for the occasion. Who became moronically eager by the mere sight of my penny areolae.

Dopesickness taught me how to detach from my body. Trickturning taught me how to disappear completely.

Duane gave our bedroom door three firm bangs. "Five minutes," he said.

We were headed out to meet some relative – a great-aunt or a second stepmother or something – at a strip-mall sushi bar for dinner. Glorianne was bringing her an African violet.

Dale's hair was washed and combed back, his face cleanshaven. He wore a button-up shirt and smelled of artificial eucalyptus. I wore a floral dress with pilled tights. With a mouth full of bobby pins, I scrambled around our room, looking under piles of floor-tossed clothes for my other shoe.

"It's ready," Dale said quietly, holding up a filled syringe. Then loudly, to the door: "Hang on!"

"Can you do it for me?" I asked. "I have to do my hair real quick."

He tied my arm off with the sleeve of a shirt.

"Hurry up!" I hissed through pins.

"Train's leaving," Duane said from the hallway.

Suddenly, a fiery pain seized upon my arm, moved up my shoulder, and fanned across my chest. My neck stiffened and my brain seared. My forearm, which I could no longer feel, swelled to the girth of a football.

The sensation was grounding, as if I had slammed back into my own body. With it came a nostalgic feeling, the memory of falling off my bicycle, the cul-de-sac's faded concrete bloodying my familiar knee. Or banging my mouth on the hot, salty crossbar of a jungle gym, dropping to the sawdust below. The surprise of those injuries, the delayed tears, my heartbeat, thrumming and huge inside my skull, behind my eyelids like fireworks.

I yelped. "I think I'm dying."

"Calm down. You're not dying."

"This is your last warning. I'm going to take this door right off its hinges tomorrow."

"My heart feels hot, Dale. My arm feels like bees."

"Count of three," Duane said. "One – two – three." Duane was in our room. Glorianne watched from the hall with the violet, peeking above its meaty leaves.

"My arm's all swolled up for some reason," I said. I was crying. Scared. "I feel weird."

Duane drove me to the ER at Palm Drive, Sebastopol's little hospital, good for not much more than stitches and casts. Dale sat with me in the back seat, his hand atop my normal-sized one. My right arm was purple and turgid, all of its creases and pits smoothed over and shiny, like a blown-up exam glove. "Turkey balloons," we used to call them.

At the hospital, I was gowned and vitaled, then told I was getting transported to the better-equipped facility in Santa Rosa. As I waited for the ambulance, I asked the nurse to call Mom.

"I let her know we're moving you to Community," the nurse said.

"Did she say anything?"

"I told her you're stable."

"But did she say anything?"

———

The first time I fantasized about disappearing I must have been around six years old. In the evening Mom and Dad had to drop me at the home of family friends Robin and Les Proteau, who had kids us kids were friends with. I don't remember the reason they were babysitting me, nor do I remember if my sisters were there with me, though I don't think they were. If they had been, they were in another room. I don't think my brother Aaron was born yet. He may have been inside Mom. Alone, I had to sleep on some strange bottom bunk with scratchy sheets and stuffed animals I could not imagine loving. I recall having a mild sense of dread — of maybe a candle catching onto a curtain and starting a house fire, or of something happening to my parents, a car accident, an abandonment. I prayed over and over again for Mom to appear, to scoop me up and take me home. When I woke to her carrying me out to the car, I knew God had heard me.

Mom put me in the back seat of the Caprice. The motor was running, the heater going. She was standing at the front door of the Proteaus' house, talking to Robin. On the seat next to me was a small wrapped package from Sanrio. That Mom had bought me a present for being so brave made my heart hiccup with glee. I tore into the Hello Kitty wrapping paper. Inside were scented erasers, peach-flavored gum, and a My Melody diary.

"Thank you, Mom!" I squealed when she returned to the car, backed out of the driveway.

She turned around and saw wads of wrapping paper all over the seat. A pink bow.

"God bless it! That's not for you! Why on earth would you think that's for you?"

"I don't know." Feeling dumb and feeling hurt were two things I felt so often as a pair that I could not separate them. They were one and the same. I was an idiot, Dad regularly reminded me. My worry could cause wrecks, Mom had said. Heartache was the instant consequence of my stupidity. "Because I thought you missed me?"

"That's for your friend Brenda, whose birthday party is this weekend. Now I have to wrap it all back up." Mom groaned. "What a shame. They did such a nice job at the store too."

I was crying. Not because I wanted the erasers and the gum and the diary but because Mom had thought it ludicrous that I could even think they were for me. I imagined stealing away in the middle of the night. Running through blue-black streets of the Coffey Park subdivision with a bindle and my Big Bird. Finding a safe place to make a home, a place where no one would ever find me. Mom would wake up to discover my empty bed, my shoes and coat gone. She'd miss me.

Some version of this fantasy played out in my mind every time she wasn't there for me: the times she'd forgotten my birthday, my rehearsal, my name; the times I'd driven miles to have her hold me only to be told good-bye, to help myself to the leftovers in the fridge because she'd be home late, can't waste the symphony tickets; the times I'd called her when on the verge of hurling myself off a bridge only to be told she was on the other line. "Is it important?" she'd ask, sighing. "Can this wait?"

I dreamed of driving away to some four-letter state, becoming forgotten in the forgettableness of it. But I didn't want her to forget. Not ever. I wanted her to weep through the night like La Llorona, the woman who betrayed her family for marrying wrong, the woman who murdered her children, carrying the pain of it forever — a pain that was entwined with her folly.

In the bright, jostling ambulance, a paramedic put tubes in my nose that seeped a slow, mind-cooling draft. He wore a heavy coat with reflective stripes and swayed above the stretcher I was strapped to. From inside, the sound of the siren was deadened by jiggling boxes of gauze, gloves, and catheters. I hoped that Mom could hear its red cries. That she too was speeding to the hospital. That soon I'd see her, hair messy, face bare.

I was wheeled into a large, hard room, and curtains were skiddled shut. I waited for what seemed like hours. Finally, a man in green scrubs hastily entered my stall, skimming a chart and snapping on his turkey balloons. He turned me onto my side and injected my butt cheek with something that burned so viciously, I told him to fuck off. Writhing beneath his latexed hand, I cursed as he proceeded to stick electrodes under my breasts and onto my ankles. He never told me what he was doing and instead talked about me to another nurse as if I weren't in the room at all. As if I were invisible. Not human.

Cellulitis. Endocarditis. Venous sclerosis. Diastolic murmur.

Heroin had made me impervious to everything: I hadn't had a cold or a flu or a migraine or a panic attack in more than a year. I hadn't felt deep sadness or paralyzing fear or boundless joy. I didn't have orgasms, food was bland, and music didn't stir me to tears or exhilaration like it once had. I thought I wasn't human anymore, and the nurses must've known it.

I sat for two more hours on the hospital bed, watching the gap under the curtain for shoes to appear, for a hand to yank it back, a doctor to walk in and tell me what was wrong with me. But I was released without any aftercare plan or paperwork. An infection, I was told. A reaction. I stepped out the gasping hospital doors into the night, dopesick with a big arm, an ID bracelet, a forgotten electrode on my rib cage. There was no sign of Mom. But I waited for her. Felt her coming. Looked at every passing car until the sky paled and Cassiopeia's softening W disappeared. Until I disappeared.

CHAPTER FOURTEEN

"The unending absence that follows . . ."

Glorianne asked if I'd seen the blue plates with the pretty ladies. She noticed they were missing from the recessed kitchen window as she washed a pan. "Well, that's funny," she'd said, shutting off the tap. She shook her wet fingers and shrugged. A couple of days later, she asked about the Wedgwood piece, the vacant spot in the curio cabinet I had tried to hide with rearrangement. I asked for a description, in case I'd seen it around.

"It would only be there," she said, her face contemplative, eyes narrowed into the middle distance. "I put it there. That's where it's always been."

She constructed narratives for the lost: She must have misplaced them, or had never displayed them in the first place; she must have left the door unlocked, allowing bad people to come inside and swipe them, perhaps the addicted ex-friends of mine and Dale's. She casually yet perniciously blamed herself because life had taught her not to trust what she truly felt — which was a rupture that demanded examination, painful both physically and emotionally, as if prised wide by a full-body speculum. She knew on some level that the shed was empty, the garage picked over, that she'd never again see her carnival bowl with the rainbow colors, the coin dot vase, her mother, for whom she still tirelessly searched.

I cleared Glorianne out. Reopened her motherless void. My void — which gaped and swallowed. Like the collapsed star Dale had told me about as we lay on our sagging mattress. A black hole. Sagittarius A* from the Milky Way. I wasn't consciously aware of it, my void. So I didn't know the loss that had opened it, structured it, or controlled it. Perhaps it was not even a loss at all but instead something I'd never had to begin with.

Trust, for one, in myself and the world, was missing. So was the language to articulate myself, the world. There was Dad, whose absence shaped his presence, engulfed it, so in my mind's eye he was not a three-dimensional man but rather a negative space, a vacancy whose bottom I couldn't reach, whose limits I didn't know. He became a symbol for my parts unknown: the mysterious blood, from a place no one could pronounce much less identify on a map; my extreme sensitivity, paralyzing frustration, obsessive fear, and overwhelming anger that seemed to have no source; his fables, embellishments, conspiracies, and insults I had internalized, folding them into my being, unable to differentiate them from truth.

The last day Dad lived with us, Mom dropped him at Grandma Coco's. It was dark out, and the four of us kids were squeezed into the back seat. I watched as he disappeared into the house with his things. I waved discreetly. Mom drifted away from the curb, flipped a bitch, and headed back toward the main road. At the stop sign, she put her forehead on the steering wheel and cried for an eternity. Her tears were loud and indulgent. They moaned and hollered and quaked, making all of us kids cry too. Pack wolves howling in the middle of a quiet street. "You don't have to divorce him, Mom!" I pleaded, revoking my vote. Mom's sadness, the dense and sunless depths of it, was unbearable to me. It rendered me lost and scared. As if it were a forest and I was all alone in it. Where was Mom? Was she the wordless tree? The invisible bird? The distant sound of cracking branches? I wanted to take her wet, beautiful, human face in my hands. To return her to her mother form. "You don't have to be sad," I said. "You can stay married to him." I carefully brushed my hand on her arm.

But she didn't stay sad. She, instead, took us, weeks later, to the county fair with the cool babysitter from church. Bought us

Mackinac Island fudge and let us go on the Zipper, whose kidney-shaped cage we rocked as it somersaulted forward and backward, our heads rushing toward the fragrant straw-covered ground and then suddenly up into the dimming sky, freckled with early stars and smeared with multicolored neon.

There was a gap between dads, between the summer after third grade and the end of fourth. Between multiplication tables and mission building,* *Like a Virgin* and *True Blue*. It was a year I recall as being candy-colored and shiny, everything smelling like sugar and shave-ice and fresh plastic. Chlorine skin and sun-warmed hair. It was a year of spontaneous trips to the coast, of experimental dinners and staying up late. Mom wore green acid-washed jeans that fit so tight, they left mean ruts around her waist. Whenever she sat, she secretly undid the top button, taking a deep, glad breath. When she bought them, she asked me what I thought, turning from side to side, one hand on her hip and the other in her hair, just like a centerfold. It made me giddy that she'd asked my opinion, considered me a perfectly capable arbiter of style. I jumped around on the bed we'd all been conceived in and she didn't even scold me to stop. She had even allowed me, once, to sleep in the bed with her. I was both nervous and overjoyed to be so close to her. So much so, I never dreamed. I just lay there, perfectly still, listening to her breathing, my heart-beat. *The awareness of full; the foreknowledge of lack.*

---

*Dad helped me build a perfectly to-scale rendition of Oceanside's San Luis Rey de Francia out of sun-dried adobe bricks made from mud we dug up ourselves from the grounds of Rancho Petaluma, General Mariano Guadalupe Vallejo's former ranch, which had become a historic park. He made the molds for them out of Popsicle sticks, then washed them in gesso once the mission was constructed. He roofed it in spliced straws painted rusty orange. Populated the grounds with plastic farm animals, trees made from real foliage. The bells actually rang. He stayed up all night working on it when I went upstairs to sleep at Grandma Coco's. He told me it was going to be, had to be, the best one. It was so good I was embarrassed by it. Ashamed of it.

The fatherless household is fun, it thumbs its nose to rules, makes up its own minute by minute. It's Cher, Winona Ryder, and Christina Ricci doing a kitchen Watusi, assembling toothpick hors d'oeuvres in the movie *Mermaids*. It's a tender and intimate matrifocal utopia. *Song of Solomon*'s Pilate Dead singing contralto over a steaming pot of country wine, her daughter Reba and granddaughter Hagar harmonizing as they braid their hair by candlelight. It's *Little Women*'s March sisters, pink-cheeked and hearth-lit, gathered around a piano. It's giggling, musing, and performing. Improvised merriment. Supple structures. Unrestricted joy. Strict father gone. It's as topsy-turvy as the Zipper: Mothers become children and children become adults.

The gap between dads was, in many ways, just like it is in movies and books. But perhaps that's because it was only a gap, not an unsustainable years and years. Not a tired and overworked forever. The gap between dads was not even so much a gap as a sliver. Not the empty space but the slim fragment that created the empty space. The disruptive matter.

It was the year Mom bared claw and fang for us. Her protection becoming fierce yet loose. She gave me permission to walk alone to Christy's apartment or to Fiesta Market for Popsicles. If anyone messed with me they'd have hell to pay.

Once, when Mom dropped us at Dad's for his weekend, he made a snide comment about the watch around her wrist, about the pink silk dress with the shoulder pads and the triple-digit price tag he'd heard about. It was me who had told. Snitched on Mom because he'd made sad eyes and bribed me with a trip to the outdoor mall in Corte Madera. He used us as spies, inquiring about Mom's purchases and gifts. Her comings and goings. The men who came around regardless of reason or association. Plumbers, cousins, didn't matter. He accused her of welfare fraud and adultery, called her a gold digger and a jezebel, sent letters rife with scripture to support his belief that she was an undeserving sinner and a hypocrite. Dad, smug, in his slippers and robe, leaned against his open door as Mom stood outside in the sundown wind – worlds apart despite the mere inches between them. "Get inside," Dad snapped at the four of us, who cowered somewhere in the center. Mom held us back with her hand. Dad demanded us with a face. Mom barred us with an extended arm. "You're not getting a red cent of child support," Dad said, smiling. That's when she kicked him. He winced and called her a bitch. It was a long game that Mom ultimately won: Dad was convicted, many years later, of violating child support laws and was sentenced to several months in jail. But that night, Dad overtook her with his fury. We were shooed inside, where we promptly ran upstairs to be with Grandma Coco, who had been standing at the top of them, eaves-dropping, both afraid of and protective of her own son.

Mothers are the protectors, the defenders of their children. They've been known to lift Chevy Impalas, stick their hands into the jaws of pit bulls, run inside buildings aflame to rescue their children, even when they are children no longer. It's necessarily the reason mothers are largely missing from fairy tales and gothics. Only in a motherless context can protagonists fall prey to evil stepmothers, envious handmaids, cannibalistic witches, and paranoid governesses.

Mom's decision to leave Dad was an act of protection. She wanted to ensure there'd be food on our plates and a roof over our heads. She still had youth and beauty. Could easily find a husband who loved her – and by extension her children – enough to (unlike Dad) put aside his pride, his endless grievances, and do his part. To leave Dad was to protect all of us against the climax of his daily frustrations – the yelling and hitting and name-calling for petty and often made-up offenses. I learned early that Dad's rage over trivial matters was commensurate with his indifference over important ones, which forced me to make predictions based on counterintuition and illogic. My predictions were rarely, if ever, right.

Once, months before any talk of divorce, we had all spent an afternoon eating ham sandwiches and green grapes on the lawn of the junior college. Dad was either taking or planning to enroll in a class there — art, I believe. I recall the textbook with its color wheels and sketchy shapes, illustrations that enchanted me, often confused me, the cubist and surreal examples terrifying me in a good way. In retrospect, the picnic was most likely all pretense; there had been serious tones, coded words exchanged across the shady blanket. When we left, all piled into the Caprice, us kids got into some typical back seat bickering. "Cut it out!" Dad spat, his eyes becoming those fiery orbs.

We kept on.

"I said stop fighting!" His voice had transformed into something guttural, animal.

"We're not fighting! We're talking!" This our regular refrain.

"That's it. When we get home, belt's coming off."

Mom dramatically swung the car off the road and onto the shoulder. "Out," she said.

A small smile crept over his face, as if he was waiting for a punch line. Or attempting to hide his shock.

"What kind of hillbilly are you, taking it out on the kids? I said out!" She shrieked in such a way I thought she must taste blood.

Dad got out. Mom took off. I turned around in my seat and watched him get smaller and smaller.

"You can't leave him!" I cried.

"Watch me."

Mom drove around the block as we protested for her to go back and fetch him, our sad, misguided dad, whom I imagined, already, as inside-out and hole-like, his head down, waiting for us to return, feeling rejected, remorseful, and self-defensively righteous.

My relationship with Dad was a series of good-byes. From me standing at the window waving to him every morning as he drove away, to him vanishing for years at a time, reappearing in letters, collect calls, and rumors – all of which I never quite trusted. Was he really alive and living somewhere I could hardly picture? Was that really his voice on the phone? His likeness on the television game show? Once, Gramma said she thought she had seen him smoking a cigarette outside a local café and my heart leaped at the thought of him so close to me. Another time, when Dad Mike had taken us all to Disneyland, a kind of fizzy gloom passed through me as we passed through Los Angeles, stopping for gas. I imagined Dad somewhere out there, perhaps even just around a corner, going about his day with no clue his babies were so near. I stared at a McDonald's across the congested boulevard as fuel glugged into the mini van. I thought I saw him in there, alone, eating a sad Egg McMuffin.

After Mom and Dad divorced, there were the couple of years he lived in Grandma Coco's basement. We'd go every weekend, as per the custody arrangement. We'd play a game with a slack red ball that slapped our skin with pink burns – pirate ball he named it (which was commonly known as Greek dodgeball, but Dad was obsessed with pirates at the time, believed he was one). We laughed and screamed and yelled, "Time out!" "Interference!" At night, we piled like sardines in his bed while he barbacked downtown. We listened to the soft talk of an AM station on the clock radio behind our heads. He left condom packets and rolling papers out on his bedside table, assuming we didn't know what any of it was. We held them up and snickered. Taunted one another with them. "Gross!" we'd shriek.

Dad encouraged us to donate the money we got in Christmas and birthday cards to the Disneyland fund, a gallon milk container he had slit with a Swiss Army knife. When it was nearly full, he carved it open and made neat stacks of bills on the spongy, permanently damp carpet. (Parts of the county had flooded on Valentine's Day in 1986. We had woken up to water above our ankles.) He told me to expect him that Monday, interrupting class to whisk me away from Sustained Silent Reading. "We'll go on Big Thunder," he said. "We'll go on Pirates!" All day I watched the door, awaiting a permission slip, hoping to see Dad's face peeking through the door's wired-glass window. After the final bell, I sat in front of the school with my Care Bears bag between my knees, waiting long after the #2 bus departed and the last children had jumped into idling wood-paneled station wagons.

I began to suspect I'd misunderstood Dad, that he was coming tomorrow or next week or never — his promise merely a figment of my imagination. A metaphor. I thought perhaps I'd missed him because I'd somehow failed to follow his directions. Or that he was mad at me for a reason I couldn't remember. I was let down. Not because I was missing Disneyland but because I'd somehow let Dad down, either already or in the near future. I waited at school until Mom arrived a bit later, a puzzled look on her face. "But what if he still comes?" I protested. I was afraid he'd still show and, seeing I was gone, would feel both rejected and remorseful. The twisting together of his actions and mine.

It had always been that way: I was responsible for Dad's emotions — for the rage he'd blaze when I'd leave a bath towel on the floor, or for the sadness from the bad luck that befell him because I'd forgotten to wave good-bye from the living room window as he left for work. Superstition filled the void left by his absence. It became the cope for his chaos. Each morning, as a young girl, I had to watch his car until I couldn't see it anymore, or else. Death, maybe, on the Golden Gate. He'd wreck. Or jump. Guilt-ridden prayers to guide him home safely fumbled around in my mouth, feeling cumbrous and dangerous, like choking hazards. Because, the truth was, I wanted him gone. Or at least part of me did. And that wish compounded the guilt I already kept for being the chief executive of his feelings. So I prayed the bad wish away, crying behind the heavy curtains, dragging my fingers through the window's condensation, drawing hearts that made my fingers stink like must, the sill full of twitchy, half-dead flies. I'd picture Dad, crying like the penguin in the cartoon who had ice-cube tears. I'd then see Jesus's face, also crying, because He knew my prayers to Him were a sham. Because I didn't believe in Him. Or at least part of me didn't. Secrets contained secrets. Guilt begot guilt. And I had sides that were at war with one another.

It turned out that Dad had used the Disneyland money to pay the water bill, or so he mumbled to us weeks later when we'd gathered the courage to confront him (we had to convince one another that the promise of the trip was, indeed, real, not imagined). It was only a year or two later when there was the backyard sale where he'd traded all his *Playboys* for quarters that knocked around in a wooden cigar box. "I'm headed down to LA," he told every person who knelt over crates, flipping through Stevie Wonder, the Doors, Simon and Garfunkel. "I'm going to break into showbiz." I remember thinking he wouldn't actually go through with the move, just like he never went through most things he pledged to do. But I feared that if he did move, I'd never see him again. "Of course you'll see me again, foondart,*" he'd said. "You'll see me on TV!"

My good-bye to him had been just a few days later, over the home phone and quick-like. He was leaving the following morning by bicycle, a tent strapped to his back, a bag of gorp in his rucksack. "Toodles," he said before having me pass the receiver. I didn't see him or hear from him for years — not when he had promised to come up for Thanksgiving, the dinner growing cold as we waited, not even at the funeral of his own father. I did,

*A lighthearted epithet he claimed he had learned from my maternal grandmother — though I'd never once heard her use it. I've always assumed it was a mondegreen, maybe an American bastardization of some French phrase.

however, watch him on *Love Connection*. Pretty sure I spotted him in the background in *Hook*.

At sixteen, I got a letter from him inviting me to come down for a visit, on my own dime. He'd been living in Venice Beach in an oceanfront youth hostel in exchange for fixing clogged drains and turning sheets. His studio came with a Murphy bed, kitchen cockroaches, and a tiny, carpeted bathroom that sat atop two stairs. He decorated with promotional posters, some of which were tacked up diagonally like a Hollywood interpretation of a teenager's bedroom: cool world, Joe Camel, Val Kilmer as Jim Morrison. A couple of bands I'd never heard of and was certain he hadn't either. He had incense and bongs and stacks of *LA Week-lys*. A refrigerator with nothing but mayonnaise and pickle juice. A hunk of old cheese. An empty Brita. He gave me a key to his apartment, a clean bath towel, and free rein.

At night, when Dad licked salt off the back of his hand and sucked limes with sunburned Europeans, I walked around barefoot and half naked with a cigarette, pretending to be local. Pretending to be older. I appreciated the aggressive gazes of nasty men; smiled when they told me to smile. Tossed my big, curly hair around and sucked my stomach in. Feeling like a new girl, I went to the apartments of people twice my age where I'd pose with a wine cooler. I rode around Santa Monica in someone's speeding jeep, standing up, hands gripping the roll cage.

During the day, I slept in. Sat in coffee shops. Hung out in a new-age store called the Psychic Eye, spending money on scented oils to rub on my neck. I walked up and down the boardwalk, where T-shirts whipped in the breeze and late-afternoon sun warmed my bare shoulders. Later, I'd walk to the convenience store across the alleyway to buy my own Diet Pepsis and dusty cans of tuna. I was pleased that I could take care of myself. That Dad trusted me to take care of myself.

My favorite memory of Dad was when he removed a piece of

glass from my foot. He called me an idiot for walking up and down Speedway without shoes and I smiled, covered my eyes. And he told me not to laugh, that he was dead serious, I could get a gnarly infection, my leg amputated. I plopped on the couch, thrusting my black-bottomed foot into his hands, which he held close to his eyes, looking for the gleam of broken bottle. He grabbed a pair of tweezers off the coffee table, ones he used as a roach clip, doused them in cherry-flavored sore-throat spray. "You trust your daddy, right?" he asked. I nodded vigorously, my face pressed into a throw pillow. "This is going to hurt, but only for a minute. Just breathe." I nodded again. I winced and cried and cussed into the pillow, inhaled its dust mites and Nag Champa and cigarette ash. I pictured having my leg hacked off without anesthesia and this still felt much worse. Such a tiny, enormous pain. "We're all done, sweetie," Dad said. "Daddy takes care of his girl." He showed me the bloodied sliver of glass. A green fang. *Disruptive matter.* I wrapped my arms around his neck and kissed his leather cheek. I was so grateful the pain was over. Pain he had necessarily made worse in order to make stop.

On my final day in Venice, Dad forgot about me. I waited in the windowsill, waited and waited, my dirty, wounded foot dangling from the third story. I was sick of Los Angeles. Sick of floating about in the wide, hazy sky like a let-go balloon. I missed my friends and my sisters and my top bunk I shared with my two-dimensional lovers – Kurt Cobain and Anthony Kiedis and Christian Slater. I missed homework and curfews and bedtimes. Missed hiding my cigarettes, sneaking my alcohol, speaking in code on the phone to Erica, telling Mom I was going to a football game when I was really headed to a party on "the hill." I missed "the hill" – a two-mile hike up a fire road to a clearing where teenagers smoked weed and made out. I missed Mom and her boxed rice pilaf and boiled chicken and soggy broccoli. Her uneasy hugs. The pay-phone quarters she'd slip into my palm before I'd head out to the turnabout dance or the matinee or the strip-mall bar and grill where a blues-rock covers band played. When Dad finally rushed into the apartment, yelling, "Let's go let's go let's go!" – the clocks that had been mocked all summer suddenly ticked with significance – I wanted to scream at him, but there was no time for a fight. We ran down Pacific Avenue, jumped on a bus that seemed to stop on every corner. Whenever someone dinged the cord I cried. I was going to miss my flight, and then what? Get a cash-under-the-table job hocking T-shirts to tourists? Help Dad with the handyman duties at the hostel? Share his tiny room with him, with lady-friends who left earrings on the nightstand? When we got to LAX, we took off running again. Dad right behind me, all the way to my empty gate. He wanted a hug and a kiss, but I denied him. No time, I said.

I'd been the last person to board, taking my seat redly, hotly, out of breath. As we tilted and wobbled into the clouds, I imagined Dad on the ground below, head down, waiting for a hug, a bus, feeling rejected and remorseful. I pictured myself standing at the window, age five, forgetting to wave good-bye. In the car backward as Mom circled the block slowly. When I landed in San Francisco my eyes were still puffy and red.

The void in me had become more pronounced when I'd returned home. Rather than filling it, I denied it, starving away the flesh surrounding it so as to release it into the atmosphere. I became increasingly sensitive to Mom's every remark, to their imagined subtexts, their accompanying facial expressions. I attributed all criticism, doubt, and fun-loving gibes from teachers, instructors, family, and peers to Mom, by proxy. I took her inability to provide adequate comfort or advice when I was down as proof that she didn't care at all. I lashed out at her for no reason, often a culmination of pain that I spewed helter-skelter. Sometimes I was preemptively defensive. I obsessed about whether she was mad at me. Or regretted me. And when she seemed proud, her spirits lifted, I worried about inevitably disappointing her. The hurtling back down to the tamped ground, the underbelly of the attraction.

Dad got off scot-free because he was inconsequential. I didn't love him the same way I loved Mom. My love for Dad pitied and my love for Mom pled, worshipped even. And Dad received my love like a black hole, absorbing it hungrily without the light of inspection or introspection upon it; Mom received my love like a mirror, reflecting and refracting it back to me in rainbow angles whose varied geometries and spatial relationships I attempted to measure and solve.

What if I was like Glorianne, having no mother I knew? Just an idea on whom I projected ideas? By whom I measured my worth? Or *was* that what I had — what all daughters had? What if the concept of *mother* was bigger than Mother herself and I couldn't tell the two apart? What if I was confusing Mom for the outsized, diametrical angel-demon of whose universe I was forever at center?

Glorianne gave the plates, et cetera, a cursory search, glancing in cupboards and across cluttered surfaces, then never spoke of them again. She concentrated her efforts on her birth mother, on whom she homed in. Using clues from a Tulsa newspaper obit, she discovered that her birth mother was living in Picayune, Mississippi, a muggy pass-through of cracked pavement and spindly pines just north of New Orleans. Glorianne was then able to procure an address and phone number from a white pages listing — which she kept written down on a worried piece of paper. For weeks she'd pick up the receiver and hold it to her ear before resting it in its cradle. Eventually, she went so far as to press the combination that made a single ring two hours into the future and more than two thousand miles away, before hanging up. "I'm not ready just yet," she said.

Joan Didion described the grief that follows the loss of a loved one as "the void, the very opposite of meaning, the relentless succession of moments during which we will confront the experience of meaninglessness itself."

Glorianne's loss was antecedent to her awareness. It was something she'd carried always, never knowing life without it. Her void was not meaninglessness but where meaning was made. She stuffed it with dreams and nostalgia. By making contact with her mother, the fantasies of her mother and her past would cease to be. She'd, in effect, suffer the loss of the loss.

Her apprehension about calling was understandable. Her birth mother was a composite. An age-processed photo in Glorianne's mind and heart. Her birth mother was in Oklahoma. Or in Mississippi. Always somewhere else. She was in the curio cabinet. The garden window. The shed. She was the pretty lady of the blue plates, prostrate on a settee, hair in a loose chignon. How could Glorianne think of misplacing her? How could she remove her from where she'd always been?

CHAPTER FIFTEEN

The Snow Chapter

Mom invited me up to Tahoe. It was out of the blue and felt like a test. When she called, I was in a fresh high watching *Northern Exposure* on A&E with my eyes closed. Glorianne padded into the living room, passed the phone over my shoulder.

It sounded like Mom was washing dishes, her voice periodically broken by the faucet's hiss. "Why?" I asked her.

"There's still snow on the mountain. Probably the last chance we'll get."

"No. I mean, why do you want me to come?"

She said it had been awhile. That she and Dad Mike wanted to have some quality time with me. That Foster and Michael did too. I reluctantly agreed to go. If I didn't, I'd have no idea how to answer her *why*. She knew there was no job, no prior obligations. To decline the invite would have been to admit I was using.

Mom said great. That they were heading out the next morning.

"Miss you," she said, her voice suddenly clear.

"Miss you too."

I missed the fragments of her. They arranged themselves like a collage in my memory. A montage of tender, softly lit moments — embellished, isolated, and incomplete. I assumed that she missed a similar version of me — the ideal daughter who had arrived in glimpses over the years. A hopeful projection. A cultural amalgamation taken from television and magazine ads and the imagined lives of other people's daughters.

I got off the phone, riled. I had to score enough to float me through the weekend, to ensure that no one would detect I was on drugs — an irony only junkies get. I needed luck on my side, to fuck someone I didn't want to fuck, to come up with a hundred bucks quick, pack up my bra cups.

I ended up hiding the dope in a vial whose contents, a valerian root tincture that smelled like dog shit, I'd dumped into the sink. I had found it in Glorianne's mirror, expired. I precooked a walnut-sized chunk of tar in teaspoon batches and trickled it all into the bottle. A preparation to cut down on time and fumes later. My only rig had a dull point and a broken plunger I'd duct-taped back together. I slid it in a cardboard tampon tube in a sixteen-count box in my overpacked duffel bag.

Mom looked surprised when she pulled into the driveway and saw me sitting on my bag on the footbridge, staring at the ragged, colorless koi below the pond's filmy surface. I knew she'd expected me to flake, confirming what she already knew.

"You sure packed a lot," she said. Her eyes scrunched as if the sun was in them, her mouth barely a smirk. "You know we're only going for two nights, right?"

I sat in the way-back, alone, sprawled. My muscles humming, neurotransmitters firing just right. In front of me, the kids: Michael, almost too tall for his booster seat at six years old, and Foster, age nine, big front teeth, big feet.

"Hi, Duckie," I said to Michael, who gripped a sticky deck of Pokémon cards. "You're so big all of a sudden!"

His smile was unsure. A twinge of stranger-danger, or maybe just shyness, tugged his upper lip. It made me feel sad and gross.

Beyond Foster and Michael was Mom's gleaming, round bob and Dad Mike's bald dome, also gleaming. Classical music was periodically interrupted with the soothing mumble of a public radio host. We bored through the borderless gray of interstate and winter sky at conservative speed. Sweet, milky coffee leaked from its lid onto the sleeves of my sweater. My pupils were still pinned.

We were headed east, slightly north, to El Dorado — the county that sits in the crotch of California's underwater angle, rubbing against Nevada. It was the site of the Gold Rush, the motherlode veining its mountains, gilding its riverbeds. As we climbed higher up the mountain pass, the patches of granular snow between the pines along the highway stitched themselves into a thick white quilt. Inversely, internally, the fuzzy blanket of my high began to unravel, exposing buried nerves and post-poned pain. Foster asked, "Can we play *I spy with my little eye?*" He asked, "Do you know *animal vegetable mineral?*" He told me that Veggie Tales was for babies. That Jason is the red Power Ranger and drives the Tyrannosaurus Dinozord but that his favorite was the yellow one because she was a girl that wasn't pink. I leaned my head against the window and told him I was too tired to talk. He offered me a blue raspberry Warhead.

Eventually, we pulled up to an unremarkable duplex on a salt-eaten residential street in South Lake Tahoe. Foster and Michael leaped out of car, which had become stale with breath, sweat, and goldfish crackers during the four-hour drive. They flung snow at each other, put it in their mouths, fell into it face down, arms out. I was envious of their delight, their healthy bodies. The cold made me suddenly aware of my bones, which felt hollow and achy and older than my age.

In a picture from that trip, I pose with my little brothers in front of the timeshare. My face is uncertain, a cross between a grin and a wince. I look like a child, but I also look old. Older, even, than Mom, who, in another picture from that trip, glows, the apples of her cheeks shiny, eyes bright, the dimple on her chin like an embellishment on a pie. On either side of me, my broth-ers hold snowballs proudly. Atop each of their outer shoulders is a hand, liver-colored and huge. Those hands were the index of my illness, announcing every spoon I held, every dirty dollar and dick, every needle that penetrated even the slightest metacarpal vein that bloomed blue under a hot faucet. And there they rested, reluctantly, on two sweet boys who called my name, tried to get me to play, to make angels and men with the material around us, unlimited and God-sent.

As we unpacked the trunk, flakes dropped from the sky in eager flocks. Every noise — the squeals coming from my brothers, the exchange of small sentences between my parents, the slam of the trunk, the crunch underfoot — was made more substantial, more intimate by the snow. I felt totally exposed. Mic'd. There we all were, so close to one another, without the obscurings of color and sunlight at play, without a vast, empty sky to carry the evidence of our footfalls, our farts and coughs and puffer-coat rustlings. I was momentarily reminded that we were all from the same place, this small, blue planet that hosts weather events.

We went to dinner at a Hard Rock Café in Stateline. The walls were lit fish-tank neon, displayed guitars and gold records and signed 8x10s of rockstars. I sat with Foster on a cushioned bench while we awaited our table. His ringlets popped from the bottom of a pom-topped beanie, and he kept a measured thunking with the back of his heels against the bench. I held a tacky, towel-wiped menu across my lap and stared at pictures of deep-fried piles and jewel-toned cocktails.

"Why are your hands like that?" Foster asked.

"Like what?"

"Like wood."

I looked at them, covered in shiny, gray sores that resembled knots on plywood. They were no longer contoured with bone and vein, the oculus of knuckle. "It's from bug bites," I said, on the spot. Puffy hand syndrome, as it's medically known, is a result of the poor lymphatic drainage and injured veins.

"Did you go to the lake?" His eyes dazzled.

"No."

"Camping?"

"There's just a lot of bugs where I live."

"And they make your hands like wood?"

"I guess so."

"Do they hurt?"

"Sometimes."

Mom came over, looking concerned. "What are you guys talking about?" she asked, her nervous smile a diagonal creep.

"I think I'm going to get a garden burger," I said.

"Me too," Foster said, looking up at me, beaming.

Over dinner, Mom and Dad Mike appraised the food on their plates and outlined the next day's agenda. The insipidness made me depressed. It revealed a taken-for-granted normalness I could no longer relate to. I wanted to feel happy about an onion ring! Bemused by a blue beverage in a hurricane lamp! There they were, the new family, chewing and chewing without a clue of heroin's hell. It made my eyes tear unexpectedly, my nose itch. I wanted to open up, confess both my love for them and my anger.

Confessions of love scared Mom more than confessions of any other kind. She didn't trust them. It was easier to assume they carried a sinister or suicidal subtext, or, less seriously, one of emotional instability or pandering. To believe there was no catch at all, that the words were plain and straightforward, was too difficult for her to handle, made her too vulnerable. So she never told us she loved us either, just as her mother, Gramma, had done. Instead, Mom would write it on napkins she'd pack in our lunches. Maybe it had been just once or twice. Maybe I only remember it as a regular thing because they meant so much to me, those three words in her left-handed slant, a heart sticker next to them. (Had it been Valentine's Day?) Napkins were safer than words because they didn't require a reply. They allowed distance. They were disposable, ephemeral. I kept mine in my smelly *Sesame Street* lunch pail as long as I could.

Back at the timeshare, Dad Mike scrolled the cable channels and found a Bruce Willis thriller in its opening credits. He sent the kids off to bed, declaring the movie was for grown-ups. I was, at that point, in a tortured state of dopesickness, pretending to be fine, contentedly engrossed in the film.

I was protecting my family through benevolent deception. Why should I have troubled them with the truth of my ever-continuing substance abuse? Make them sleepless with worry, guilty they'd somehow failed as parents? How could I have placed such heaviness on my little brothers, who so clearly looked up to me? Introduce the strange, forbidding, and adult topic of drugs into their pure minds?

I fidgeted in the unfamiliar living room. It smelled like discount-retailer potpourri and water damage. Mom and Dad Mike were absorbed in the drama unfolding on the television set. Every time I sighed or whined Mom glanced at me. "You all right?"

"Stomachache," I said.

"There's a Tums in my purse."

After the movie, after the light in my parents' room went out, I knelt by the window on the far side of my bed, where the moonlit snow lent a uniform, grainy dim to the room my eyes slowly adjusted to. I removed my gear from the innermost depths of my duffel bag and made a shot.

To the person addicted to opiates, relief doesn't come as the orgasm portrayed in movies. It comes as a surfacing, a breath to long-emptied lungs. It's the end of panic, not the apex of pleasure.

A quiet shored me as my organs and circuitry flickered back to life. Standing at the window, I watched the stillness. Only the sky moved, and just barely – smudges of cloud skimming over a lean moon. The snow was phosphorescent blue and barred with the long shadows of pine trees. The street was renewed, its tracks covered. Such beauty! I wanted it to stay that way forever.

I had the impulse to slip out the front door and walk around ever so gently in that moon-bright silence, to be part of the temporary perfection, the illusion. Simply looking at it through a pane of glass was not enough. But I wasn't a snowshoe hare, blurring into the background, soundless as a ghost. I couldn't hide like a sidewalk. I stood out despite my attempts at camouflage. And stayed invisible when I yearned to be seen.

The next morning, we drove up to Heavenly, a ski resort that straddled the state line, boasting slopes in both California and Nevada. I hadn't skied since I was sixteen. Dad Mike had taken us up a few times when we were younger, each time enrolling us kids in ski school, where we learned and relearned to pizza-plow on bunny slopes. My body remembered how to look over my shoulder to grab the chairlift's beam, how to swerve the slope and get up from a fall. I took an easy run again and again and again, familiarizing myself with its rhythms and ruts until I no longer had to think. I was pure body. When I started to feel dopesick, I continued, concentrating only on the sensation of slicing, weaving, whooshing atop a perfectly blank layer, temporary and deceiving though it was. I ditched my hat, my gloves, and my jacket. My stiff fingers numbed, my nose leaked, and my bowels cramped. Being in nature – even the semi-simulacrum of it – helped me tolerate the pain a little bit longer.

On groomed trails of machine-made snow, sculpted by snow-cats and dynamite, behind a pricy paywall with a pass clipped to my coat, I pretended to be in the comforting arms of the wild. But real nature isn't safe. Its cloud-cycles and crust-rumblings cause disaster. A slab of sliding snowpack is murderous. The untouched mountain is a place to disappear without a trace, buried until spring's thaw, identified by teeth.

That night, twitchy, urgent, I slipped my gear in the waist-band of my pants and announced I was taking a bath. I limped to the bathroom, locked the door behind me, and made my shot as the water rose in the tub. Once I settled into its warmth, the doorknob began to rattle.

"Why is it locked?" Mom asked on the other side.

"I'm taking a shit," I said.

She didn't let up. Progressed to pounding, gripping, kicking, threatening to bust in with a bobby pin. Blood streamed down my wet arm, tinging the bathwater pink. I licked its metallic drips and quickly hid my rig back into the tampon tube, damp now from my fingers, smears of blood on it. I flushed the empty toilet and ran the sink for sound effects. Then I opened the door – buck-naked and bruise-covered. Mom's lips tremored and her eyes avoided mine. She looked terrified. I realized, at that moment, she was more afraid *of* me than for me.

"Where is it?" she demanded. "Where is it hiding?"

She frantically rummaged through my stuff, hurling lip glosses and compacts, turning the pockets of my wadded clothes inside out. She looked tired – not late-night tired, but years and years tired. Defeated, she knelt on the bathroom floor looking somewhere in the distance. She was disappointed. Not because she found the evidence of my addiction, but because she didn't.

CHAPTER SIXTEEN

Abandon

After the drama up in Tahoe, the tense drive back home where I lay in the way-back, feeling Mom's apology to Dad Mike for having invited me, or for having given birth to me, like a stiffness residing within me, my neck especially, keeping me alert to the sparse words and thick silences whose meanings I gathered and piled atop myself, alert too to Mom's stiffness, doll-like and ever-perfect, as she watched Dad Mike's face for meanings she gathered and piled atop herself, I was dropped off in my rotting little corner of Sebastopol, where addicts and dealers hid beneath the bucolic surface.

They were there all along, within a mile radius of where I'd been living at Duane and Glorianne's. But their presence hadn't become known to me until I learned to recognize them. Until I became recognizable to them. A mutual Baader-Meinhof phenomenon. Down the street, in the house perched on the hill with the American flag, was Danny — a heroin addict in his sixties who drove past me and Dale one day as we walked to the market. He circled back, called for us from the window of his pickup. Offered us a gram for half off. There was Simmie, the forty-something-year-old grandfather who lived in the worn-out house on the highway with all the worn-out cars and the big aluminum gate. He was a Black man who lived with generations of relatives, with children who jumped all day on the sagging trampoline out front. He shot his dope straight into his marred biceps, wincing as he did it, his yellow eyes weeping, a picture of his newest grandson tucked into the corner of his mirror. Then there was Craig, a senior in high school, blond with a military jawline. He was an ambitious dealer who stepped on his dope with dirt from his driveway, learned the ropes from his hippie mom, with whom he lived in a red farmhouse, down the way from Simmie. Down the way from me. All of them in houses I'd walked past hundreds of times as I waited for Puppy and the others. I never would have guessed how close to me it had always been, melting in spoons behind windows that glowed warmly on frigid, dopesick nights, obscured behind scenic pastures, ancient trees, those wild pink lilies.

I stayed there, in the hidden image embedded in the pixels, in the sailboat that revealed itself to walled eyes that trained focus both on and beyond the anticipated object of desire. Like the ones at the mall I'd stood in front of, a teenaged salesman telling me to look through the chaos of the art as if it were merely a screen, not really the art at all.

If I stayed hidden and holed in my own little world, I could prevent sadness. Sadness in Mom. Sadness in myself. And when I was ready, I'd emerge. I'd be clean and healthy and honest – except to say, "What? I've been this way all along, Mom. Don't you know I've been over here making you proud?" And her stiffness would relax, the gathered and piled intimations, under which festered guilt and shame and fear, would blow away like leaves, her hair becoming slightly messy in the process.

Glorianne's mother had been hidden by space and time. Concealed by layers of sky, a stack of decades in a pre-internet world. One blue-skied Saturday or Sunday, Glorianne glided into the living room with the receiver clutched between her breasts, braless under her muumuu. Her hair was done in a long braid down her spine, ending at the curve of her buttocks. The windows were open and the honeyed smell of mimosa poms floated into the house. Taking a deep breath, she said, "It's time." Dale, Duane, and I gathered in the family room, taking seats on the scratchy

couch. Glorianne stayed standing, fretting her hands and swaying to the amplified hum of the anticipatory open line, on speaker
for all to hear. Finally, she dialed.

I imagined an old rotary phone, heavy as a weapon, echoing
through a weathered farmhouse, each unanswered ring deep
and bright in an otherwise silent, sepia-toned room, dusk-lit and
speared with dust motes, a King James Version on the kitchen
table. Finally, a woman answered.

"Hello?" Glorianne asked, "Is this Edith?" She stood with one
hand on her décolletage, the other midair, palm open. An oath.
A halt. A heart attack.

"Yes. Who's calling?" the birth mother asked, her voice brittle,
thorny. "Who is this?"

"My name is Glorianne Carter. Do you know who I am?"

A wobbly, diphthonged "No?"

"You're my mother," Glorianne said. The declaration, made
aloud and alive to its intended, was itself a birth. Glorianne,
already tear-streaked and pink, seemed to be cleaved wide open
by that final, out-of-body push after years and years of emotional
and investigative labor. "I'm your daughter!" she cried. Her
mouth yanked downward in agony, ecstasy.

The expanse of silence on the other end made me think the
connection was lost. Then the mother said, "Oh." The single
mouth-shaped vowel, clipped, creaky, sounded like an escaped
ghostlet. It was quickly swallowed back into intestinal darkness.
"Please don't ever call here again," she said. All of us heard the
fumbled click.

Glorianne looked at us, surprised, as if she'd forgotten we were
there. She managed an embarrassed smile, then let it collapse
into a bawl.

"She asked me not to call again," she said. "She's abandoning
me all over again."

We hovered around her, floating our hands over her back,

mirroring her expression of grief. I was not expecting her mother to reject her. I had been certain the woman, after a few seconds of processing, would sob every emotion – some joy, some pain, some possible regret, her wailing blending with Glorianne's like it had fifty-five years earlier – not handle Glorianne as though she were a telemarketer, a reaction that was, presumably, for a golden-anniversary husband sitting across the room, oblivious of the secret child, gave birth to before him. The confusion in the woman's voice, however, was sincere, as if she had completely forgotten the baby girl, *had* to forget in order to move on. The unexpected breach in amnesia was, maybe, an intrusion, a thrust into her hippocampus that left her in an emotionless state of shock. The phone call had reopened both women's wounds, too ragged to ever cleanly heal.

Glorianne stayed in bed for days, maybe weeks. The search was over. She no longer needed to spend afternoons on the phone, requesting newspapers and phone books and documents she'd scour for clues. She forwent the TV. The ice cream. The catalogs. The house whiffed of rotting broccoli. Dog pee. The mimosa outside had already dried up, becoming ammoniac too.

Dale and I ratted around lavishly, making piles of dishes and smoking inside by the cracked slider door. We shot up in the living room while watching adult pay-per-view, chip crumbs in the couch. As if Glorianne was never going to emerge from her room, I shopped the house, no longer limiting myself to the inconspicuous. I took pieces of the special-occasion china, the good silver. I took cookbooks and self-help books, Duane's collection of classical CDs. The rest of the Wedgwood from the cabinet. The rest of the Fenton.

I couldn't even zip my backpack. Sharp corners and odd shapes bulged from its mass, jabbed into my spine as I rode to Bill. From the handlebars, plastic grocery sacks containing fragile artifacts swayed.

I burst in, bells chiming, backpack getting caught in the door, bags hanging from frenzied limbs. Bill pressed his temples. Squinted at me.

"What's going on with you?" he said.

"What do you mean?" I asked, panting, sweating, clanging.

"I mean this." He motioned at me. Or maybe at the piled and dangling stuff that had me clamoring around like a one-man band.

"I told you before. My grandma."

He narrowed his eyes at me.

"What do you *think's* going on with me?"

"Haven't the foggiest." He took a sip from a mug of coffee. "You got some trouble in your personal life, is that it?"

"My boyfriend's an alcoholic," I blurted without thinking. Just a slight fudging of the truth, edited it to be legal and commonplace, removing myself from culpability.

"Goddamn it." He took a sharp breath in and closed his eyes. "I knew it was something like that. Thought maybe drugs. I take it you're funding his habit with this stuff?"

"Sometimes I have to drink too. Just to deal."

"Figured as much. You don't have to hide anything from me." Then: "You need a place to stay? I can talk to some people. I can help you out."

"It's not like that," I said. "He's not violent."

"Abusers abuse. Doesn't have to be violent. Can be mental. Emotional. Codependence, it's called."

I nodded again, my eyes downcast. I was such a piece of shit.

Bill gave me quick, beckoning fingers, fed up though they were. I freed myself from the weight of the bags, crowded everything onto the counter. He gave the whole lot a quick once-over. Didn't bust out his loupe or consult his coffee-ring-covered buyer's guide. Didn't seem to notice or care about the minor chips and stains. He handed me a lowball and told me to get out before he changed his mind. He crossed his arms. Frowned at his own foolishness.

I knew I'd never go back. His trust in me was gone. Anyway, so were the antiques. I felt rash. Destructive. Like I could hold up a bank. Hijack a car and drive to Iowa. Ohio. If I changed my name and dyed my hair would I still be me? And how far backward would this bottle-blonde with a nom de guerre have to drive in order to arrive at that first place she'd made a wrong turn, start anew on the right fork?

All of my wrong turns had been abandonments, by every definition. I had deserted the things that required too much of me – the jobs and hobbies, the relationships, the nascent hopes and dreams that were snuffed out before they were even hopes and dreams. I recklessly indulged in increasingly hazardous behavior. Silenced the strident voice in my gut with a violent stripe of duct tape before tossing it into the trunk of my Iowa-Ohio-bound hijacked Buick. Which sank slowly in a pond. Motivated by fear and shame, I avoided, rejected, and fled so regularly that I never gave myself the chance to develop my own thick skin or steady voice, a gut I actually trusted. I could never truly *know* anything, myself included.

The word *abandon* connotes an imprudent, inexorable resolve that seems always to be accompanied by denial, shame, failure, and frustration. Though it comes from the Old French term *à bandon*, which translates to "at will" or "at discretion," it had come to mean, by the late fourteenth century, its inverse: "to relinquish control" or "surrender." You abandon the car that broke down on the highway, the house whose mortgage you've fallen behind on, the child you cannot take care of, the job that's killing your soul. You could even call suicide an abandonment of the self, of some self, preserving then a different self – trapped forever in time's amber memory. To that point, all abandonment carries the paradox of self-preservation and self-destruction.

I think of David, the central figure in James Baldwin's *Giovanni's Room*, who exemplifies this paradox. A gay American expat living in mid-century Paris, David abandons his homosexuality through public-facing heteronormativity while simultaneously abandoning self-control and caution when he becomes romantically involved with Giovanni, an openly gay bartender. To perform as straight was survival as much as it was death; to honor his natural homosexual impulses was also survival as much as it was death.

In the novel's opening, David attempts to pinpoint the precise occasion that prompted his "flight" – the string of abandonments from his homosexuality and, essentially, himself. He recalls his first love, Joey, who, after a sexual encounter, one of discovery and tenderness but also self-disgust and terror, David abandons, ignoring the boy and denying his own feelings. He later abandons his home, his plans for college, his country, his desire. Acknowledging his "elaborate systems of evasion [and] illusion," David confesses the determinants of his flight: "This is certainly what my decision, made so long ago in Joey's bed, came to. I had decided to allow no room in the universe for something which shamed and frightened me. I succeeded very well – by not looking at the universe, by not looking at myself, by remaining, in effect, in constant motion."

In 12-step programs, this is called a geographic – the avoidant personality type's escape fantasy with the attached caveat: "Wherever you go, there you are." This perpetual fleeing, whether from a place or a person, a commitment or a conflict, is a way to circumvent the unbearable pain of knowing oneself, of discovering and defining personal boundaries. I adopted nonconfrontational behaviors because confrontation requires a sure sense of self. I had blurry edges that ran together with whatever or whomever I was confronting. As such, my fear of confrontation was actually a fear of myself.

———

Pedaling away from Bill's, I knew, somehow, the jig was up. I took myself to the Sequoia Burger for a milkshake because of this. A last meal of sorts. A way to stall and self-soothe. I ordered a black-and-white, which was a chocolate shake made with vanilla ice cream and chocolate syrup. It wasn't on the menu; you just had to know. The girl at the counter used her whole body to scoop, then thrust the metal cup up and down on the machine's buzzing wand disinterestedly. She was big-boned with homecoming tendrils, bottom eyeliner. Had an FFA look. As she handed me my shake she told me, somewhat timidly, that she liked my pants, which were fake leather, so cheap they had become warped and scaly. Her compliment read as a secret longing, a wink, a rejection of her farminess. It was one I would have given a few years before to someone with a nose ring or a studded belt.

I sat at a picnic bench, moving my straw around to the thickest clumps, lifting them to my mouth, shake dribbling on the plastic pants. I listened as people placed orders at the window — a Sequoia burger, no tomato. Onion rings. A large diet. It smelled like charbroil and pine needles. Duane's bike relaxed against a handmade sign for free horse manure.

After a long sit, I walked the bike back home. Up the big hill. Past pothole. Flagpole. Woodpile. Cat. I chain-smoked two and a half, putting the unsmoked half in my pocket. When I got to the house, Dale came down the driveway at a clip, pantomiming his own decapitation.

"They know," he said.

Mom told me that when I was a baby she had the urge to kill me. I was so small and helpless yet the most enormous thing in her life. This was a confusing and unsettling discrepancy. One time, at the mall, she had to grip her own hands to refrain from pushing me, in my stroller, off the balcony. ("The cradle rocks above

an abyss," Vladimir Nabokov said.) She imagined me splat, like
a cantaloupe, in front of Miller's Outpost. It was a disturbing
thought she wanted banished from her head, a cross between the
high-place phenomenon and catastrophizing. She didn't yet realize that the urge wasn't uncommon, that it didn't make her evil
or crazy. The thoughts kept on until one night she found herself
with a can of Hershey's syrup. A can that would not cooperate.
A husband who would not cooperate. A baby who would not
cooperate. Screaming and laughing, she flung its sticky contents
all over the ceiling. A high-fructose Jackson Pollock in the cran-
nies of asbestos vermiculite; a bitch to clean, but what reckless
abandon!

Mom's behavior had been the result of crashing estrogen and
progesterone levels. Of spazzing neurotransmitters. Of swelling
stress and zero sleep. Of having a preemie, a tiny living thing,
suddenly, demanding her exhausted body every moment. Mom
had only experienced postpartum depression with half of us. It
was, fortunately, short-lived and well managed. Antidepressants
were prescribed following two of her subsequent pregnancies to
dampen the intrusive impulse to abandon her babies (if not her
better judgment with regard to the ceiling). Self-preservation.
Self-destruction. Kill the mother (by way of the babies), save the
self was, perhaps, her unmedicated and irrational logic.

Who was I saving by killing myself off?

I went into the house. Glorianne sat in a chair, her hands fuss-
ing in her lap. Duane stood, his chest puffed, belly taut, lips flat.
He did most of the speaking, which was measured and cool. Bill
had been notified. The police would be too if we stepped foot in
any antiques store within a ten-mile radius. On the floor in the
middle of the room was the footstool, repurchased. Some of the
Fenton was back. The silver.

The entire confrontation was brief and anticlimactic. There
was no yelling. No tears. Just long faces and low tones. Glorianne

kept her gaze outside the darkening sliding glass door, at those four cane chairs purchased years before, left in the rain all that time to rot. As the sun dipped below the tree line, the chairs disappeared.

I remember when I first met Glorianne, how she had told me that nothing was ever garbage. I think of her boxes full of her children's schoolwork. Permission slips. Handwritten receipts on carbon paper. The sheds of newspaper-wrapped Depression-era glass. The chairs in the backyard. I think how for her to ignore the candy dish at the welfare shop or the vase at a garage sale or the beanbag owl at the pharmacy, for her to toss Dale's elementary school dittos in the trash, would be for her to enact an abandonment. Her own abandonment, replayed over and over again. The stuff amassed because she couldn't bear to do the very thing done to her.

I don't know if that evening, when Duane told me plainly and unequivocally that I was no longer welcome in their home, Glorianne thought of herself as the abandoned or the abandoning. Or if they were always the same thing in her mind. Duane offered me a ride to somewhere safe. My mother's, he suggested. He gave me time to collect my things, which, fewer now, went back into the same blown-out trash bag they'd arrived in more than two years earlier. As I passed back through the living room, Glorianne was still sitting, silently, facing the glass, which by then had caught the kitchen light's blazing rectangle. "I'm sorry," I whispered to her back, hoping she wouldn't hear me. Then I fled, knowing I'd find another picture in which to hide.

PART TWO

Other
Comforts

CHAPTER SEVENTEEN

The Name of the Father

My first night with no home to go home to, I threw rocks at Aly's window until a lamp went on. She lived in a granny unit behind a wooden side gate with a string that made the latch go. She opened the front door in a big T-shirt, squinting from the porch light, her face flickering, worried and annoyed. Inside, running shoes by the door, an electric piano, cardboard cups of dehydrated soup on the counter, and a small white cat. Aly insisted that I take the bed, said she preferred the couch, anyhow. The bedroom was up a ladder, and she warned me to watch my head. I woke up confused and disoriented, the ceiling too close, a warm cat lumped on my feet. I left in the backlit black of predawn without waking my sister. Or maybe she only pretended to sleep. It was easier when we didn't have to speak to each other.

The next night I went to an extended-stay motel off the 101 to meet a dealer. In the parking lot, there were a bunch of guys whose cars had bass that made my teeth rattle. I waited just inside a second-floor room, sat near the door, my backpack in my lap. A man with tattoos on his face placed chunks on a digital scale. Boys in clean, pressed white tees with new mustaches came in and out. Someone handed me a Zima. Someone offered me a hit of meth. Someone asked me to suck his dick.

I slept on the couches at friends' apartments, on the floor of friends' bedrooms, smuggled in past parents or grandparents or straitlaced roommates – that is, if we slept at all. We'd instead drift in and out of nods all night, *Celebrity Deathmatch* in the background, *The Powerpuff Girls*. Once, I hid in a closet as a suspicious mom padded down the creaky stairs to the partially finished basement, the temporary bedroom of her hardshipped and retrogressed daughter.

At some point, Dale asked me to visit. I crawled through his window, clashing the blinds, scraping my legs, the shrubbery snapping beneath me. We argued in whispers as he hovered over the muddy spoon, the lighter burning his thumb. We had lazy sex to test our love, our loyalty. The next morning, I slipped through the front door unnoticed, the quiet rooms feeling uncannily altered since my eviction, as if they were only staged to look like the real rooms, kept undisturbed behind thick velvet ropes. Even as I walked back down the street, I felt like a trespasser.

I continued along the shoulder of the highway because I'd missed the bus into Santa Rosa. I was headed in the general direction of the headlands, and though the coast was too far off to walk to, the air smelled danker and mushroomy as I went. Maybe it was the swish of passing cars that tricked my ears, reminding me of the slow breath of the sea.

I was in no town – just the length of a song when I drove, but a long in-between by foot. I think the area is called Bloomfield. Or Cunningham. Or perhaps something else. A census-designated place that's rarely referred to by its actual name – instead taking the name of the nearest real town. Even the rare mailbox had no associated home in sight, and perhaps at the end of the adjoining gravel drive that disappeared into trees and beyond yellow pasture was an entirely different zip code altogether.

As I walked, dump hauls curved me with sputters and groans, their wasted shocks jouncing. A chicken truck passed – stacks of jam-packed cages, a pandemonium of clipped and beakless birds, soon boneless, skinless. Feathers confettied the road like the white apple blossoms of spring. But it was somehow already fall. The county fair and its horse races had come and gone. Kids filed off school buses with *Rugrats* backpacks. Some porches already had pumpkins.

A reddish car slowed and stopped ahead with a single blinking light. I heard my name from a voice I recognized. It was Dad. He stuck his head out the passenger-side window and flapped his arms around. He had a beard. Lost some weight. "My baby!" he cried.

As I got closer to the quivering car, Dad leaped out, slightly crouched, his arms wide as if to catch me. "Get over here!" he yelped. The guy driving was ponytailed, and his hands were sheathed in ratty sleeves. Dad introduced him as Dave, his roommate. They had just dropped off Dave's girlfriend somewhere. Dad pushed his seat forward, motioned to the back seat.

He was like a child. Kept turning in his seat to look at me, his face aglow, eyes wide.

"Would you look at you?" He grinned and mussed my hair.

I watched out the window as the countryside flew by. We passed the old red roadhouse with the dollar-bill ceiling, trembling walls of eucalyptus, cinder-blocked fifth-wheels, and silvery, tumbledown barns.

"Seems like it's been ages," Dad said. "Hardly recognized you."

"I haven't gone anywhere," I huffed. "I've been here the whole time."

"Oh, well, you know. I've been so busy these days. Working two jobs. Two jobs! Can you believe that?" He snorted. "Three if you count taking care of your grandmother. She gets worse each year, you know, since Grandpa died. But you don't visit her anymore, she tells me."

"I've been . . ."

"Busy, I know. We all are. But you need to visit her, Karleigh Anne. You understand? Show some fucking respect." Like that he flipped. His eyes bulged. Gums foamed. Voice rose and hardened. All because I obliquely reminded him of his absence.

In his window's reflection, I saw the flared nostrils, mouth like an anus. Exactly how he looked fifteen years earlier when Mom, after circling the block, made him get back in the car after kicking him out of it.

"Sorry," I said.

Dad reached back with his hand, blindly groped for mine. I took it, held it firmly, then let it go.

Dad had moved back to Petaluma from Venice a couple years beforehand, blocks away from his mother, from the house he'd grown up in and later returned to. I was living in that punk orphanage at the time, had invited him to a few living room shows and attended a single birthday party at his apartment. Mostly, we were mere acquaintances who ran into each other occasionally. It was as if, by avoiding each other, we minimized opportunities of disappointing each other. But the strategy of prolonged absence on both parts only created, ironically, a chronic, low-grade disappointment in the other for doing exactly that. "You never call me," Dad would say. "You never call *me*," I'd retort. When either of us were confronted with the guilt we kept for being absent, this baseline disappointment flared up into resentment and anger that only justified our continued absence. And so the cycle went.

Dave's car smelled like weed and gasoline. The clutch stuck and brakes ground. With the windows rolled down, it was both hot and cold — a shaft of heat from the vents that made me sweat under my big jacket, the frigid whip of outside air that blasted my ears and crazied my hair. Red-orange sparks from cigs flew past my face, were sucked out the window and trailed behind us before their incandescence was snuffed out on the asphalt.

Soon, we pulled into Petaluma — the quintessential small town with a clock tower, a riverfront, a grand old bank building on the corner. Festive banners arced the puttering boulevard. There was a plaza with a fountain. It looked like a Hollywood set because it often was one.* And like every charming good-ol'-days small town, it possessed a subtle creepiness. There were huge Victorian houses with bent rooftop finials, peeling paint, and turrets that looked to accommodate ghosts. There were buildings whose upper stories had been sealed decades beforehand, only the ground levels used, offering some consumer delight. And between the commercial drags was a narrow, tortuous alleyway of brick and graffiti. Mice and garbage cans.

As a child, Petaluma felt like the shadowy cities of children's movies: *The Aristocats'* Paris, *Mary Poppins'* London, *Annie's* Manhattan. I was enchanted by it. I'd stare up through our rainy windshield at lit-up lightbox signs – bakery, surplus, radiator, fine foods, shoes, singer service sales – words that filled me with an ineffable sense of the world I didn't yet understand. It was all very mysterious and grown-up. I gazed into the big curved windows of historic buildings, imagined what secrets were kept behind them. I associated Petaluma with Grandma Coco and Grandpa Jim since it was where they lived. Like their home, it was a place of different smells and flavors and textures and colors.

Dad's apartment was behind a house, above a garage. Its address had a fraction in it. His front door was covered in all manner of decals – question authority and nader la duke. SoBe lizards. Bumper stickers cut up ransom-note-style to say clever, filthy things. Inside, a mishmash of found objects arranged like tiny art installations: a radio station's mug atop which sat a promotional teddy bear who wore both a political pin and a single dangly earring and held a five-hundred-hour AOL CD. Our wallet-sized school pictures were wedged into the corners of framed art, some of it his own, which hung willy-nilly, adja-

---

*American Graffiti, Peggy Sue Got Married, Pollyanna, Inventing the Abbots, The Zodiac, Phenomenon, Tucker, Mumford, Pleasantville, Howard the Duck, Cujo, Basic Instinct, The Sweetest Thing, Lolita ('97), et cetera.

cent those diagonal posters I remembered from Venice. He had houseplants whose long, yellowed tendrils were pinned along-side tracks of year-round Christmas lights. There was some sort of crude clay sculpture one of us had made him in elementary school, a supermarket's freebie calendar, furniture he'd found curbside on trash night, dragged home in the dark. "God looks after me."

Dad poured rum into jars with crusty label gum for the three of us — me, him, and Dave. I took a sip and felt my innards heat.

"Why don't you move back home with your papa bear?" Dad asked. "After all, what are daddies for?" He glanced at Dave with a praise-seeking smile. I'd learn later that Mom had something to do with the plan. Had maybe told him I was struggling and suggested that he ask me to live with him.

"You don't have to do that," I said.

"I know I don't. But you're my baby. I'd do anything for you. Give you the clothes off my back."

Dad balanced a blue Danish cookie tin filled with schwag atop his knees. He went at it with a pair of tweezers, removing stem and seed. Eventually, he gutted a cigarette, mingled the tobacco with scraps of bud, and rolled it all into a spliff to pass around. Said he learned it from the Europeans.

"I only have one condition, and that's staying off that heroin bullshit you're into. You can smoke all the ganja you want. Eat some magic mushrooms for all I care. Anything God made for us. I don't like drugs that come from a lab."

"God made poppies," I said.

"Don't be a fucking wiseguy."

Dad extended his arm, wagging the joint at me. I showed him my palms, shaking my head. "Pot gives me panic attacks," I said.

Dad frowned. "Probably because you're not smoking it right, foondart," he said. "You have to start slow — a puff here, a puff there. Build up a tolerance."

That night, I claimed the papasan chair. Dave had the couch.
Dad slept in the other room, on a mattress with a hole cut into its
underside where he kept all his cash. Dad didn't trust banks.

As I tried to settle in, my nose dripped and I coughed violently.
"Knock it off," Dad said. I told him I couldn't help it. He made me
toss back a heavy pour of the rum to help me sleep. It made me
nauseous. When I told him I was going to puke he got angry.

"I'm starting methadone tomorrow," I said, hoping to please
him.

"You don't need that meth crap," he said, screwing the lid back
onto the bottle. "You don't even know what they put in that stuff."
He went on a rant about doctors and so-called experts. He didn't
trust them either.

Dead set on starting treatment, I told him I had to go into Santa
Rosa in the morning for a meeting.

"One of those 12-step ones?" he asked, scoffing. "You're too
smart for those. You know they're just replacing one addiction
for another, don't you? Sugar. That's why they always have cookies at their meetings. Doughnuts. Why they're all so fat."

"Court-mandated," I said, interrupting.

"Ah. Well, can't argue that. I'll leave you some bus fare on the
counter in case I'm gone before you wake."

The rattan saucer in which I tried to sleep creaked under every
thrust and twitch. I sat still in the darkness, afraid to wake Dave,
who sawed away inside his nylon sleeping bag. High beams came
down the driveway and blued the kitchen, momentarily illuminating our rum jars we'd left on the counter. A door whumped,
and anonymous feet found the path up to the front house by
heart. I listened, both envious of and comforted by the regular,
trusting sounds made by some unknown neighbor.

Thinking another small pour might knock me out, I edged into
the kitchen, running my hands along the length of the counter,
using the memory of those fleeting headlights to find the bottle.

I took one chug and promptly vomited into the sink. I pulled the bulb cord to see the mess. The counter scrambled with ants over a curl of cold cut. They all so desperately went for it, for the tiniest takeaway to schlep back into the crumbling grout. I wiped them effortlessly, rinsed their bodies off the sponge, and watched them whorl down with my barf. No one woke up.

In the morning, Dad sat outside the front door, at the top of the stairs, soft with rot, refolding his crossword gently so as not to disturb me. His cigarette drifted in from the cracked window. Dave's bedding was stuffed under the couch.

I stepped outside and waved shyly. Dad was in Velcro slippers and a robe. He cleared phlegm and tapped his pen in time to his mindwork.

"Hi sweetpea," he said. "You're up early. Sleep okay?"

"Yeah," I lied.

"There's coffee."

"I'll grab some in a sec."

"Here. Want the pink section?" He waved part of his newspaper at me.

"Can I snag one of your smokes?"

He lit it for me like we were in an old black-and-white, then leaned back and smiled his broad smile, a single missing tooth near the back. He had no idea of my discomfort. How would he? It seemed he thought it was all behind me now – I had kicked last night and now was clean, bing-bang-boom. Baptized in discount rum. Saved. We went inside and he showed me where the towels were, how to make the shower go. I stood under its stream, letting hot water pummel my back. "Toodles," Dad called from the front room.

I began sleeping in Dad's bed with him. When he invited me to, I scrunched up my nose. "That's weird," I said.

"You're my fucking daughter for Christ's sake. My flesh and blood. People think it's weird because they're all a bunch of perverts. They all have their minds in the gutter. Do you have your mind in the gutter?"

"No."

"Well then. No reason to keep sleeping in that chair."

For the next couple of weeks, I'd go from the clinic straight to the smoke shop where Dad worked. He'd ask how my meeting went and I'd shrug. Then I'd sit on a brass-legged stool and chain-smoke, thumbing expensive fashion magazines from Paris or London or New York, shoving them into my backpack. Dad introduced me to everyone who stepped foot in the place. "This is my baby girl," he'd say, rattling my shoulders from behind. "She moved back home with her papa." He'd sermonize about how the American expectation to be out of the house at eighteen was based in capitalism, greed, and whiteness. How in his culture, people lived at home until they married. Sometimes after – three or four generations in one house. He frothed. Swayed gently. His eyes unblinking. "I believe in family, see? In open doors." People would applaud Dad, and Dad, scratching waxy tickets with a quarter just below his audience's sight line, would beam. Dad would talk all day about the government, about God. His customers would nod their heads, even if just to be agreeable. And I'd seen how he was with people who weren't agreeable, even if accidentally. Once, to a woman who had just bought a couple of quick picks, Dad asked, hypothetically: "Lump sum or annuity?" "Annuity?" she said, unsure, the bud of a captivated smile forming on her lips. Dad called her an idiot who was no doubt too stupid to handle a lump sum anyway, let alone a jackpot. I felt awful for the woman, tried to catch her eyes and communicate my apologies on behalf of his behavior to her. But she was shocked blind. "How dare you!" she screamed. "You crazy person!" Dad stood calmy behind the counter, beaming all the same. Then resumed his scratching. Twenty, thirty, forty scratchers until he made enough to pay back the till and have a chunk of cash left over. He'd toss me yellow packs of cigs. "On the house," he'd say.

Dad's other job was in a tree. His cousin Ray, the son of Grandma Coco's best friend Isabel from Nicaragua, was an arborist who owned a chipper and a chain saw. Dad loved getting up high in the treetops, his saw's wheeling teeth wailing through dangerous or ailing limbs – those gone rusty to bugs or fungus. He was offended when Ray assigned him to the ground, tasked to shove branches into the grumbling maw of the chipper. Dad would curse Ray and threaten to quit. "That jerk's gotta show me some respect! He knows I'm his best guy!" Ray and Dad regularly went through spells of not speaking to each other. But they always made up with great slappy hugs at some convenient point, both pretending there had never even been an issue at all.

When Dad walked through the front door after work, it was as if a TV had been turned on. His volume swallowed us – us being me, Dave, and whoever else happened to be hanging out. There were always people hanging out – local stoners and girls from the bar whose thong panties breached their jewel-encrusted jeans, fellow conspiracy theorists and undergrad Marxists in their wool caps and fatigues, smoking rollies. Often, it was other tree men, still dressed in hi-viz yellow and steel-toe boots. They'd drop heavy tool belts crowded with carabiners onto the floor, release their weary bodies into scooched chairs, rubbing their palms anticipatorily as Dad reached for the grinder, the rolling papers. They'd shake their heads to Dad's stories, always about some fool he'd encountered that day. Some exaggerated fable that made Dad look like the hero.

Dad, his eyes becoming lazy and his smile dopey, would introduce me to the room. "This is my beautiful baby," he'd say, his hands open and pleading. "Looks just like her mother! I'm so proud!" Sometimes he'd cry because he couldn't hold his liquor. He'd be weepy-drunk after two swigs. The men, afraid to look at me, would raise a couple of fingers or sternly nod with a grunt before hiss-cracking a Coors. And around that time of night, when Dad was quoting the Old Testament or talking about how the moon landing never happened or mawkishly reminiscing about Mom's icy feet (he'd sing a song called "Popsicle Toes"), I'd violate his sole condition and relapse over and over again, each time telling myself I'd get back on track with the methadone the next day. I'd announce to the room my plans to shower and excuse myself. Then, swiveling the showerhead away from me, water spattering all over the warped faux marble, I'd squat into a steamy corner, allowing the heat to cultivate the blue crazing on the top of my thighs. It was in those shy leg veins I'd find ways back in.

The guilt I had was not only for disobeying Dad but also for fooling him so thoroughly that he put me on a pedestal and paraded me around like a show pony. It made me forgive all the past lashes and varied bruises (buttocks, forearm, heart, ego), all the times he'd called me an idiot, all the times he'd left me waiting. But I'd always had the guilt. Since age five at the living room window reciting prayers, tracing hearts.

When I'd emerge from the bathroom, skimpy and vanilla-scented, my hair in a towel, the men slyly glimpsed me as I passed through to the main room to fetch some needed thing. To fetch their imaginations in some way or another. I wasn't interested in any of them. I was only interested in interesting them.

Three weeks had passed. Methadone was over, and I was no closer to being clean than I'd been when I'd started. I was worse off. My tolerance had grown robust, requiring more drug and more money for an equivalent high. Dad, clueless, convinced his friend Dixie to hire me at the coffee shop she managed. For a few weeks, I ran the register and washed dishes. Poured heavy cream into stainless-steel canisters. Spent my lunch breaks in the employee bathroom where I'd shoot up in a squirrelly foot vein, calling, "Just a second!" every time someone knocked, needing napkins or nitrous oxide from the supply shelf. Dad showed up nearly every morning, right at open, filling his own mug with drip and eating Saran-wrapped day-olds. Then, sensing that I was about to be confronted if not canned, I stopped showing up for my shifts. Dad was pissed. I told him that everyone there was an asshole.

One morning, while Dad was out, there was a timid knock on the door.

"Your pop around?" the man asked. He was prematurely mature, his meaty hands paint-splattered, eyes dingy. I recognized him from the living room.

"He's still at work," I said.

"Imagine he doesn't get much work this time of year," the man said, gesturing to the open door behind him. It was raining.

"Who knows," I said, leaving the door open so he'd follow me.

"Hey um," he said, rubbing his eyebrow. "I heard some stuff about you. Probably just some bullshit."

"What stuff?" I asked, thrilled.

"Drug stuff, I guess." He crossed his arms over his chest and looked at his steel-toes. "I'm no rat. I won't say nothing to your pop. I was just thinking maybe if it were true maybe you could get me a little. Of course, I'd pay you. I just gotta get my back right." He put his hand on his lower back and winced to show me what he was referring to.

I had known from the second he knocked that he wasn't there for Dad. I dead-bolted the door and retrieved my stuff from the bottom of my drawer.

"I don't go near needles," he said, putting his hands up defensively. "I'll just smoke off some tinfoil if that's cool."

I called him a scaredy and made a show of cooking up right then and there, of hiking up my nightshirt and feeling around with my fingertips the contours of my leg veins. I wanted to show him that I was braver than he was.

I snagged a pen and took it apart, removing its ink reservoir, its ball point. "You gotta grab the smoke through the pen," I said, demonstrating.

He lit the foil from underneath, and the smoke went everywhere.

"No, man, you gotta suck harder. Try to grab all of it."

He coughed. "It's sour," he said. "Hot."

As the months passed, he and then a couple of others started coming around before Dad came home, their wads of cash wrapped in ATM receipts. Sometimes they nervously drove me to parking lots where I slid from their trucks into slowing cars to buy. If they came over to get stoned with Dad, they didn't acknowledge me when I opened the door. They kept their eyes unregistered, unfamiliar with, in some cases, the body they'd been inside of mere hours before: a transaction, a humiliation, a pleasureless motion for sixty or forty or twenty during which I held my breath so as not to smell their boyish stinks, the mask of cool sport. Their calloused hands pretended to love me, held me like I was an egg. But their faces, strained and shamed, hated this, their weaknesses. They came anyway.

I told myself, just like I had with Puppy and the rest, that it was no different from putting a finger in an ear. And how could it have possibly meant more than words in an ear, which, to me, was far more intimate. Those men actually knew me less than they had before, as I'd only confirmed what they'd already assumed about me. I knew them less too, had reduced them to a *them*, though they had never been anything more, never even Dad's real friends, though Dad didn't know that.

My guilt became so thick I couldn't bear to be around Dad, especially when he was jauntily going about, whistling a tune, making us a fifteen-bean soup, folding our laundry, my panties into tiny parcels. The guilt was no longer just a heavy sensation at my solar plexus; it encased me like a full-body cast from whose hardened poultice I peeked. It was immobilizing, attempting to reset my wayward bones, to correct me. Worse than my lies to Dad was my betrayal of him, my disrespect. I was making him the fool he absolutely dreaded to be, the fool he already was, unknowingly wearing the fool-suit passed down from his father. He embodied every application of the word, from the clowning court jester to the naive wanderer of the Major Arcana, from the religious fanatic to the haughty scoffer of Proverbs. He, ironically, made foolish choices in work and in love and in everything else because he wouldn't be made a fool. Not by a pastor or some idiot boss. Not by some "big-titted ditz" with a Today sponge in her purse. Not by society, the media, our institutions. Not by his mother, his ex-wife, or his children ("April Fools!" we'd shouted). Not by the daughter whose forbidden and selfish desires could both collapse and strengthen patriarchies.

There's a Nicaragüense folktale about a girl named La Mocuana — a legendary beauty, daughter of a legendary chief. She came from the green valley where the Río Grande de Matagalpa and the Río Viejo meet in Nicaragua's Sébaco Valley, which was known for its fertility, its cacao and corn. She was likely Cacaopera, an indigenous people who were skilled with bows and arrows and the ways of war. Her tribe was rumored to be unconquerable, and the conquistadores feared them.

Whenever Spaniards passed through Sébaco, La Mocuana's father was genial to them, fed them and gave them placating gifts of skins and gold pieces. They'd eventually go on their way without trouble, taking with them another rumor — one about the tribe's vast fortune. On salty wind, word of it moved over the ocean, back to Spain, to King Charles V and the holy men in their robes. One of them, a studying priest and son of a conqueror, set sail to the New World, ten weeks from Seville to San Cristóbal de la Habana, then from Habana to the isthmus, and finally north-ward into what is now Nicaragua. The chief welcomed the young man into his home, and everyone feasted on beans, squash, pino-lillo. La Mocuana fell in love.

The chief was concerned. He didn't want his daughter marry-ing this white man in an embroidered jerkin and nether-hose, a showy cross at his breast. La Mocuana told the young Spaniard that her father disapproved of their union. Crying, she suggested that they run away together. He told her that she must first prove her love to him.

She promised to take him to the spot where her father stashed their tribe's entire fortune, a location only she knew and was trusted with years before, in case something should happen to him, struck with an arrow or with smallpox that came in on galleons.

Later, in the darkness, the moon behind a scrap of cloud, La Mocuana dug and dug until she saw a glimmer. As she pointed to it, the young man took her within his arms, his kiss an ambush. Atop her now, he bound her wrists and ankles with lengths of silk he'd ripped from his gown. He threw her into a cave. Sealed it off with large rocks that absorbed her screams. Then he robbed the tribe of their fortune.

La Mocuana's fury was, at first, in that cold and musty cave, directed at the man she thought had loved her, betrayed her. But soon, it turned on herself. *She* was the betrayer – for how could she have done this to her father? Her people? She dug her way out of the cave, using her fingernails, her teeth, her inward outrage. She dug and dug till she saw a glimmer.

In eternal limbo, La Mocuana drags her guilt around, heavy as chains. She wanders the dense jungles and ancient ruins, the dark alleyways and dusty roads, seducing men with her unfad-ing beauty and irreparable sorrow. The men who leave with her disappear forever. I'm sorry, she says in the forced tongue. "*Lo siento.*"

Because she betrayed her father, the patriarch, La Mocuana deserved to be fatally betrayed by her beloved — her eternal punishment to punish men for their desire for her. Her story was a cautionary tale that warned not of greedy, deceitful men but of the loose women who had the power to enfeeble them. Because a woman's passion, beauty, and devotion were bigger weapons than a man's crossbows, cannons, and coins. Because *she* is, symbolically, to blame for the death of her people, the disappearance of her race through marriage and motherhood. She is the key to colonialism.

This tale was not passed down to me in the oral tradition sense. Its gist I gleaned through real-life examples and attitudes. Patterns of behaviors I'd spied out of the side of my eye. Words I'd heard hurled around.

One morning, I woke to a loud, persistent banging. I was not at Dad's but at some dude's apartment. He was nineteen years old, six five, with long fingers and a goofy smile. I was in his bed, wrapped in a cheesy satin bedspread, muted porn still flickering on the television from the night before. The next thing I realized I was being grabbed by the hair, dragged across cold, slippery sheets. The guy said my dad's name. Asked it, rather, in a shaky, high pitch.

"Put some fucking clothes on!" Dad yelled, shoving me onto the floor.

"What are you doing here?" I cried.

"What are *you* doing here? You never came home last night! I was worried sick. You ever think of anybody besides yourself? Huh?"

"I'm almost twenty-five years old!"

"I said put some fucking clothes on! Have some decency! You look like the town whore."

Horror.

The guy apologized, putting his big hand on Dad's shoulder. He said it was completely his fault, completely his idea, which was only half true. I wanted the guy to love me, had trapped him with my eyes the night before at a house party. When, later, up in his room, he called me a good little slut and flipped me around, I was both hurt and contented. He had choked back my affectionate words with his cock, his big hand engulfing my skull.

Dad grasped the dude's forearm in a tender, respectful way. Called him a good kid.

Dad and I walked through town, our strides rushed and ungainly. He put his heavy wool coat over my shoulders, the *I AM* lapel pin catching my hair. Then he shoved his hands in his pockets, perhaps to keep them restrained, hidden. People flipped around open signs and rolled out doormats. A woman placed a four-cup tray of Starbucks on the roof of her car as she unlocked it with a beep. Dreading recognition, Dad and I kept our eyes low. I waited outside the smoke shop while Dad punched in the alarm code. Once inside, the click-hum of lights, the roar of till drawer. Dad counted bills, the whisper of paper, the whisper of his voice to himself. He whacked rolls of coins and let them clatter. Then, the clonk of the safe. The ringing slam of the till drawer shut. He looked up, everything suddenly silent.

"I said I'm sorry," I said.

It was as if every expression landed on his face at once. Fear, confusion, rage, humiliation, hurt, even humor. "People have been saying you're still doing heroin," he said, finally, puffing his cheeks, blowing.

"People talk," I said. "You say that all the time."

"They're probably just trying to piss me off," he said. He bit his thumb, moved his gaze to the room's empty middle. His lips were so tight they whitened, but his eyes were soft. His eyelashes like a cow's. I was sad for him.

———

Before God had He/Him pronouns and was depicted with a white, flowing beard, before God sat above the clouds, looking down on earth, judging and enforcing, God was the earth itself – the great mother from which all life rose and eventually returned. She was named Gaia and Ki and Vasundhara and Mama Pacha and Houtu and Akka and Danu and Kali and Cybele and Papahānaumoku and Bhumi. She was a Venus figurine carved from limestone or tusk, an assemblage of engorged spheres. She was a bell-shaped terracotta goddess with a crown of opium poppies atop her head. She was a cave painting. She was the moon.

But then the gods and their incarnates became male, became singular. Women lost their status, becoming subordinate to and even the property of men. There are many theories as to why this happened, and they are probably all correct, working in concert, enforcing and begetting one another: It was the rise of agriculture, the ownership of acreage and assets, a budding profit-motivated economy; it was monotheism and monogamy; it was the emergence of empires and nations, of lines drawn, lines that demanded defending by warriors, by men. To quote Angela Saini from her book *The Patriarchs: The Origins of Inequality*: "Ultimately, [the rise of the patriarchy] is a story of individuals and groups fighting for control over the world's most valuable resource: other people." And who produced this resource but women.

Woman is mother and mother is factory. Woman is yanked from heaven and shoved inside a home. Made to make soldiers and workers and leaders. Good citizens.

And this plays out in a microcosm within the family. Father's rule supplants Mother's protection. It severs the phantom umbilicus, the insular bond, catapulting the child into the greater environment, a society made functional with law and order. Lacan called this process *le nom du père*. Freudian theories about the father figure, a symbol that could inspire anti-authoritarian impulses on unconscious minds, developed into popular ideas about human behavior – shaped by parental images that have colored our expectations, have populated our projections, demanding replays in every relationship we forge.

Counter to Mother's amorphous, squishy love is Father's hardened love. He is structure and context and function and rod. Ergo, the absent father makes an aimless and delinquent daughter. But Dad was neither absent nor present. He was a man of rigid and impenetrable convictions yet also lax, lysergic. He was artsy-fartsy, anti-establishment, yet severely dogmatic – uncharitable and intolerant to those who questioned him. He was cruel but also a clown. He confused the fucking hell out of me. I craved the unambiguity of either a deadbeat or an involved father. I wanted hard lines, clear-cut definitions because I was exhausted from always having to guess where he stood. Where I stood. I was always either the apple of his eye or the thorn in his side, never anything in between. It was in that baffling atmosphere that my guilt bloomed: It was my fault I couldn't keep Dad happy. In my mind's eye he was a morose figure, a tragic, pitiful man I needed to take care of.

Later that night, when I returned to Dad's, I saw a bunch of bags piled at the top of the stairs. Paper sacks from Grocery Outlet, tipped and rain-sogged. From one, the dangling sleeve of a familiar sweater. Not until I saw a scattering of hypodermic needles did I realize that it was all of my stuff, dumped from my single drawer. There was a note on the door:

> I am sorry I have to kick you out. I hope you can get off (bad) drugs. Someone once said that good girls don't make history. This is probably true! But there are less dangerous ways you can rebel. I love you and want you around a very long time.
>
> Love eternal, Daddy Bear

His letter put a feeling in my chest. Similar to the expansive lightness I'd felt from dope in the beginning, but different. It was pure, came from somewhere inside of me. It was a puffy, blue hydrangea blooming big where my lungs were, tickling my ribs, dewing my eyes. I was, for once, not sad for him. Instead, I felt an overwhelming peace when I imagined him, alone that night, behind the locked door. Maybe it was because he didn't belittle me. Or, instead, smother me with unearned exaltations. It was the equilibrium of the message — mellowed discipline and steady love. It was the fact of the letter at all. It was like I could finally see his edges. The void of him took shape, filled out, became real. And he was going to be okay.

CHAPTER EIGHTEEN

Gimme Danger, Shelter,
A Man After Midnight

The new millennium came without incident. Dad had warned of a digital apocalypse that would shut down modern life as we knew it, making conditions ripe for Jesus's sequel. I had half hoped the electricity would go and money would become null. All of us picking apples and building fires.

On New Year's Eve, I had gone to a park and found a bench to get high on. Then I wandered Petaluma's residential streets, hoping to discover a house party I could slip into before midnight. I don't remember where I ended up going. I just know I was disappointed when, upon waking the next day, nothing had changed. There was no chaos in the streets, no traffic lights out. People sat in front of the coffee shop shaking out their newspapers, flicking packets of Equal like any other day.

I wanted something to change so badly, but I couldn't figure out exactly what. I thought the problem was external and extensive, not something within myself. So I awaited a metaphorical second coming, some large-scale devastation that would hit the reset button, leave us all looking for some kind of shelter and grace.

Dad moved into a new place — a big, spooky house that had been hacked up into several apartments. Mom and Dad Mike would soon move into the brand-new McMansion on the street they'd named after themselves. I'd haunt dive bars and pool halls, looking for couches to sleep on, beds to share, dangerous men who'd protect me from dangerous men.

One of them had a pretty face, but his mind was ugly. He lived at home with his parents though claimed to have once briefly lived in Seattle with a much older girlfriend who apparently had better tits than me. This young man smuggled me into his room, tied me to his headboard with wimpy rope because he said it was hotter that way, when I couldn't push back against the play-rape, which wasn't really play at all because when it hurt, which it often did, I had to take it. I couldn't tell him to stop because that would mean to stop forever, to stop whatever we were. *Are we boyfriend-girlfriend?* I asked him. *Are we star-crossed lovers?* No, he'd say, scoffing, laughing. You look like a tweaker, he'd say. I also couldn't say stop when, bound, he'd shoot me up in the shoulder muscle with Demerol he'd stolen from his father, a retired carpenter with a bad back and disability insurance, who watched *Loveline* in the next room from a recliner chair. The mom was quirky and frizzy-haired, wore clinking jewelry even when she relaxed with a piece of Nicorette gum. They didn't care to get to know me well because they knew I was only temporary. There had been other girls before me and surely after me, padding into the kitchen in borrowed boxer shorts and scrunchies, bruises on their wrists, fetching glasses of water.

Then there was the unlicensed masseuse who slapped the fat of graying women in his tiny cottage, which hid behind a thick mat of blackberry and a wall of tule fog on a narrow road crosshatched with cracks. I lived with him for a year but never unpacked the plastic bags I'd left outside. Everything in them became blotched with mold. My journals and sketchbooks had swollen, their pages sticking together in clumps I could never take apart – my words and drawings, dreams and aspirations, sealed up forever.

I was madly in love with the masseuse. I was terrified of him too. He had pewter Buddhas and brass incense holders; baggies of benzodiazepines, Ecstasy, cocaine, and ma huang; big, wild eyes, a big nose, a big mouth. He took me to sketchy parties where he made me show off my skills in fellatio and phlebotomy. Called me a cunt when he lost his boner or his vein. Threatened Dale when he had stopped by once for a visit. I even watched him kick a man to the brink one night after too many drinks and a handful of shrooms. The man, who had brambles in his hair and blood all over his shirt, was limp, curled in like a knocked spider, as the masseuse's foot made repeated contact with his body. The man was beyond the point of screaming, so I screamed for him – "Stop!" – this time not worried if it meant stop forever, but the masseuse ignored me. He was doing this for me, after all, he had said. For my honor. The masseuse had caught the man, who was also extremely drunk and tripping on shrooms, hiding in the blackberry that pressed against our bedroom window. "What the fuck are you doing back here, my man?" the masseuse had asked. "Trying to peek at my woman?" He called him a peeping Tom, a pervert, a piece of shit, a racial expletive. Said he couldn't look at me without his permission. I told the masseuse I hated him and that I was leaving him, but my fear of being alone and unhoused and unprotected and unloved was greater than my fear of him, so I stayed.

There was the drummer in the cover band, yellow-eyed and pre-cirrhotic, with whom I cuddled platonically after the bars closed; the Coast Guard whose bomber jacket I'd slip on, whose bed I'd slip into uninvited, begging for sex because I thought he was only playing hard-to-get; the fifty-something divorcé who frequented peep shows in lingerie stores; the gypsy-punk who dumped his girlfriend for me, who fantasized about poisoning his mother, changed his name to Our Lord and Savior's.

I loved those men. Wanted to lick their wounds, to shelter them with my uglied arms. I snared some of them with heroin, gave them burning habits because I needed them to need me as much as I needed them. I'd shoot them up for their first times, and they'd look at me like I was God. They'd take me into their chaotic and broken lives, and I'd display all my chaos and brokenness right back to them. I'd confess my sins, beg for mercy. We'd sit in gone-cool bathwater, staring at each other, feeling like we were the only people in the world who understood each other. We'd cry.

I didn't want to die, but I had lost the will to live. I could not see a way out of addiction, and I wasn't sure I even wanted to. My whole purpose for existence had become using, which I trusted would eventually take me. In that sense, I no longer regarded myself as living but as dying a potentially long, slow death. Any self-care was palliative; I used heroin and men to make myself as comfortable as possible, to keep the pain at bay. It was the drug itself that made me feel this way: the whiplash of endorphins; the sustained physiological and psychological stress; the growing isolation and alienation. But I couldn't remember what had come first – the apathy and anguish or the drug. I couldn't tell if heroin was the cure or the cause.

Between the various men I shacked up with, I slept in the car I'd acquired from the masseuse, one my brother Aaron and two of his buddies pried from a muddy rut and push-started when I'd finally fled the masseuse's rage forever. I parked in a garage near the second-run theater that moonlighted as a punk venue. I drifted off to the intimate sounds of laughter reverberating off concrete walls, the whir and clatter of boys practicing ollies on hand-me-down decks. Once I woke to the face of a man peering into my window. He was as startled as I was. "You're a girl!" he declared. I couldn't tell if he was delighted or concerned. If he was going to harm me or save me. If he thought those things were one and the same.

Today, there's a woman I know from work. She brings cans. She has burgundy hair and freckles on the bridge of her nose. Wears baggy men's clothing and rides a bicycle. She's addicted to heroin – strong, fentanyl-laced heroin. The first time I ever saw her I was startled. It was something about her girlness. Her me-ness.

I projected onto her my past desires, fears, and motivations, believing I knew exactly who she was. Believing she was me. She brought me the maximum 144 that first day. Many of them were nonredeemable, but I took them anyway, turned them into dimes.

I started to see her regularly. She lives in a sprawling encampment near my apartment, and I often find her digging through our building's recycling bins. Or sitting on the curb with her sketchbook. Or in the cosmetics aisle at Fred Meyer, shoving toiletries into a reusable shopping bag. We acknowledge each other with quiet smiles, both of us seemingly apologetic, uncomfortable with ourselves toward each other. At some point, she told me her name: Nichole. I don't know if it has an *h* in it, but for some reason that's how I picture it in my mind. Maybe because my name contains a silent *h*. I noticed her belly had expanded beyond the waistline of her pants. She told me she was pregnant as she lovingly rubbed her abdomen, held it under her hands.

I want to find housing for her. A women's shelter. But she says she could never live inside again. That it makes her claustrophobic. That it's too confining. To me, walls represent protection. But to her, they represent oppression. Depression. Only outside is she at peace.

Chicken or egg, I don't know if drug addiction led to her homelessness, or if it was the other way around. Though I'm wary to conflate homelessness with drug addiction, as many folks without housing do not have substance abuse problems at all, there is an undeniable correlation between the two.*

*Because the data we have are often based on self-reporting, the statistics are not accurate in their representations. For example: In 2019, the *Los Angeles Times* conducted a study that found that almost half of the city's homeless population had a substance abuse disorder — a percentage significantly higher than what another agency, the Los Angeles Homeless Services Authority, had found earlier that same year. The California Policy Lab at UCLA determined that 75 percent of LA's houseless citizens had substance abuse issues.

With housing and healthcare becoming increasingly unaffordable and inaccessible, jobs with livable wages becoming harder to secure, and generational wealth and social safety nets disappearing, it seems more people are winding up on the streets. More people are resorting to drugs, finding refuge in them.

There are countless reasons a person might turn to drugs, multiple factors that compound one another, becoming greater than the sum of their parts. I can speak only from my own experience. I felt beat down in a rigged game. Underprepared, overwhelmed, and ill equipped. I felt unheard, unloved, and completely unable. I was, in a sense, internally homeless. The distillation of all this was my self-doubt, my low self-worth — even self-hatred. Having no idea how to survive in the wild, I looked backward, back to when I was a helpless, blameless thing. An infant in my mother's arms. I homed in to heroin. I knew, somehow, intuitively or coincidentally, that it would return me to the only time I ever had everything I needed. To a time I can't even remember.

After I fled the masseuse, my sister Molly invited me to stay with her on a futon mattress on the floor of the kids' room. She had a newborn and a preschooler. A new husband. A new house in a new subdivision where everyone drove RAV4s on lease, had kids zipping around on scooters, hung framed Monet prints in their living rooms. I hated it there because it forced me to become aware of myself. I could smell myself. Could see myself spilling against the pristine carpet and fresh walls. Could hear my histrionics and profanities, to which Molly put a finger to her lips.

I was uncomfortable in her comfortable home, so I only stayed a week or two. Then I was back outside, wandering the streets like La Mocuana. Not knowing that I was a predator because predators were only men. I thought myself a gift giver. Generous with my body, my hard-earned substances. I only hoped my gifts were reciprocated with love and protection and companionship; if they were not, I moved along.

Then I met Ronnie, with his long, black hair and yellow, nicotine-stained fingers. He sat on the ground, in the tiled entryway of a shoe store on Petaluma's main drag, an acoustic guitar in his lap. His raspy falsetto and open chords earned him dollar bills, cups of coffee, friends.

Though it was hot out, he wore a heavy leather motorcycle jacket with sweatpants. He played a song by the Beatles about two people, comrades or lovers maybe, on their way home.

When I walked by, he shrieked at me, tongue out and devil horns. The gesture was for my T-shirt, the new york dolls. "Johnny Thunders!" he cried. I went to him. Sat next to him on the sidewalk. Asked his name, where he was staying. He pointed to the store.

"My dodo brother bought this place when the geezer who had it croaked. He's totally fucking manic, man – my brother. Gacked. Keeps pumping out these little alien babies, you should see them. Spooky as shit. They all sit in there and don't say a word."

He removed a cigarette butt from his pocket and lit it. Then tuned his guitar. His rings – tarnished skulls and goat heads and pentagrams – were tight on his swollen fingers, left green shadows. Old track marks poked out of his unzipped jacket sleeves.

"Wanna get high?" I asked.

"I'm clean, man," he said, putting his guitar pick in his mouth, squinting the sunlight.

"Sorry," I said, standing, brushing the seat of my pants.

"Why you leaving?"

"Going to my dad's." I pointed with my chin up the boulevard. "Wanna come with?"

Ronnie strummed as we walked. Little bits of vaguely recognizable songs. He talked the same way, never finishing his stories or thoughts. No beginnings, no ends. He told me he'd been in a successful sleaze-rock band. Their video was filmed in a junkyard, was featured on *Headbangers Ball*. They opened for Motörhead. Toured in Europe. Then the band broke up and he came home to no home. No work. He refused to pivot from pyrotechnic arena stages to Burger King. "Fuck that shit," he said. "I'm a musician. Not some pizza-faced teenager." He had been homeless in San Francisco for the better part of a decade, squatted in a service station on South Van Ness. Wound up in the ER with an infection in his heart, nearly died. His brother, one year older and years estranged, retrieved him, took him to Walmart for sweats and tighty-whities, told him he could live in his shoe store so long as he kept an eye on it. Ronnie still had the hospital band around his wrist. The no-slip socks on his feet. The jagged, pearly scar across his concave chest.

My car was parked in front of Dad's. Its tires needed air, the windshield wipers no longer worked. I opened the trunk, which was jam-packed with my stuff. I rifled through balled-up clothes, sniffed pits and crotches for clean enough.

"You living out of your car?" Ronnie asked.

"Yeah."

"Can you stay with your old man?"

"He lets me come over and shower. Buys me coffee and smokes. He's got two roommates right now. This couple. They're pretty cool."

No one was home at Dad's. I took a shower and then made Ronnie take one too. He left a ring of grime, a mat of hair swirled atop the drain, a sour stench. He admitted he hadn't showered in months. I dressed him in a pair of Dad's shorts, fresh socks, and one of my T-shirts. He cursed when I worked the snarls out of his hair with my brush. Then he slipped back into his squeaky leather jacket, his off-brand running shoes.

That first night together, we slumbered under a canopy of ergonomic footwear. Clogs and Birkenstocks and putty-colored comfort loafers. The shoe store was not typical. It had a pool table smack in the middle of the sales floor. Ronnie's brother impulse-bought it while overly caffeinated and sleep-deprived. He had nowhere else to put it. That's how he had purchased the store too. It had been a place called Keig's Shoes since 1900. The old sign was still there. Before that it had been yet another shoe store that had opened in 1870, serving those who'd settled during the Gold Rush. When Ronnie's brother took over the store in 1990, after the last Keig in the business had passed, he inherited all the inventory. All the debt. The store's leftover merchandise was a combination of ancient deadstock loafers whose insoles had turned to yellow crumbs and Danskos in unpopular sizes and colors. The only regular customer was a man who came in for shoe glue, several tubes at a time, to huff.

In the morning, Ronnie switched on the sign and unlocked the doors. We shoved our bedding into the stockroom, where I took a whore's bath in the cold-water sink. A customer moseyed in and almost immediately left. Ronnie's brother showed up, double-parked on the boulevard, dragged in some paintings wrapped in blankets he'd scored at an auction. Lenders and debt collectors and old ladies looking for resoling services kept the phone ringing. In the afternoon, teenagers came in and played pool, some still in their Catholic school uniforms. And in the evening, we dragged the bedding out all over again.

Sleeping on the floor of the shoe store, atop the hard carpeting and under a cloud of synthetic down, was more comfortable, comforting, than any proper bed or bedroom I'd known. It was such an unlikely place to find perfect slumber, but it was precisely because of that unlikeliness that I did. Every night, I had to consciously and intentionally prepare the comfort I would otherwise have given little to no thought. There was something, too, about the way the muffled joy of nighttime revelers seeped in through the walls, the way passing headlights made me aware of the life surrounding me, going ever on as I slipped into my most vulnerable and passive state. For eight or so hours a night the shoe store was not a shoe store at all. Just like how in pitch darkness red is no longer red and blue is no longer blue because the very thing that makes red red and blue blue, light, is not present.

After a few days, Ronnie and I told each other we loved each other. I said it first, in a San Francisco bus shelter, on Fillmore and Chestnut, where he had just taught me how to play a Cheap Trick b-side. We were on our way to busk in a bar on Haight Street. Later, we kissed in front of a Chevron. Then ate gas-station taquitos in greasy sleeves.

We spent our days together in the store's entryway, atop the chipped tiles, playing covers, harmonizing. Our voices, growing and merging, disembodied from the wounds and scabs and scars, from the dirt and sweat and stink. *On our way back home.*

CHAPTER NINETEEN

The Lie of the Bottom

People in recovery speak of their bottoms as if they're concrete and once. Past tense. Immediately recognizable voltas that separate before from after. They often resemble trainwrecks, take place in jail cells or hospitals, are formed in the vacuums left behind by lost custodies, dissolved marriages, and job dismissals. They become the stories told in 12-step meetings, stories shaped like sharp-peaked mountains rendered in broad strokes, trimmed to emphasize cause and effect, action and consequence.

My bottoms continually fell out. They had trapdoors that swung open under the weight of my fall, taking me endlessly lower to lows I never imagined I'd go, sometimes nearly six feet under the cold and indifferent earth. My bottom, if I was forced to pick, was the aggregate of feelings that permeated me during the wear-off, the meantime between well and sick, when I had become drafty and open somewhere. The feelings were like the dots of daylight that puncture dense forest canopies, spear all the way down to the understory, revealing the scutter, dankness, and rot. The feelings were often beautiful. They were always painful. While having them, I'd count my wounds, every abandonment, large, small, and imagined. I'd feel sorry for myself and cry alone, in my car, in a bed with a stranger, or as I walked, head down, the sun taunting me. The rain matching me. I'd interpret the lyrics of songs as confirmations, corroborations, of my grief. I'd ache for something I missed, something I never actually had to begin with. I'd become disgusted with myself, berate myself for my need and greed and foolishness. I'd scream. Break things. Harm my body with the sharp edges of those broken things. Make pretty, wimpy nooses out of chiffon scarves. Hate myself even more for such theater, theater for only two observers: myself and God, if there was actually a God. I'd pray anyway. Make vows to get clean: for a day, a week, a month. I'd go back and forth to the methadone clinic. Tell myself I was only chipping. That smoking it didn't count. That Percocets didn't count. That Vicodin didn't count. That relapse was normal. That sex work was ancient. That rape wasn't rape. That abuse was deserved. That a big shot of black tar was deserved. My bottom was not a hard pivot. It was a chain of very slow turns.

I was doing my makeup, kneeling and leaning into a slanted shoe mirror, when Ronnie said he'd marry me.

A few nights before, I'd told him I wanted to marry him. I said it to almost everyone I dated. Meant it every time too. They mostly told me I was nuts. Or played along, saying they wanted me to be their wife because saying it turned them on. They gave me their mothers' rings.

The ring Ronnie bought came from an antiques shop. It was silver or maybe platinum and had a blemished diamond. I put it on my index finger so it wouldn't slide off. Held it up to the quivering fluorescent lights.

"Here's the thing, man," Ronnie said. "No fucking around. You gotta be clean."

"I can be clean."

"Not even methadone."

"Fuck you, Ronnie. What if I'm on methadone forever?"

"Then I'll marry you the day after that."

Ronnie kicked a rubber wedge under the front door and daybreak spilled in. So did a breeze of nearby bakery, of sidewalk plums. A few customers poked around. Ronnie smiled and strummed, his leaky Styrofoam cup of coffee by his side. The day after forever felt soon. It felt possible.

Methadone has always been a substitute. It was never meant to be a forever medication. German scientists created it specifically as a cheap and accessible alternative to morphine during a global opium shortage due to prewar stockpiling.* It was to be primarily used on wounded soldiers but was ultimately sidelined because of the adverse effects it exhibited during clinical trials. In 1947, after the Allies were given access to German patents, the drug debuted in the United States as a long-lasting and less addictive† synthetic opioid painkiller.

Methadone didn't really make a splash until 1964, when doctors Vincent Dole, a researcher at New York's Rockefeller University, and Marie Nyswander, a psychiatrist and addiction specialist, conducted an extensive study wherein heroin addicts were administered doses of it as a segue to detoxification and eventually abstinence. Participants, while on methadone, returned to school, found gainful employment, and took part in "socially-useful activity." It became apparent to Dole and Nyswander that methadone was not necessarily a means to an end. Under a long-term maintenance model, patients could resume or in some cases begin functional lifestyles without the regular nag of dopesickness, the threat of medical complications and death, and the engagement in criminal and/or dangerous activity. Methadone

---

*The United States, under direction of Federal Bureau of Narcotics commissioner Harry Anslinger, stashed three hundred tons of opium in the vaults of the US Treasury in DC on the cusp of World War II.

†Though methadone is just as physiologically addictive as morphine and its derivatives (heroin), it is not characterized by the euphoric rushes or sharp drop-offs of those drugs. Because of this, subjects were less likely to seek the high from it, thus reducing the reinforcing behaviors that propel addiction.

afforded addicts a way to participate in society, to move from psychic isolation and self-preoccupation to community and utilitarianism. This was both its strength and flaw.

Since its widespread application as a treatment for opioid dependence in the 1970s, it's been met with criticism and controversy.* Policymakers, government officials, the medical establishment, the media, and the public see it not as a solution but as a stopgap — a hastily applied Band-Aid that soon loses its stick. Because methadone is itself an opioid, opponents argue that its users are merely trading one addiction for another.

Dole and Nyswander were the first to propose the idea that opiate addiction is a disease and should be managed accordingly. Just as diabetes is treated with insulin and hypertension with diuretics, long-haul and possibly lifetime usage of prescription medication should be supported and encouraged. Never stigmatized.

But substitutes have always been stigmatized. It's in the word itself: *sub*par, *sub*ordinate, *sub*human. They are under, inferior. Perversions. Weak, harsh, evil, slapdash. From Similac to Spam, synthetic fabrics to stepmothers, substitutes are rarely recognized in their own right, for their advantages or differ-

---

*Other grievances have included the following: Methadone clinics are a nuisance to communities, as they encourage loitering and lingering in public spaces because addicts now have entire days that would otherwise be filled with trying to score drugs; methadone treatment center NIMBY-ism results in clinics being built in lower-class/poor neighborhoods, which makes them inaccessible to many and is also damagingly classist; methadone is a Schedule II drug that is federally regulated and keeps its patients highly monitored and controlled (one must comply to supervised dosing, done daily, out of the home, and during strictly enforced hours; one must submit regular yet random urinalyses); because addiction disproportionately affects minorities, methadone is a racist solution meant to keep these minorities "drugged out and peaceful" (*New York Times*, March 16, 1975); methadone was invented by Nazis, was endorsed by Nixon; "Methadone is a terrible, terrible perversion of drug treatment because it leaves a person dependent" — New York City mayor Rudy Giuliani, 1998.

ences. Instead, we tend to regard them only in comparison with whatever they're filling in for: breast milk, ham, wool, or Mom, respectively. We give primacy to what's natural, to what springs from the ground over what's created in a lab. We equate the natural with moral goodness, and this affects everything from policy and ideology to the consumer goods we buy. "There is a veritable law," Cicero said, "a true rule of reason, in harmony with nature, unchanging and eternal, which by its command should summon us to our duty, and by its prohibition warn us from doing wrong."

Further, implied in the substitute is temporariness, and we loathe the temporary. We want the seemingly fixed nature of the "real" thing, not some transitory replacement that leaves us unsettled and anxious. We demand the purity of poles – the arrival of sick or well, clean or unclean, good or bad, here or there. We need outcomes we can picture, not the imageless abstractions of neither/nor. Essentially, we need our worlds to be well defined so we know how to define ourselves within them.

When I lived with Glorianne, I could only distinguish her in contrast with my own mother. The things Glorianne did for me only magnified what Mom didn't. Because Glorianne's love was a balm, it was also a threat. I regarded her kindness as audacity, her blind-eye ignorance as deliberate, her announcements of love as condescension. I tried to deny the love I had for her by continuing to hurt her. By hurting her I was allowed to continue hurting myself with heroin.

And if heroin was a substitute for Mom, a substitute for her approval, trust, and love, then methadone was a substitute for all of that. When I went back to the methadone clinic, for what was the fifth or sixth time, it wasn't for one of their hasty twenty-one-day detoxes. At the behest of a dosing nurse named Nancy who'd seen me start over too many times, I signed up for maintenance with an extremely gradual wean, still unsure how I'd come up with the twelve bucks a day. Mom said I obviously had no problem coming up with much more money than that every day for heroin, but I argued that I wasn't going to do illegal or demoralizing things for methadone, as that would've defeated the purpose. Methadone was not just a way to get off drugs, but a way to get out of the life. After much convincing, she agreed to pay for my treatment. I promised her that she wouldn't regret the investment. That I was turning my life around.

I got a job up the street from the shoe store at a place that cashed suspicious checks and gave payday loans with a 400 percent APR. I worked eight-hour shifts behind bulletproof glass and within a self-locking cage. After work, Ronnie and I played music in front of the shoe store, drawing small audiences of new pals, locals who crossed their arms over their chests as they gazed out onto the boulevard, mumbling about the new crosswalk lights or drought or Barry Bonds. Teenagers with David Bowie pins and Hot Topic shirts spent all afternoon in the store, homework splayed on empty chairs. They clicked balls into pockets. Drank Bawls, bummed smokes, goofed in shoes with springs at the heels, tied shoelaces around their wrists. I gave them haircuts, taught them how to tune their guitars, showed them minor sevenths. Nearby business owners brought Ronnie and me coffee and newspapers before flipping their signs around for the day. It seemed everyone in town kept their protective eyes on us.

One time, I sat straight up in the middle of the night, crying out like a coyote. "Shhh, shh, shh," Ronnie whispered, petting my arm. "You're having another bad dream."

In the darkness, Ronnie's features were scrambled. His ear was an eye. His belly button a nipple. I was in a mausoleum where boxes of shoes were drawers of bones. Our bedding was a cloud about to break, to return to the ocean from whence it came, racing through gutters, quickly around oak leaves and trash, into the storm drains, the sewers, where all the pennies lived in gleaming piles. "It's not a dream," I said.

I cried all the time, dry though – as if all the liquid in me had evaporated, was up in the clouds too. With every lost milligram of methadone, parts of myself loosened, broke off, slipped out, bit by bit. I became slowly rawer. Sharper. Water had a taste. Fear had a taste. Love was an actual feeling. When I looked up, I could tell the vastness of the sky, could see the blue beyond the blue.

Something happened during that time on methadone: A person who was capable of both giving and receiving love, of both giving and receiving, who had dreams and desires, who laughed and slept and returned the things she borrowed, who fed herself and brushed her teeth and showed up to work and actually worked snuck up and replaced me when I wasn't looking. I was tricked into it, like the secret let-go of a parent's hand from a bicycling child.

A bottom assumes a top, or at least that which is not the bottom. It assumes a line. A loss. Or what one perceives as a loss. One's bottom, to be such, has to trespass one's personally held boundaries. Has to challenge one's belief about oneself. Has to disprove. Diverge. Scare the daylights out of. My bottoms only confirmed what I already was convinced of. They didn't break my narrative. They merely granted permission to keep on as I was keeping on. It was only when I rose up a tad that everything changed. I felt the feeling of impossible and wanted more of it. I was off the ground, ascending, wobbling, tossed around even. I couldn't look back down or I'd crash. I had to keep my eyes pointed up. At the blue beyond the blue. Just as using reinforces using, rising reinforces rising.

CHAPTER TWENTY

The Bottom of the Lie

Mom, like me, had endless bottoms, except she called them last straws: the second or third or fourth time Dad lost his job and she was forced to ask, again and again and again, for help – from her parents, from the government, from her work, from babysitters, from friends, from God; the eighth or ninth or tenth time Dad beat us kids, the twentieth, the fiftieth – "Out!" she demanded again and again and again; the millionth time she felt disrespected by her husband, her mother, women on the street who glared at her for publicly breastfeeding, men on the street who whistled at her for publicly existing, society, which lied to her again and again and again.

Mom started seeing the butcher while she and Dad were still married. He, the butcher, had a dinner-plate belt buckle and a wet cigar. I assumed he was a repairman or a cable guy when I found him behind our television after school one day. "Now you got your MTV," he said, cracking open a new beer. There was suddenly a remote control and good channels to keep us distracted while he and Mom giggled behind her locked bedroom door. Once Mom came into the room, I knew he wasn't a TV repairman. It was the way she held herself around him, the way she spoke. "He's a friend," she told us. He was a way out.

The butcher told Mom he loved her. Told her, "Hold on a little longer, little lady." He was married to an old woman and had old kids. Lived in a big house that was filled with soft and dreamy pictures of the old woman and the old kids in gold frames, looking sideways. He had stairs carpeted in white or maybe it was powder blue. We played on the stairs because they were exotic. He had cows he named and later ate. He had quads, a couple trucks, and I'm pretty sure a boat. In a fantasy, I was the wheat-haired youngest daughter from the pictures, slim-hipped in blue jeans, driving the quad across the fields, past the cows and some horses. My bedroom was up the plush stairs, behind a door I'd never seen open. I imagined it to have Duran Duran posters and dried homecoming roses and a see-through phone. A canopy and a vanity.

Mom had fantasies too. She imagined herself as the new missus, the angel of the thirty-five-hundred-square-foot house. She wanted to be the soft-focus, double-exposure bride on the wall, lily of the valley, brimmed hat and all. She wanted the handsome, robust family. The meat-faced charmer with dazzling teeth, a wallet fat enough to feed her kids.

One afternoon, Mom was out with the butcher, and Lisa, the cool girl from church, was babysitting. In her blue-and-white cheerleader uniform, she twisted crispy ringlets into her ponytail with a curling iron and rubbed a kohl pencil she had burned with a lighter into her waterline. At some point, the doorbell ding-donged and a couple more cheerleaders strutted in, filling the bathroom with laughter and Valley slang and a haze of hair spray. "Grody!"

When Mom wasn't back when she said she'd be, Lisa paced around the kitchen, making phone calls to everyone she could think of, the long telephone cord entwining her ankles, her pom socks. The football game was about to start and she needed to be at the high school's stadium, but she also couldn't leave us by ourselves.

"Is Mom okay?" I asked, feeling sick to my stomach.

"Go back to bed, Karleigh," Lisa said.

"Did something bad happen to her?"

"She's fine. Just late."

I lay in bed, straining my ears to hear what was going on, praying for Mom's voice, for key jingles and the front door shutting to silence. I imagined Mom gone from me forever, and I cried for what felt like hours. I wondered if the butcher had stolen her from us. If they got on an airplane and went somewhere across oceans, never to come back. I cried until my brain throbbed. At some point, I must have drifted off, because when I woke the house was dark and all I could hear was a wobbly clip-clop coming down the hall. I leaped off the top bunk and saw Mom holding on to the wall as she walked toward her bedroom. All she wore was a pair of pumps and a men's short-sleeved button-down shirt, unbuttoned, nothing underneath. Her naked body was alarming. I needed to cover her, protect her, shelter her from nasty, lying, charming men who only saw her as a naked body and nothing more. I ran to her and hugged her, kissed her madly. She squatted down, then sat on the linoleum floor, her head against a closet door. Her décolletage was red-hot and her cheeks bloomed from too much wine.

"Oh, my sweet baby," she said. Her breath reminded me of fallen, late-summer apples. "Why are you crying?"

"Are you okay?" I asked.

"Yes. Mommy's just fine." She smiled faintly, her eyes closing.

I gazed at her with care and caution. Gently smoothed her hair with my hand.

"Go back to sleep," she said.

Her affair with the butcher ended dramatically. He stopped coming by, stopped returning her calls. His wife phoned and threatened Mom, called her names. Mom cried for days, taking swigs of liquor and reading the Bible. One time, she packed us all into the Caprice, hastily, with a bale of Charmin and a bottle of bottom-shelf tucked between the front seats. "You can't drink and drive!" I said, terrified, exhilarated.

"Know how to teepee a house?" Mom asked. "It's like decorating for a birthday party." She laughed giddily. "It'll be fun!"

The plan was to toss the toilet paper rolls into the trees and bushes that lined the butcher's drive, let them unfurl like streamers. Mom drove so fast out to his ranch, she got pulled over by a cop on a motorcycle. She blamed her speed on a Chaka Khan song that played on the radio. The cop gave her a warning only. Winked at her.

Mom, after all the last straws, after weaning off Dad with the butcher and manifesting Dad Mike, Mercedes-Benz and all, climbed. Quietly and passively strove. The images from her long-tossed vision boards slowly materialized: palm trees, passport, hot tub. Chunky house in the hilltop neighborhood of chunky houses. She refused to be reminded of handouts and canned milk, all of us crammed in a single room trying to kill one another with our baby teeth, our bunkbed rods.

CHAPTER TWENTY-ONE

Merge

I told Mom first. "He proposed to me," I said, even though it was me who had popped the question, not on a bended knee but under our comforter, a curled tail pinned onto an impulsive statement. "I want to marry you," I'd said. "Do you want to marry me?"

As I paced around the shoe store, the phone wedged between my ear and shoulder, I ignored the persistent beep from another incoming caller – someone needing their money, our hours. Nothing mattered more than Mom's reaction to hearing that I was about to join her ranks as a wife. It would make us closer. More related than blood. I'd also be nearer her desires for me, if she squinted. Our patterns a near match at our shared seam.

"He's good for me," I told her. "He won't marry me till I'm one hundred percent clean. So we're going to have a wedding the day after my last day of methadone. I'm down to just fifty milligrams."

I wanted the real deal. Punch bowls and rice sachets. A dress that looked like fondant and a cake that looked like a cathedral. A bouquet dense with white roses, which I'd fling behind my back to eager, ringless hands.

What better way than a wedding to announce to the world my redemption, my recovery, my acceptance within my family and community? What better way to announce that to myself? And how better than to pretend to be the kind of woman I never thought I could be, the kind of person I never wanted to be but was becoming, generously. This was my gift to Mom. A gift that cost her several grand. A gift that said we were the same.

Mom asked, "Don't you think this might be a bit soon?" and I said, "Your first husband was soon, Dad was soon, Dad Mike was soon." She sucked her teeth. Thrice she'd been a quick bride, why wouldn't I be too?

"If you're happy, then I'm happy," she said.

Mom was also first to know that we were moving into a proper home. The cops had barged into the shoe store during the night, waking us with their flashlights and walkie-talkies. Because it was hot out, we had left the back door, which opened onto the alleyway, ajar. They ran our names as I yanked the comforter over my boobs, then directed us to leave even though we told them over and over we were allowed to be there. They called Ronnie's brother to confirm we weren't trespassers, told him he was violating zoning regulations.

Dad hooked us up with his landlord, who kept a hidden hamlet of tiny homes in a backyard behind a house, one that was Section 8 designated, its renters' Rent-A-Center couches and TVs in the process of being repo'd the day we moved in. We had the biggest unit back there — a flat-roofed rectangle with a salvaged stove range, a toilet, and a shower. Its thin all-weather carpet sat right atop the earth, and ants marched through its seams, making trails up and over the network of extension cords that kept our lights on and our space heater running. I was proud of the place. I tacked up postcards of Man Ray art, draped patterned scarves over lamps. Burned incense and votive candles. All the time I had guests over: Aly and Aaron and Aaron's girlfriend Raina, my cousin Jordan and our friend Patrik. I'd make pancakes, burgers on the George Foreman. We'd all sit on the mattress on the floor, surrounded by ant traps, listening to *Abbey Road* or *Marquee Moon* or *Music for Zen Meditation*. "Who wants another?" I'd ask.

Ron became lonely and aimless without the shoe store. He preferred living in public, taking song requests, compliments, day-old pastries and dollars, not to be hidden away behind some hidden-away house on a hidden-away street staring at the oppressive walls while I counted out payday loans into desperate hands.

He was frustrated that I didn't see the irony of handing over most of my income to live in a place that, like the shoe store, violated zoning regulations. That I unquestioningly gave whatever money was left over toward our cut of the electric, which was collected by the front tenants, who now had no furniture and alleged pill habits. I reasoned that I'd rather pay to play house than stay hidden in a place that wasn't ours, where we had to conceal any evidence of ourselves.

"I want to be real," I said.

"You are real," he said.

"No, I mean I want to be *considered* real."

"You care too much what other people think."

I began to resent Ronnie for not contributing to the living expenses and pointed out that the Wendy's down the street was hiring. He called me an asshole for even suggesting it. I reminded him that it was his idea to be on the up-and-up, his ultimatum for me to get clean. He reminded me that being addicted to heroin and choosing unconventional housing were two entirely different things. I told him that I refused to be a homeless wife, especially considering that Mom was sinking money into me – reluctantly footing the bill for both the wedding* and my methadone. I was an investment, of sorts. He said he would have been fine with the courthouse. That all the conventional pageantry was wasteful and purposeless. "Talk about wasteful and purposeless," I said, pointing out his defunct glam-metal band and their borrowed ethos of excess: the alleged (or aspirational) hotel penthouses and mounds of coke, the bespoke leather pants and custom guitars. He said I

---

*One she initially refused to give me, which hurt my feelings, so I unintentionally hurt her back by accusing her of not loving me as much as Molly – for whom she threw a posh country-club wedding a year beforehand – an accusation I sincerely believed.

sounded like a capitalist pig, caring about the cost of a thing. "Newsflash," he said, "you're just like your mom."

Then 9/11 happened. We heard about it on the clock radio. The panicked voices of live coverage seeped into my sleep and filled my head with nightmares. Then I was wide awake, not sure if I was wide awake, not sure if the nightmare was just a nightmare. Ronnie and I sat on our mattress, my hands enclosed in his, listening rapt as the second tower was struck. I thought the world was ending.

Yet I had to drive to Santa Rosa to get my dose. The sunrise, which limned the distant wall of trees with a golden thread, was heartlessly beautiful, as ignorant as the many souls who still slept, still rested in yesterday, the catastrophe not yet real. At the clinic, counselors and dosing nurses told us to stay strong, to seek support if we felt like relapsing. To go to meetings. Back in Petaluma, everyone in town, it seemed, gathered at the smoke shop, where the big-screen TV had the news going all day, after hours, even. People brought their dinner there – slices of pizza, sub sandwiches – food that seemed impossible because how could a pizza or a sandwich get made by hands that no longer knew what to do with themselves? It was days or maybe weeks of this, communing in the smoke shop. We'd watch over and over again the swell of smoke. People leaping from a thousand feet. The slow collapse of the skyline. Of the horizon. Of reality. Of differences.

I had a nightmare about the *Titanic*. In it, I sat in a life raft and the water was eerily still and held no reflections. I watched as the stern of the ship, severed from the bow, rose to its terminal position. In the pause before its descension to the ocean floor, I believed that it could avoid complete destruction. That it could stand like that forever, brutally wounded, defiant of everything – glaciers, terrorists, physics. The ship became the towers, and the towers, gashed and spewing and momentarily calm, surrendered. Steadily, orderly, the towers went down, the ship went down, all the people trapped in those constructs buried under ash or fathoms, all the pride and promises and secrets and symbols too.

It was a haunted time, made more so by the curtailment of my methadone, the regular reshaping and remaking of my person. I was confused in my body and confused in the world. I put an American flag sticker on my car. I told the clinic to bump my dosage back up a few milligrams. Dad started to say it was an inside job. My friend's brother was on the front page of the paper, unrecognizably gaunt and bearded; he was named the American Taliban. Mom left checks for my methadone under the doormat. Everything felt too near yet too far, both inside of me and unreachable. I held tightly to Ronnie with all my might.

I went every Sunday to Mom's to pick up my checks. She made them out to Santa Rosa Treatment Program and left them on the porch. I hated going to fetch them. *Do I sneak up the steps?* I'd wonder. *If not, do I knock? Wave?* I cringed to imagine Mom watching me from a dark window as I bent over to snatch her arm-twisted mercy from under the welcome mat.

One evening, I pulled up to the curb a few houses away, as I usually did, headlights killed early, door shut gently. The pristine sidewalk, lined with saplings, was illuminated by moon and streetlamp. A roly-poly bug inched across its washed expanse. I was careful not to disturb it. There was nothing at all to hear, nothing to smell but the atmosphere, which carried no moisture or bloom, just stars.

As I ran my fingers along the mat's underside, the front door opened.

"Oh!" Mom gasped.

"Did I scare you?"

"Did I scare you?" We said it at the same time.

She wore a velour robe and her bangs popped over a headband. Her face gleamed with night cream. "I was just going to get the mail. I forgot to bring it in yesterday. Probably junk."

We stood looking at each other.

"You doing okay? You look good."

"Oh thanks. Yeah, I'm only on twenty milligrams now. I get take-homes."

"Your eyes seem brighter. Pretty." She smiled.

"Not everyone gets take-homes. But my pee's been clean, so."

Mom swatted the mail onto the top of her other hand. A coupon mailer, a Triple-A offer. She looked out onto the street. "Where's your car?"

I flung an arm in the direction of it. "I didn't want to bug you guys."

"Oh," she said, waving off my concern. "Dad's playing a video game."

I wanted her all to myself then — as Dad Mike was lost in the stereo-sound blasts of *Halo* and Foster and Michael got ready for bed. I wanted to be whisked into her bathroom, not her present bathroom, which I hardly knew and couldn't picture in my mind, but one from an earlier house, the carpeted en suite I remembered from junior high, where sunlight entered in soft amber-colored slants. There, side by side, in front of the mirror, we'd gaze at each other's reflections. It would smell of hot hair. She'd be putting on makeup or taking off makeup. We'd talk to each other like we did so many times before while she blurred her eyes with Vaseline or defined her mouth with rose-hued pencils. Our conversation would be the same as the sunlight coming in, and I would forever associate the two. By the end of it, she would be transformed — from private Mom to public Mom, or vice versa. From my creator to my peer. Jarring, then, when she'd cut our laughter to remind me, somehow, inadvertently, that I wasn't her peer. That I was always her child, with much more learning to do even when I knew more than she did sometimes. And how irate I'd become when I'd realize I wasn't a child. I wasn't her center. I was a woman she needed to nudge away for my own good.

"Do you have Triple-A? All that back and forth for your metha – for your medication. What if your car breaks down? I'd feel less worried if you had it. Dad and I will pay for it . . ."

All I heard was that methadone was a verboten word and my car was a piece of shit and I caused Mom to worry and I was poor and incompetent, requiring even more money than what they were already doling out for the wedding I had guilt-tripped her into giving me just to prove to me her love. "I don't need it," I said, irritated.

"Did I say something?" A crease between her eyes formed, her mouth went small and round. "I just wanted to help."

"No, you didn't say anything," I said as I walked down the steps. "Don't worry about it."

"You know, you can knock next time. If you want."

Historically, I'd retreat from Mom when I was hurt or ashamed or harming myself, usually all three at the same time because one usually led to the other. And then, as surely as the rhythms of the tide, I'd return to her, needing her so much I'd create some great excuse because to tell her I needed her was inadequate and queer. In high school I moved into my friend Erica's house because I was unhappy at home. Her parents gave me the room that had previously belonged to a great-aunt with dementia. The "reason" for my return was my runaway eating disorder, which I hoped Mom would reverse by making me pancakes and sending me to therapy and talking to me in front of the bathroom mirror as she swiped silvery-blue over her eyelid. There were many returns. I'd come home to her when I got pregnant by my unfaithful boyfriend, when my niece got cancer, when I discovered bedbugs in my Echo Park apartment, when I stopped sleeping during my first year of grad school, when Santa Rosa burned down, Mom's house included. Whenever I was back with her, I examined her face and movements and words and tones for their hidden meanings, for reasons to pull away again.

"We merge and separate, merge and separate," Jamaica Kincaid wrote in "My Mother," a story comprising nine dream-like vignettes about the dance between mother and daughter. The first one starts: "Immediately on wishing my mother dead and seeing the pain it caused her, I was sorry and cried so many tears that all the earth around me was drenched." The mother, as a result of her daughter's distress (which is a result of the mother's distress, and so on and so forth), comforts her daughter by drawing her into her breasts until she, the daughter, suffocates. In another, the daughter builds a "beautiful house" over a "deep, deep hole." She decorates the house in a way that will make her mother happy – latticed windows, yellow paint. The daughter invites her mother inside, asks her to assess the house, yearning for her approval. When the mother enters the house, the daughter hopes her mother will fall down the hole atop which the house was constructed. When her mother doesn't stumble, and instead expresses satisfaction, the daughter "fill[s] up the hole and burn[s] the house to the ground."

Each vignette depicts not only the perpetual cycle of repelling and receiving between mother and daughter but also concedes to their fixed proportions: "I had grown big, but my mother was bigger, and that would always be so." The vignettes also reveal the ephemeral places the mother and daughter are forever bonded: their shadows, their voices, their food, and their tears. "What peace came over me then," the daughter says upon reuniting with her mother, "for I could not see where she left off and I began, or where I left off and she began."

By my read, Kincaid portrayed a relationship that is neither dysfunctional nor unique but typical and healthy. The push-pull is the necessary process to find equilibrium between the enmeshment of our identities and individuation, how we find ourselves within the context of each other. An over-and-over again snipping of the umbilical cord, one that both feeds and strangulates.

———

Another Sunday. I parked right in front. Shut the car door with confidence. Knocked.

"I'll pick you up at noon tomorrow," she said in her velour and cream.

At a bridal shop in San Anselmo, she helped me step into a whirlpool of satin. Standing behind me, she carefully fastened a hundred buttons up my back. At the top, she brushed aside an errant hair, and the feeling of her fingers on my skin, fidgeting with the last, stubborn hook-and-eye, made me cry. I blamed it on the weaning. The rawness of each subsequent day.

"Should we go home?" she asked, her face mirroring mine.

"No!" I hissed. "I'm fine."

She tucked my bustle and had me turn this way and that.

I was waiting for her to say something about my tattoos. Or the price tag.

"You look so pretty," she said.

"I look like you."

The day after forever fell on an overcast December day, exactly thirty-one hours after I had drunk my last dose of methadone. I was on my knees on our bathroom floor when I had pushed down on the lock-top lid and put the container to my lips. A fraction of a milligram suspended in room-temp water tasted like nothing. Felt like nothing. I knocked the last drop onto my tongue, licked the edges, refilled it from the tap, shook it, and did it all over again. Then I prayed I would be okay.

I hadn't slept in three days and Mom, buttoning the hundred buttons, said it was nerves and was normal, but I knew it was my brain rewiring itself and my body becoming something unfamiliar and vast. Spun out on my own norepinephrine, my spooked-out eyes watched from somewhere inside a body that clonked around, trying to remember how to regulate, how to think and talk and walk and sleep and eat.

In a musty church, I passed through a gauntlet of crinkle-eyed smiles, past old relatives I hardly knew and new friends I hardly knew and old friends who no longer knew me to a man I hardly knew. I glanced at Mom – front row, dry-eyed – and didn't know yet that she knew I didn't know myself-yet either.

I wonder now how Mom had felt when she married that first husband whose name we hardly ever put in our mouths. Did she know, already, that her marriage was not to a man but to some notion? A convention that came with the contradictory promises of community and independence, of tradition's holding back and maturity's moving forward? And what about, then, her marriage to Dad – in a courthouse, a handsome blouse, a nursing bra. Rushed and hush-hush. Was it to legitimize me, the love child in the incubator? Was it to legitimize herself?

At the altar, Ronnie, in his rental tux, twitched and beamed. Behind him, his brothers clasped their hands at their groins, rocked on the balls of their feet. My sisters, in green dresses and flower crowns, watched with tilted heads and barely-smiles. I stood across from Ronnie, my eyes searching his to find something I could hold on to, knowing already I never would. I wasn't in love with him, but that was no longer the point.

The pastor read from Ecclesiastes. A hot flash zipped through me, leaving the taste of electricity in my mouth. My bones ached and my brain fuzzed, and I wondered if Mom could tell from her pew. I was terrified to look at her. Then I heard clapping. Ronnie and I pressed our lips to each other's and we hustled back through the semi-strange faces. I made a beeline to the ladies' room, where I ate half a Klonopin and hid in a stall. I listened to two women agree that the ceremony was beautiful as I tried to minimize the sound of my diarrhea.

At the community-center reception, people I knew from the shoe store, people I'd handed blank invitations to, whose names I'd misremembered, lined up to hug me. They sat at tables with acquaintances and ate steak, drank wine. They shimmied and shook to Al Green on the dance floor; spun my nieces around in circles; coaxed Grampa up and Uncle Brad up and Aunt Stacey; Grandma Coco, who snapped her fingers in her silk pantsuit. My sisters kicked off their heels and ditched their wilting crowns, did the locomotion and the limbo. Ronnie's brothers danced. My brothers danced. Dad danced, his smile like a jack-o'-lantern's. My friend from the methadone clinic danced. My friend from junior high. The American Taliban's brother. I danced. Through my fever. Through fear and pain. I danced with a joy I'd never felt before. Maybe I wasn't in love with Ronnie, but I was, I knew, in love.

CHAPTER TWENTY-TWO

Final Rests

Ronnie and I spent the night in a cozy upstairs bedroom in a Victorian house, blocks away from the reception. One of my aunts had made us a reservation at the bed-and-breakfast during the champagne toast. Apparently, it pained her to imagine us returning to our cold, ant-infested hovel in the afterglow of matrimony. We walked over, husband and wife, the hem of my wedding dress dragging on the sidewalk. People honked as they passed – departing guests, enthusiastic strangers. Ronnie flopped atop the bed in his tux, already hungover. I ran a bath in the claw-foot tub. We didn't have sex. Instead, I lay all night with my eyes wide open, little tremors rippling through me.

Methadone had allowed me to separate from heroin – from its ritual and romance, its demand on my body and time. Now I was separating from methadone, a merely chemical attachment, but one whose torture was protracted and, counterintuitively, worse over time. I could feel the hollow of every bone, an astringent ache I visualized as actual liquid methadone leaving my fibulae and ulnae, the crests of my hips and hinges of my fingers, as if it had pooled in my marrow during the eight months of taking it and now was being slowly expelled on beads of sweat, in streams of pee. My muscles felt wrung. Their burn was gritty and raw, like the fourth-grade forearm prank with a racist name. Indescribable sensations zapped through me, stole my breath and heartbeat, left me terrified and distrustful of the body I was trapped inside.

I could not locate myself within myself. Even my brain, where I had always assumed I resided, became unfamiliar. It thought weird thoughts. Made emotions that didn't fit the situation. I pictured myself as something entirely separate, something pea-sized and powerless that peered out of the wild pupils of a grotesque mascot.

After the wedding, I stopped going to work at the check-cashing center and was subsequently fired. I stopped going outside. I skipped Christmas. Hibernated under smelly sheets, the empty refrigerator moaning behind my head. The ants had left. The water in the bowl atop the space heater evaporated, leaving a ring of white residue. Outside, impossible snow. Ronnie splurged on soup from the Whole Foods hot bar for me, brought new-release movies that seemed to play all night, sound muted, their images becoming the stuff of my bizarre half-dreams. Or perhaps they were hallucinations, the delirium of impending death. I thought I was dying.

There had been countless times I'd brushed against death and imagined the aftermath of discovery – of being found slumped in a bathroom stall or beneath an overpass, stripped of any dignity like it was copper wire. I pictured Mom walking into my posthumous room, stumbling upon the instruments of my disease, the spoons and needles and plastic baggies, the evidence of a truth she already gut-knew. Sometimes, those images became the scenes of a revenge fantasy aimed at Mom that filled me with self-pity and grief. I'd wallow in the belief that only in death would I be missed, gratified that I finally "showed her." Most of the time, the images caused me to shudder and bite my hand, squeeze my eyes tightly closed so to make them disappear. "No no no no no!" I'd cry, grieving now for Mom and the eternal sorrow I'd be handing her, the woman I had elevated to God-like status, who I couldn't see as a normal, flawed mortal, whose faults I took personally because I'd become deranged in my estimation of her. I'd picture the pile of hypodermic needles she'd find, still traced with my blood, its

helical code that linked me to her long lost. I knew how she'd feel:
haunted, nauseous, angry at God.

My second hometown, Santa Rosa, was named after a young
saint. So was the school for rich girls and the stone church on the
quiet street that smelled like citrus. I'd gotten high on its steps,
under its gothic arches, under Jesus's sleepwalking arms, the big
sleeves of his bronze robe. It was blocks from the soup kitchen,
appropriately, as St. Rose had dedicated her life to serving the
hungry and the destitute.

As an infant, she suckled a table linen sopped in guava juice
when her mother's milk had failed. It was around that time that
her head had legendarily metamorphosed into a rose the size of
a large pomegranate. Oliva – her mother – and the maid had
witnessed the fleeting phenomenon as the future saint slept in
her crib. Believing it was a message from God, Oliva immediately changed her daughter's name from Isabel to Rosa. (This
remained a source of contention between Oliva and Oliva's
mother, Isabel, after whom Rosa was originally named, an act of
amends between the ever-quarreling matriarchs.)

Throughout Rosa's childhood, Oliva and Isabel fought over
Rosa, vied for her affection. They used her as a threat, a prize, a
lure. Oliva adorned her daughter in crowns of fragrant flowers
and dresses made from mill ends of the finest fabrics, donated by
merchants who were struck by Rosa's otherworldly beauty. Oliva
proudly paraded Rosa around, gathering endless compliments
about her daughter's delicate features and silken hair, hoping
someday they'd win her the hand of a "noble caballero."

Isabel did not drag her granddaughter to shops and dinners,
but rather to mass. She granted Rosa permission to take communion. To vow virginity. To behold sweating statues, smiling
iconography. Sister Mary Alphonsus, in her hagiography of St.
Rose, noted that Rosa "grew up . . . in an atmosphere of miracles."
And so it was that these two worlds – the superficial world of

mother Oliva and the supernatural world of grandmother Isabel — shaped Rosa into who she would become.

Both of those worlds served as antidotes to the chaos of Peru in the late sixteenth century. The Spanish conquest had collapsed the last Inca state. There was widespread rebellion and revolution. The forced labor of indigenous peoples in the *Mita*. Rampant smallpox and typhus. Rosa was six years old when she became obsessed with St. Catherine of Siena and her ascetic practices. Rosa hacked off all her shiny hair with a dull knife. Prayed for ugliness. Unmarriability. She starved herself. Refused water. Drove the pins that held her crowns of flowers deep into her scalp. Plunged her hands into a vat of corrosive lye. Blistered her cheeks with hot peppers.

Eventually, Rosa demanded a private room where she could perform the extreme acts of mortification and deprivation that eventually took her. She scourged herself with a cat-o'-nine-tails. Wore a heavy chain around her diminishing waist. Slept atop a bed of logs that had been embedded with shards of glass and broken pottery. When she began exhibiting strange fits, some called it epilepsy. Others, ecstasy. Her hallucinations were either a result of madness or malnourishment, or proof of divine guidance.

Oliva did everything she could to intervene, but Rosa refused to stop. Even Rosa's various religious directors dropped their endorsement of her, warning that her penances were too excessive and taking a dangerous toll on her health. Oliva grew afraid of her daughter. Couldn't bear to glimpse the festering wounds and protruding bones. Couldn't bear to watch the self-destruction of her own creation.

Near the end of Rosa's short life, Oliva discovered all the hidden tools of her daughter's decline: the glass fragments with blood-crusted jags; the busted plates and vases; the spikes and pipes and rope whips; the heavy chain that kept the flesh of Rosa's wasted waist. Oliva felt sick. Faithless. Broken. She collected everything into a sack and dragged it down to the Rímac River. When she flung the bag into the water, the weight of it slammed her body down onto the hard, unyielding earth. Her screams and cries of grief were silenced by the river's roar.

On her deathbed, Rosa's last request was that her mother find strength. "Lord," she said. "I return her into thy hands. . . . Do not permit her heart to be broken by sorrow."

Mom was the reason I got clean. I didn't do it for Ronnie, though his conditions for our marriage set everything in motion. I didn't do it out of fear of homelessness or incarceration or flesh-eating bacteria or overdose or rape or violence at the hands of johns or boyfriends or cops or dealers. I didn't do it for myself, because I still hated myself, and had I been completely estranged from or disowned by Mom, or had she been no longer alive to witness my recovery, I probably would've kept right on using. I did it for her until I realized I was actually doing it for myself.

On what I believed to be my deathbed, my body in a state of fight-or-flight, my neurotransmitters out of whack, I took some comfort in the fact that my death would not be the result of excess — namely, overdose or its complications — but of dearth. I didn't see yet that those were the same, that lack is the inevitable consequence of glut. That either way, my death would be of my own doing, and would trouble Mom just the same.

Perhaps I was peaceful with the idea of passing, of returning to Mother Earth, because I was tired. Maybe it was a survival mechanism that allowed my body to rest and heal. Maybe it was old depression rearing its apathetic head after years of being buried in opiates. Or maybe it was because I was finally myself, pure and unadulterated.

For years, I lied. No one could love or accept who I truly was because no one knew who that was. To Mom I was sober. To friends I was hardcore. To strangers I was innocent, pitiful, even dutiful. I had a "sick mother," a "dead grandma," a "drunk boyfriend," a "shut-off furnace." To johns I was turned on. To lovers I was in love. I was whomever I imagined the person next to me wanted me to be.

Perhaps it was with Glorianne whom I'd been most honest. I stole from her, yes. Cooked odorous dope right under her nose. Fed her fibs about where I'd been and what I was doing. On some level she knew everything, but to confront me would mean to confront herself. So instead, we colluded. We stood across from each other, carefully balancing a great glass surface between us. It was a heavy thing — fragile and transparent. Like a window, maybe. It was shame and grief and the scrambled-up love of women who believed themselves unlovable. It was heroin and Fenton glass. It was my mother and it was her mother. This was how Glorianne and I held each other. Neither of us could let go.

One afternoon, while Ronnie was gone, I picked up the phone. I put it back down. I went into the bathroom to practice. "I'm sorry," I said to the mirror.

Glorianne and I had learned to decode each other's words, our gestures and silences. When I told her I hated her, she knew I meant that I hated myself. And when I told her I loved her, she hoped it meant that I loved myself.

I tried again. Dialed the number. Hung up. Outside, a construction crew built another shack over the concrete-filled swimming pool. There was buzzing and pounding and a Van Halen song blasting from a fuzzy rooftop radio. I sat on my bed, lifting the blanket up over my head to muffle the noise. Sunlight filtered through it, creating a golden cave with cottony walls, the excretions of detox trapped in its fibers. I couldn't die before apologizing. I reached out my hand and found the phone.

The span of time between rings felt eternal. I wondered if I was making a mistake. If contacting her would only upset her. Or upset me. What if she told me to never call her again, as her mother had done to her?

"Hello?" Glorianne said. "Is anybody there?"

"It's Karleigh," I said. And then: "I'm sorry."

She asked if I was Making Amends and I said yes because I was afraid of coming on too strong, of admitting how much I cared for her and scaring her off. It was less weird if she was just a name on a list,* a step in my recovery.

She was warm but cautious, allowing long silences to lapse. I knew she, like me, was in her bed, bulwarked by blankets, sorting the emotions that spilled around her and onto the floor with the Gump's catalog and the CitiBank offer and the wee-wee pad, staring down some sort of death, the release of a former self, a farewell to the old, defective comforts.

She told me it meant a lot that I had called and wished me the best. Then was the click. Our line severed. The snip of the cord.

---

*"Step 8: Made a list of all persons we had harmed, and became willing to make amends to them all. Step 9: Made direct amends to such people wherever possible, except when to do so would injure them or others." – taken from *The Big Book* of Alcoholics Anonymous.

CHAPTER TWENTY-THREE

New Green Car

Green sprang up from the ground, sudden and eager, mocking the chain link of empty, neglected lots, the hardness of concrete sidewalks. Overhead was sweet-smelling blue, and I thought an airplane's engine was the sound of the sky bending. I rose into it, as if by a soft, gentle mouth at the nape. It had been 114 days since my last drink of methadone, almost a year since my last shot of heroin. Though I still couldn't sleep without Klonopin, I was down to just half a milligram just before bed.

On Easter morning, I went outside to find that the new car I had leased – a 2003 forest-green Honda Civic – had been vandalized. At first, I couldn't even tell what I was looking at. It looked gruesome, gory, as if splattered in blood and guts. Up close, I realized all of its paint, from hood to trunk, was flaky and bubbling, like the scales of a dying mermaid. Ronnie was close behind me, and when he saw the car he went quiet. I asked him what he thought had happened, and he shrugged. "Maybe you shouldn't have boughten it," he said. I called the police and a pair of them came out to file a report. One of them said it looked like paint thinner or some kind of corrosive acid had been poured onto my car. "Do you have any enemies?" he asked.

I took my car to a shop. The five-hundred-dollar deductible maxed out my new secured credit card with the unreasonable APR – which the shop had to run as two transactions a day apart because of its daily spending limit. The damage to the car was so extensive, it was considered totaled. The familiar overwhelm rinsed over me, left me nauseous. Ronnie and I were due to move into an apartment with Aly in Santa Rosa. I'd already signed the lease, given notice at the old place. I needed every penny. And I needed a car to get to work to get the pennies.

The new apartment had coin-slot windows, blistered walls, concrete breezeways that smelled like piss and dryer sheets. Aly and I spent an afternoon lining the cupboards with checkerboard contact paper, tacking up posters of Wes Anderson movies, the Strokes, the Velvet Underground. We bought a velvet couch at St. Vincent de Paul, a hexagonal end table with a little door, a few torch lights that didn't stand completely straight. We slung our damp beach towels over our second-story railing, slipped our legs between the balusters and let our bare feet dangle above the pool whose turquoise beckoned. It felt like Venice.

Ronnie couldn't stand it. He kept to our bedroom with a pillow over his eyes. Told me he liked me better when we first met. "You mean when I was on heroin," I said.

When I was finally able to go pick up my car I was elated. Its green was again gleaming and smooth; its seals, which had warped, were flush and tight. I cruised it through a drive-thru, careful not to drip ketchup on its upholstery. I smoked my cigarette outside of it to keep it smelling new. When I got home, I parked it in its designated spot for the first time, under the carport, between a truck and a custom vintage hot rod.

Later that evening, Aly, Aaron, Raina, and I walked through the parking lot. The concrete acoustics made our voices echo, our shoes clack. We were on our way to a live show. Aaron was ahead of the rest of us by a few paces. He turned and faced us, a crease between his shocked eyes, sorrow on his mouth. "Oh fuck," he said.

My car, again, had been vandalized. Covered anew in scales, its fresh paint job hardly even dry. There was even a gash in my hood, from a foot, maybe, a baseball bat. I was floored. My brother held me steady as I sobbed. "Who would do this to me?" I cried. Aaron asked if I had any unpaid drug debts, if it could have been a past dealer, some junkie. I shook my head. "No way," I said. "We don't do that shit to each other."

I realized that nobody even knew where I had moved yet anyway, not to mention where I parked my car for a mere three hours. Only family knew. Only Mom and my siblings. Ronnie.

I never confronted Ronnie about having found the empty gallon containers of lacquer thinner in his brother's front yard.* Or the baggie that looked to have crank residue in our bathroom garbage. I was too afraid to, so, instead, maintained a cold and constant glare on him. One that made him roundhouse-kick the windshield of the loaner I'd been driving. I was sitting behind its steering wheel when it happened, the motor idling. His body, jumping forcefully atop the hood, was alarming, but the fracture itself was wimpy. It was quiet and self-contained and anticlimactic. A blunt crunch. Suddenly my view was crazed, crystallized.

The last time I saw Ronnie before I left the state, he was wearing my flannel pajama bottoms with kittens on them and being prodded into the back seat of a squad car, his wrists cuffed behind his back. He had come after me earlier that night with a kitchen knife, a wedding present he'd removed from its wooden block and threatened to ruin me with. Aly screamed at him, covered me with her body. I grabbed the phone and ran outside, down concrete steps that were cold on my bare feet. I crouched in someone's front door and called 911. Some neighbors came out and, seeing me hunched and half naked, brought me a blanket. Dispatch kept me on the line till officers arrived. I watched as

---

*It was Mom's idea to go looking there; she drove me over that same night, got out of the car and tiptoed around his messy, junk-filled yard in the darkness with me.

they filed up the stairs, their dark and bulky figures alongside our bright, flung towels.

I quietly grieved the onslaught of losses. Of heroin, then methadone, then Ronnie. Of life as I had known it for more than five years, the bulk of my adulthood, a fifth of my existence. I learned that the masseuse had died of an overdose and I shrugged because that is how I grieved. As time went on, there were so many more — men I had loved, if only for a night; girls who still had baby fat, who still laughed and danced and told me their secret crushes. One friend's ashes were mixed with purple glitter, which I wore around my neck.

It was as if I were climbing Everest, passing those who had perished on the trail, morbid signposts still wrapped in Gore-Tex, preserved forever in endless snow. I could hardly glance at them, their partially buried bodies, or else I might collapse, might run out of air, might give up too.

I stumbled. Found footholds. Then loopholes. Found a doctor who prescribed me Vicodin for my very real pain, so what if that pain leaned more existential than physical? I told myself it wasn't relapse because it was legal and legitimately procured. But then it wasn't. Then, I snooped behind bathroom mirrors for pills leftover from wisdom-tooth extractions. I was fortunate when I didn't find anything, when I was forced to forget again the warm-blanket feel of opiates, to ignore and push through the letdown, my crawly restlessness. To find something else instead: my drawings, my writing. The vibrant green of a pair of fast-fashion short-shorts; the rusty lace of an antique sash; the supple weight of silk velvet draping off a bolt and over my hand, one yard the same price as a gram.

I didn't yet have a sewing machine, so I did everything with a needle and thread. I handstitched big satin bows onto the cheap green shorts from Forever 21. Sliced up and knotted old T-shirts so they looked like soft cages, then paired them with stiff, itchy skirts whose linings hung intentionally from their bottoms. I made blouses out of white eyelet and pastel diaper pins, mini dresses out of polyester nighties.

I could manipulate fabric to tell a story. Create garments and whole outfits to create worlds. I went to thrift stores and fabric stores and off-price stores like Marshalls to gather raw material, the basic units, the words that would come together to convey ideas or inspire emotions. My technique was made-up, messy and improvised. I worked the same way with actual words, which I strung together in a spiral-bound notebook that had an erupting volcano on its cover.

I was obsessed with words. It was an obsession born from lack. Words gleamed like rare jewels in my ears. I wanted my tongue to be familiar with their syllables, my mind with their meanings and connotations. Neither of my parents were college educated, and, other than my pharmacist maternal grandfather, neither were my grandparents. The words that flowed through me and around me were simple, economical, and multipurpose. They were incorrectly applied or mispronounced. They were non-native and TV-learned. They were grunts and ums. And there wasn't a paucity just of vocabulary in my household, but of adages and allusions and common figures of speech, of the sharing of complex ideas.

Keenly aware of and embarrassed by my weak vocabulary, I'd break into a sweat when, in conversation, I grasped for the appropriate adjective, my red face betraying my anxiety, my deficiency. I was envious of friends who took words for granted, who could snatch them without thought and express themselves precisely. It was safer to write because I could take my time with each sentence without the pressure of an awaiting ear. I could try out various words, consulting dictionaries along the way. I could invent them by smashing two together with a hyphen, or by turning a noun into a verb. I could turn a color into a thesis. Or a description of my day into a universal truth.

Later, when I went back to school for a bachelor's degree at nearly forty, I kept lists of the words I didn't know under the covert heading l/u, which meant "look up," at the tops of my pages of notetaking during lectures and discussions.

I grieved wrong and sewed wrong and talked wrong and wrote wrong. I typed wrong, watching the letters below my fingers, always favoring my right hand. I even held a pen wrong, a bulbous callus on my finger since kindergarten. I embraced wrongness because it made possible the things I wouldn't have been able to do had I had to do them right. And it was in the very wrongness I found inventiveness and play and fulfillment. In wrongness I found what was right for me.

In the year between Ronnie's arrest and my departure I jumped headlong into everything that turned me on. I learned how to spin records and, with some friends, launched a weekly dance party at a strip-mall tavern. I played Le Tigre and Miss Kittin and 50 Cent for suburban hipsters in skinny jeans who sipped vodka crans and smoked American Spirit yellows. We called it Sunday School. It became so popular it eventually outgrew us. I took a position managing a chain beauty store, in the same shopping center where Mom had long ago bagged groceries. My job was to erect the planograms emailed from corporate. To build displays that showcased our sales events, buy-one-get-ones on jumbos of shampoo. I'd spend the bulk of my shifts experimenting with color, with shadows and glosses I'd apply to the wrong features of my face.

One of my new friends told me about an event he was participating in. It was to be held in an Oakland warehouse and would feature DJs, acrobats, dancers, and poets, art installations and sculpture. He said there was going to be a runway show and urged me to send some of my creations down it.

In the days leading up to the event, I stayed up all night drinking diet Red Bulls, my five-year-old niece, India, sneaking into my room, watching with awe as I affixed ostentatious bows to the butts of cutoffs, ruffles to flight jackets.

I packed a dozen outfits into a suitcase with a wonky wheel and a floral tapestry pattern I'd scored from the Goodwill and rolled it into the warehouse just as the party was getting started. The interior of the warehouse was dizzyingly byzantine, with zigzaggy stairs that led up to various levels and mezzanines, somewhat Escherian. There were tiny nooks, walls made from wooden pallets and parachute cloth. A trapeze hung from the center of the main room. Around me, people danced, hula-hooped. It was a circus of humans that smelled of armpits and privates. Of metabolized molly seeping from wide-awake pores. Of Tibetan incense. Electronic music pulsed from a DJ's decks. A man wearing nothing but paint offered me a back rub and a cookie made with psilocybin, but before I could decline I was whisked away by a coordinator who needed me to dress the models.

Girls with asymmetrical haircuts, with gauged earlobes and jewels dangling from their navels, shoved their lithe, playa-tanned limbs into my clothes. They strutted down a slapdash plywood runway in mukluks and short-shorts, ripped-up T-shirts and face paint. From the back end of the stage, I peered into the crowd that had gathered to watch. Front and center was Dale. He was almost unrecognizable. The hollows of his face had filled out, and his plaid button-down shirt fit snugly against his torso. As if lit from inside, he radiated a soft luminosity.

We'd been back in touch for a few weeks, after I "bumped into" him at a potluck I knew he'd be at. He was going to UC Berkeley, studying his numbers and stars. He'd gotten sober in the wilderness, with Duane, detoxing in a tent while listening to the

Stones' *Let It Bleed* on a Discman. He joined a dojo. Went to Japan. Shopped at Wild Oats. Learned how to sail. How to play Go.

When I approached him at the fashion show, his blue eyes glimmered impishly like they had when we first met, when we kissed amid the scream of a leftover Piccolo Pete. We tried to talk, plugging one ear and yelling, reading each other's lips. I suggested we go outside where it was quieter. The night was cooling off. I took a thin sweater from my purse and tugged it over my bare shoulders.

"This isn't really my scene," I said.

Dale laughed. "Yeah. Not mine either."

He asked me if I wanted to bail, to go somewhere, maybe grab a bite. I did. I followed him in my car to his house, tailing his flashing blinkers down industrial side streets. I already knew we'd never actually go out for food. That we'd stay in his house, his roommates gone. That we'd have sex, both of us wondering if there was anything still there, if there had ever been anything at all, and if there could be something now. If, through our reunion, our renewed intimacy, we could make sense of our past together – the drug addiction, the lies, the fears we tried to ameliorate with misapprehended love. If we could right it all somehow. Redeem it; revise it.

There we were back in Oakland, back where we'd started, where the sky was terrifyingly endless to me, a gutless youngster too wrapped up in myself, swaddled in my own self-absorption and fears. Where I did heroin for the first time, Dale's fingers carefully assessing my veins, pressing them gently, like a nurse. How poetic would it be if we fell in love now? If we made it all worth something?

After we had sex, we stared at each other and laughed. Nodded at the awkwardness, the awareness of our mutual appreciation, the deep and undeniable affection we had for one another. It seemed that our motions of lovemaking, both of us clear-minded for the first time, was a closure.

Though so much had been opening up to me, it all carried the cast of closure, a wistful happy-sad, a deep gratitude that felt already removed from the impromptu afterparties held in sultry kitchens, the now-regular dinners at Mom's with the sibs, the familiar sun-bleached streets of Santa Rosa, the oak trees and grapevines and golden hills and pink sunsets.

Mom couldn't understand why I wanted to leave. "We've been here for generations," she said. "No one ever leaves." Then: "I want all my babies near me." She made a sad face as if holding the green rubber ball.

I didn't want to be near her. I didn't want to be near her because I wanted more to show her that I didn't *have* to be near her anymore. I was strong and brave and ready.

"But you're going to be so far away," she said.

I told her I'd been far away already. That by moving, I'd be closer to her than I'd ever been.

I left before sunrise one morning in September. Before the noise of life began. Before words could be exchanged, my mind changed. I had packed up my new, green car the night before. Had two months of cashed paychecks in a paper bag, a MapQuest printout on the passenger seat. Soon, I'd be one of millions on the open interstate. I'd zag mountain passes. Cross Mount Shasta, the state line, the Willamette River.

But before that, I pulled into the Valero where I'd stood six years earlier with an empty gas can and a pocketful of spare change. As I pumped my gas, the ghost of the girl I'd once been approached me, begged me to help her.

"I'm sorry," I said.

PART THREE

Holding Out, Holding On, Holding Her

CHAPTER TWENTY-FOUR

Regrowth: An Epilogue

I landed in Portland, Oregon. Not Iowa, not Ohio. Because I no longer wanted to be lost. Though Portland was the farthest I'd ever been from home, it comforted me to know that I shared an ocean, a sunrise and sunset, with my past. With Mom. I found an apartment in a fortress of brick with thick plaster walls and hot, banging radiators. My bathtub had talons and my bed tucked inconspicuously into the wall. There were honeycomb tiles and curved doorways and all these clever little built-ins I'd eventually fill with books or spices or sweaters. It was nothing like the motel-style apartments of California I was accustomed to. It felt like I was in a real city, Brooklyn or Boston or something, someplace old and out east I'd never been. Yet it was all so exaggeratedly western with its snowcapped mountains and giant firs, which encircled me, the sky a lid of heavy gray that broke in spring to feverish sunshine and the potent scent of blossoms.

I still called Mom regularly, to tell her the weather, that I was getting my tires rotated, that I had a weird mole, a famous neighbor. "Welllll . . ." she'd begin, and I'd let her go with ease. Slide back into the world where nobody knew the old me, the various versions I had shed. I imagined them, the moltings, those empty outsides, as fragile and transparent skins that dissolved into meaningless dust underfoot.

In Portland, in the early aughts, anything was possible. I had a fashion show on a real runway in a downtown event space. Someone even wrote about it, took pictures for his webzine. I wrote religiously – a novel that was a stack of loose papers I binder-clipped and lent to friends, a chapbook of short stories, a two-part memoir for the street paper, a blurb about a big indie band for a music festival's website. I could afford yards of nice fabric and Copic markers and daily soy lattes because my rent was actually affordable. So were my bills: rates from another era. No longer did I feel overwhelmed and hopeless as I had in California. Life in Portland had a gentle, comfy ease that was simultaneously energizing and inspiring.

I got a job at a coffee cart inside an art school, and then at a late-night falafel joint where I shaved shawarma from a spit and stuffed it into pitas for people leaving the bars or the nearby movie theater. One night, I confessed to a regular customer who wore a name tag that said jim that I often stole the industrial one-ply rolls of toilet paper from the restaurant's storage closet. They only paid me minimum wage, I complained, even though I scraped grills till two in the morning, hefted trash into a dumpster much taller than my arms could reach, de-escalated drunk arguments, and chased after people who didn't pay for their pitas. He told me his grocery store was hiring and I could use him as a reference. He also told me you could buy a dozen two-ply rolls there for just a few bucks. I went in the next day and put Jim's name on my application and was hired later that same afternoon.

I still had my struggles, but they were different. Subtler. Little shifts into sadness I'd muffle with the buzz of new love interests and cheap wine and SSRIs – first Lexapro, then Zoloft, then Lexapro again, which I still take today. I ran up exorbitant debt by enrolling in a for-profit art school, where I majored in fashion design, then dropped out after a year. I moved back home for a three-month spell and lived on a sagging air mattress in the bonus room, misted my hair with drugstore body spray to mask the cigarette smoke Mom loathed. I moved to expensive cities, Brooklyn and San Francisco, and lived on spoiled groceries I filched from my work's donation boxes, took subways and bus lines to the farthest extremities, to flat, windy shorelines where I stood cold and alone for only long enough to have made the trip worth my while. Then I'd return to makeshift bedrooms in moldering apartments where the presence of my roommates was only verified by the leftover steam in the bathroom. Moist ghosts, they were. I had a therapist call me immature and a community-college professor call me sexy. I told both of them to fuck off, which felt good. And when I felt like giving up, I told myself to fuck off too. To stop being such a coward. And then I'd smile inwardly as I braved the task. All of this was living. And to live was much riskier, much more extreme, than to die slowly on drugs.

One does not grow out of addiction, nor does one arrive at recovery alone. For me, it took a constellation of support: It took the social worker who checked a box to approve me for state-funded services, the dosing nurse who wouldn't give me an inch; it took Mom, my dads, and my siblings; it took Glorianne and Duane, who let me stay in their house and then who kicked me out of their house; it took the guy at the check-cashing center who gave me a job despite my spotty employment history, the slumlord who handed me house keys despite my risky rental history; it took the guy who told me I could use his name as a reference, the grocery store that believed in me; it took the people in AA rooms, the coworkers, the customers, the therapists, the friends; it took Ronnie, it took Bill, it even took the owner of the coffee shop and her big hands; it took the cop who didn't arrest me, the boyfriend who didn't kill me; it took methadone, Lexapro, exercise, reading, sleep, vitamins, vegetables, and ice cream; it took self-help books and soaking pools and deep-tissue massage and meditation; it took my own understanding of God; it took art: the clicky purr of my sewing machine, the drape of fabric over my hand; the drawings that filled the cardboard portfolio I toted to classes; the music I played from tablature I'd printed from the internet, from the crackling records I began to collect again; the writing, oh how it took writing – the words I'd stay up late arranging into stories, into feelings I couldn't otherwise articulate; it took the MFA program that accepted me, the professors who encouraged me, the literary journals that published me; it took the loving, supportive, and patient man I'd marry in 2019. It took the luck I'd had and the grace I was given.

Mom goes, "When are you gonna be rich and famous?" She goes, "When are you going to quit the grocery store?" I've worked there for more than twenty years now. And when I'm there, I'm still somewhere in between. I'm neither the customer with the nine-to-five and the kids and the house, nor am I, any longer, the bottle-redeemer, whose pinned eyes and scarred arms I know so well. I watch these people with something like eager infatuation, hoping they might recognize me. I focus my love on them because maybe that could help. Maybe I'll be a single, anonymous star in their crowded constellation someday. I've realized that the feeling of not belonging anywhere is, at last, fulfilling. It's freeing. Because it means I can be everywhere.

Mom goes, "When are you going to move back home?" and though part of me will always wish to return, another part can't bear to. I'm afraid it will undo me. Reverse me. Unfurl it all back out again. I need to keep some distance between us so I can maintain perspective. So I can see her clearly, see myself clearly.

In 2013, Dad moved back into Grandma Coco's, into her garage, where he fashioned walls out of bungee cords and bedsheets so he'd have some privacy while she was running loads of laundry. He became her legal caretaker, collecting checks from the state with which he paid for her frozen meals and medical copays. His Powerballs and Mega Millions.

The last time I visited Grandma Coco was in 2015. She was wearing a fleece bucket hat with a plastic rose on it to cover her bald head, her thick helmet of steely hair lost to chemo. She was a grayish pale, and her legs were so skinny that her pants looked empty. When I walked into the room she cried, "I thought you were your mother!" and then went on to tell me that her former daughter-in-law was the most kindly and gracious and classy woman she'd ever known. "She loves you kids so much," she said. Then she offered me soup and juice. A piece of last year's Almond Roca whose nuts tasted like the cupboard. She shuffled over to the old hi-fi and crouched tenuously over her records, flipping through them. "Here," she said. "This for you. You remember. It was your favorite." On the cover, Natalie Cole with a neat Afro, her eyes and teeth and sequined top sparkling.

Grandma Coco slowly lowered herself back into her chair and winced. Dad and I helped her into her bed, and he gave her her pain medication. I called her a few times after that, from Portland, and she told me she hated Portland because it was cold and dark and wet and it was where her tarty mother-in-law had lived. We laughed. Then she told me she was laughing at the monkeys outside her window, and I asked her where she was, and she said Managua, even though she was in Petaluma. She referred to me by my mother's name a few times during our last conversation. I was at work when I learned she had passed. I can't remember who delivered the news — Aly or Aaron or Dad — but it was just as I had punched out for the night. I sat in my car and listened to "Heaven Is With You" on repeat, bawling for what seemed like hours, long after the last employees had left.

A year after Grandma Coco had passed, in 2017, Mom moved back to Gramma and Grampa's black ranch house, Dad Mike too. They took the bedroom Mom had once had as a child. She hadn't even processed her own mother's rapid decline and subsequent death, was just starting to numbly sort through Gramma's Calico dishes and Beatrix Potter music boxes and the photos that spanned decades when the Tubbs Fire tore through Santa Rosa on high-speed winds, taking her and Dad Mike's house, their storage unit across town, their whole neighborhood, their city.

Mom became old that year. Her lips disappeared, and her eyes looked perpetually startled. A subtle trembling of her spirit took hold. When I'd ask her if she was okay she'd say she was fine, fine. As if she'd only forgotten she wasn't fine, her grief a misplaced key, a blanked name. I returned home because I was worried about her. I didn't trust her reports of fineness, which were neither falsely chipper nor tellingly morose, but guarded and afraid.

She'd driven through flames, after all, in the middle of the night, after she and Dad Mike were woken by the clang of some blown-over equipment in their backyard. Only then did they smell the smoke, hear the commotion of hollering neighbors, of motors revving and horns honking.

I cried for days, weeks. I cried for the gone baby books, the locks of hair and little teeth. The letter Mom had written to me when I was in the NICU. I cried for all the photographs, of young Mom and us kids as kids, of Gramma and Grampa. Of Disneyland trips and Tahoe and summers at the lake. I cried for her handwritten recipes in the wooden box; for the ones snipped from *Woman's Day* and *Family Circle*, from the back of a Bisquick box. And when I arrived in Santa Rosa, I cried for the ruins. The miles and miles of ashes where homes had once been, the homes in which I'd spent my entire youth – doing makeovers, making crank calls, making out. All those kitchen dance parties. But mostly, I cried for Mom.

Mom didn't cry once. Though weary, she kept her head up and did what she had to do. She put Grampa in a memory-care facility. Sorted through pages of insurance paperwork, made a detailed inventory of everything lost to the fires, down to the spare toothbrush in the guest bathroom. She dealt with her parents' finances and wills. Her own. She bought shoes and underwear and laptops and bar soap and face cream and pillows and heart medication. She had so much to do. Her beloved errands. No time yet to mourn the loss of her mother or her home or all those irreplaceable things inside her home, our concretized memories.

Without the hard copies that had been stored away in closets and crawl spaces, that hung from walls, rarely noticed anymore, she relied solely on her mind for our faces. She learned the futility of trying to capture people and experiences and feelings in pictures and souvenirs, in rubber balls and glass candy dishes and commemorative beanbag animals, of lazily assigning some reductive meaning to these representations of moments. Of communicating to others, herself especially, that her worthiness was based on material stuff. It had all become ashes anyway, as we would eventually be too. But now, we were all here, mother and babies.

Mom took me to where the house had been. Everywhere I looked: lone chimneys, tangles of rebar, concrete steps leading to nothing. Rusty, burnt-out cars tagged in Day-Glo orange with identifying digits. Cleanup crews in hazmat suits wading through the toxic ash, through cadmium and arsenic and lead. There was nothing left of Mom's but the mangled garage door. The fragments of the bright-blue Calico dishes that popped from the rubble like blossoms. The wiry guts of Dad Mike's piano. Trees were charred and leafless, but already tiny, vibrant blades poked from the scorched earth. The furry curlicue of an ambitious fern seemed like a miracle. "It's so nice out today," Mom said, sighing dreamily. "Want to go somewhere?"

There was a nature trail halfway between Sebastopol and Santa Rosa. It crossed the laguna – a marshy wetlands that was usually underwater during these winter months. We parked at the Grange hall, where we used to attend pancake breakfasts where old ladies sold crocheted tissue-box covers and raffle tickets for cords of wood. The day was bright and crisp. We headed north, away from the highway, the tack shop, the gas station and rusty mailboxes. The path was narrow and sun-bleached, flanked with tall grasses and bare oaks whose crowns were clumped with mistletoe. In them, those collared doves sounded like owls. Who-whooo-who, who-whooo-who.

It had been fifteen years since that last dose of methadone, down to the week. But I didn't mention it – Mom didn't like to be reminded of my druggy past. Wanted to pretend it never happened. So, as we walked, we talked about little stuff – the health advice of an internet doctor, the show on Netflix we were watching, whether to do pizza for dinner that night or Thai. She smiled, but I could sense the dense grief that vibrated inside of her. It had deepened the lines on her face, changed the texture of her dyed hair, which shone a dull copper in the hard winter sun. I wanted her to break open in my arms. To hold her emotions that quivered like a bright, perfect yolk beneath a cracked surface. I wanted to hold her. It was my time to hold her. Instead, I gently brushed my hand against hers, gave it a little rub, pretended it was an accident, merely the swinging motion of our arms that had created the gesture.

"What's this about?" she asked, her eyes reflecting the perfect sunlight, her lips my smile.

Still walking, she took my arm by the sleeve of my coat and pulled me in. We laughed as our feet bumped and tangled and synced. As our long shadows became one.

Portland, Oregon, December 2024

Over the past ten years or so, I've connected with Glorianne on many occasions — in person, over email, and through old-fashioned, chat-for-hours phone calls. It must have started when I ran into her in the grocery store when I was home visiting my family over the holidays. She invited me up to the house on Christmas Day, told me that Dale would be there but was unsure if he would eat the dinner she'd prepared because he was always on some trendy diet. I made an excuse not to go because I felt it would have been inappropriate for me to do so — I would have been a bad memory haunting Dale. But Glorianne and I did get together shortly thereafter, meeting up at a little bistro in Santa Rosa for lunch.

We kept in touch over email, and about a year or so later she invited me up to the house, said she had some things for me. When I made the drive out there, I realized I hadn't been up that steep road I'd once spent hours walking up and down in nearly twenty years. Everything about it was the same: the concrete's craquelure — evidence of sun and rain and then sun again, the mildew-freckled fifth wheel with its nose in the dirt, the rusty barrels of fuel, the address signs nailed haphazardly to trees and telephone poles. *Pothole. Flagpole. Woodpile. Cat.*

When I got to the house, I parked out of sight, my car concealed behind a bush. I didn't want to announce myself before I was ready. The koi pond still tinkled and hummed, and the tarpaulin-covered woodpile where the opossums lived looked like it hadn't budged in years. But as soon as Glorianne opened the front door, I realized at least one thing had changed.

Behind her, the house was airy and sparse. Gone was the chaos of stacked glass and corner-stashed shopping bags. Glorianne looked younger, brighter. She said it was because she had started dyeing her hair, but that wasn't all of it.

It was so strange being back there. In some ways, despite the lack of clutter, it looked and felt exactly the same, launching me twenty years into the past. I could smell the heroin — my brain completely bypassing the need for a nose. And though being in that house triggered all sorts of feelings, I had no desire to leave. In fact, I was strangely comfortable.

Glorianne handed me a large box.

"Should I open it now?" I asked, as if it were an early Christmas present.

"It's up to you," she said.

I tried to see through the rectangular aperture at the center of the interlocked flaps, afraid of what might be in there.

"If you just want to do away with all this, I can get rid of it for you," Glorianne said. "I don't want to dig up any painful memories for you."

"No, no," I said. "I appreciate this."

I didn't go out there that afternoon to retrieve any old belongings. I went out there to see Glorianne. I like to think that her impulse was the same — to reconnect with me, if only briefly. The box of stuff merely pretext.

When I opened the box, the first thing I saw was the Beanie Baby owl I'd rescued from the trash can and kept on my dash. He was sun faded, disturbingly cute, and still carried a faint whiff of cigarettes. Seeing him gave me a gross feeling. An icky déjà vu that made me squirm in my chair.

Underneath the owl were photographs taken in living rooms that no longer existed in my memory, all of us pale and smudgy looking. There were piles of journals and letters I didn't want to even thumb through. And, at last, there was the stainless-steel kettle — its whistle gone missing — from Mom, a strange birthday gift for a girl who was essentially homeless at the time.

Glorianne apologized when I quickly pushed the box's flaps down and kicked it away with my foot.

"Please don't feel bad," I said. "I want these things. I just don't want to look at them right now."

Glorianne went into the kitchen to get me a glass of water.

"Mostly, I wanted to see you." I took a sip of water and waited for her to settle back into her chair. "I know I've said it before, but I can't tell you enough how sorry I am for everything."

Glorianne cut me off by shaking her head and putting a finger to her lips. "Please don't apologize anymore. You have already. That was all in the past."

She told me she had gone down to Oklahoma to meet her aunt Anna, who had remembered the brief period with her baby niece before she was Glorianne. Aunt Anna remembered how Glorianne was there one day and gone the next; how she was forcefully forgotten, to speak of her verboten. Aunt Anna lived on a hundred acres in the upper corner of the saucepan, right below the rimmed lip that pours into Missouri. The gray crosshatch of hickory, whose late-summer debris left the ground crackling, was strangely familiar to Glorianne. She sat on the edge of the Spavinaw Creek and said to herself, *I have been here before*.

During that trip, Glorianne met her siblings: two brothers and a sister. She became especially close with one brother and visited him and his family numerous times afterward. She described him as a mirror.

"When you're adopted," she said, "you never see yourself reflected back. Not just eyes and mouth and all that, but the small acts, the ways you do things." She looked over at Duane, who joined us in the living room. "Dale looks exactly like Duane when he sleeps. As a baby even. I often wondered if I looked like anyone when I slept."

I asked her if she ever got to meet her mother.

Glorianne shook her head. "We spoke a couple of times. But it wasn't good."

"Is she still living?"

She snorted. "That woman's too mean to die."

I was happy to see that Glorianne could now laugh about her mother's hard-nosed refusal to see her, even if the laughter was merely a coping mechanism.

I told Glorianne that her house looked lovely, and she explained that she had donated all her stuff to church charities. To Glorianne, the comfort that came from buying and saving things she bought was gone. Their meanings now mean. Broken. No longer providing her with substitute love. She turned all of it into something good, though, by giving it to those less fortunate. Before I left, Glorianne handed me a wrapped present. It was a book of poetry written by one of her friends, a well-known poet. The poems in it are about Nefertiti and Jeanne d'Arc and Princess Diana. They are about mother figures.

As I drove back to Mom's later that afternoon, I hoped Glorianne truly knew how much I loved her. I feared my expression was inadequate. For many years, I assumed that my preoccupation with her had everything to do with the guilt I carried for having taken advantage of her. Or that my love was purely narcissistic, based on the reflection of myself I saw in her. I wanted my love for Glorianne to have nothing to do with me, to be reasonless, like the love you innately have for your mother even if she, literally or figuratively, abandoned you.

We conducted interviews over the phone several months later, when I was developing my MFA thesis. The last time I saw her was at the same grocery store I had found her in a few years before. I was back home because of the fires. She hugged me with all of her body, swaying a little like she had when she'd visited me and Dale in rehab. She patted me twice. *There, there.*

Selected Bibliography

Association for Psychological Science. "Harlow's Classic Studies Revealed the Importance of Maternal Contact." June 20, 2018. https://www.psychologicalscience.org/publications/observer/obsonline/harlows-classic-studies-revealed-the-importance-of-maternal-contact.html.

Baldwin, James. *Giovanni's Room*. Vintage Books, 2013.

Benarroch, Eduardo. "Endogenous Opioid Systems: Current Concepts and Clinical Correlations." *Neurology* 79, no. 8 (2012): 807–14. https://doi.org/10.1212/WNL.0b013e3182662098.

Carey, Benedict. "Addicted to Mother's Love: It's Biology, Stupid." *New York Times*, June 29, 2004. https://www.nytimes.com/2004/06/29/health/addicted-to-mother-s-love-it-s-biology-stupid.html.

Coogan, Michael D., ed. *The New Oxford Annotated Bible with the Apocrypha*. Oxford University Press, 2018.

Davis, Kristina. "What Does the Future Hold for Mexico's Opium Poppy Farmers?" *San Diego Union-Tribune*, July 3, 2020. https://www.sandiegouniontribune.com/2020/07/03/what-does-the-future-hold-for-mexicos-opium-poppy-farmers/.

De Quincey, Thomas. *Confessions of an English Opium Eater*. Ticknor, Reed, and Fields, 1852.

Desmond, Matthew. "America Is in a Disgraced Class of Its Own." *New York Times*, March 16, 2023. https://www.nytimes.com/2023/03/16/opinion/poverty-abolition-united-states.html.

Didion, Joan. *The Year of Magical Thinking*. Vintage Books, 2006.

Doyle, Nora. *Maternal Bodies: Redefining Motherhood in Early America*. University of North Carolina Press, 2018.

Espinoza, Martin. "1 in 4 Sonoma County Residents Has Prescription for Opioids." *Press Democrat*, January 17, 2016. https://www.pressdemocrat.com/article/news/1-in-4-sonoma-county-residents-has-prescription-for-opioids/.

Fass, Sara. "Measuring Poverty in the United States." National Center for Children in Poverty, May 1, 2009. https://www.nccp.org/publication/measuring-poverty-in-the-united-states/.

Frontline. "Transforming Opium Poppies into Heroin." PBS, n.d. https://www.pbs.org/wgbh/pages/frontline/shows/heroin/transform/.

Gladwell, Malcolm. "Lost in the Middle." In *Half and Half: Writers on Growing Up Biracial and Bicultural.* Edited by Claudine Chiawei O'Hearn. Pantheon Books, 1998.

"The Goose Girl." In *The Original Folk and Fairy Tales of the Brothers Grimm.* Edited and translated by Jack Zipes. Princeton University Press, 2014.

Gruber, Valerie A., Kevin L. Delucchi, Anousheh Kielstein, and Stephen L. Batki. "A Randomized Trial of 6-Month Methadone Maintenance with Standard or Minimal Counseling Versus 21-Day Methadone Detoxification." *Drug and Alcohol Dependence* 1, no. 94 (2010): 199–206. https://doi.org/10.1016/j.drugalcdep.2007.11.021.

Halpsern, John H., and David Blistein. *Opium: How an Ancient Flower Shaped and Poisoned Our Ancient World.* Hachette Books, 2019.

Hodgson, Barbara. *Opium: A Portrait of the Heavenly Demon.* Chronicle Books, 1999.

Holden, Janean E., Younhee Jeong, and Jeannine M. Forest. "The Endogenous Opioid System and Clinical Pain Management." *AACN Clinical Issues* 16, no. 3 (2005): 291–301. https://doi.org/10.1097/00044067-200507000-00003.

Inglis, Lucy. *Milk of Paradise: The History of Opium.* Macmillan, 2018.

Kerényi, Karl. *Dionysos: Archetypal Image of Indestructible Life.* Translated by Ralph Manheim. Princeton University Press, 1976.

Kincaid, Jamaica. *At the Bottom of the River.* Farrar, Straus, and Giroux, 1982.

Lacan, Jacques. *Book X: Anxiety.* Polity, 2016.

Landau, Julia. "For Uninsured, Methadone Treatment Hard to Secure." *California Health Report,* August 15, 2012. https://www.calhealthreport.org/2012/08/15/for-uninsured-methadone-treatment-hard-to-secure/.

Lerner, Gerda. *The Creation of Patriarchy.* Oxford University Press, 1986.

Lopez, German. "From Portugal to Portland: Oregon Decriminalized All Drugs, and Overdoses Have Surged." *New York Times,* August 4, 2023. https://www.nytimes.com/2023/08/04/briefing/portugal-portland-decriminalization-overdoses.html.

Lorde, Audre. *Sister Outsider*. Ten Speed Press, 2007.

Martel, Frances, Claire M. Nevison, F. David Rayment, Michael J. A. Simpson, and Eric B. Keverne. "Opioid Receptor Blockade Reduces Maternal Affect and Social Grooming in Rhesus Monkeys." *Psychoneuro-endicronology* 18, no. 4 (1993): 307–21. https://doi.org/10.1016/0306-4530 (93)90027-I.

McPhillips, Deidre. "US Drug Overdose Deaths, Fueled by Synthetic Opioids, Hit a New High in 2022." *CNN*, May 18, 2023. https://www.cnn .com/2023/05/18/health/drug-overdose-deaths-2022/index.html#:~: text=Monthly%2520updates%2520to%2520the%2520provisional,com pared%2520with%2520109%252C179%2520in%25202021.

Moran, Mark F. *Warman's Fenton Glass*, 2nd edition. Krause Publications, 2007.

Nakamoto, Kazuo, Ayaka Taniguchi, and Shogo Tokuyama. "Changes in Opioid Receptors, Opioid Peptides and Morphine Antinociception in Mice Subjected to Early Life Stress." *European Journal of Pharmacology* 881 (2020): 173. https://doi.org/10.1016/j.ejphar.2020.173173.

National Institute on Drug Abuse. "Drug Overdose Deaths: Facts and Figures." Updated August 2024. https://nida.nih.gov/research-topics/ trends-statistics/overdose-death-rates#:~:text=Drug%2520overdose %2520deaths%2520involving%2520prescription,involving%2520 prescription%2520opioids%2520totaled%252016%252C706.

NCHS: A Blog for the National Center for Health Statistics. "Provisional Data Shows US Drug Overdose Deaths Top 100,000 in 2022." CDC, March 18, 2023. https://blogs.cdc.gov/nchs/2023/05/18/7365/.

Neumann, Erich. *The Great Mother: An Analysis of the Archetype.* Translated by Ralph Manheim. Princeton University Press, 1963.

New York Times Print Archive. "Methadone." March 16, 1975. https://www .nytimes.com/1975/03/16/archives/article-21-no-title-methadone.html.

Nutt, David. "Why Are Drugs Illegal? You Asked Google—Here's the Answer." https://www.theguardian.com/commentisfree/2015/oct/28 /why-are-drugs-illegal-google-answer.

PBS NewsHour. "A Secret Look at a Mexican Cartel's Low-Tech, Multimillion-Dollar Fentanyl Operation." YouTube, September 14, 2021. https://www .pbs.org/newshour/amp/show/a-secret-look-at-a-mexican-cartels-low -tech-multimillion-dollar-fentanyl-operation.

Pew. "Overview of Opioid Treatment Program Regulations by State." September 19, 2012. https://www.pewtrusts.org/en/research-and

-analysis/issue-briefs/2022/09/overview-of-opioid-treatment-program
-regulations-by-state.

Powledge, Tabitha M. "Addiction and the Brain: The Dopamine Pathway Is Helping Researchers Find Their Way Through the Addiction Maze." *BioScience* 49, no. 7 (1999): 513–19. https://doi.org/10.2307/1313471.

Pruitt, Sara. "How Early Church Leaders Downplayed Mary Magdalene's Influence." *History.* Updated March 18, 2024. https://www.history.com/news/mary-magdalene-jesus-wife-prostitute-saint.

Rich, Adrienne. *The Fact of a Doorframe.* W. W. Norton, 2002.

Roane, Kit R. "Legislation for Those with a Methadone Clinic Next Door." *New York Times*, April 6, 1997. https://www.nytimes.com/1997/04/06/nyregion/legislation-for-those-with-a-methadone-clinic-next-door.html.

Saini, Angela. "How Did Patriarchy Actually Begin?" *BBC*, May 29, 2023. https://www.bbc.com/future/article/20230525-how-did-patriarchy-actually-begin.

Saunders, Nicholas J. *The Poppy: A Cultural History from Ancient Egypt to Flanders Fields to Afghanistan.* Simon and Schuster, 2013.

Schultz, W., P. Dayan, and P. R. Montauel. "A Neural Substrate of Prediction and Reward." *Science* 275, no. 5306 (1997): 1593–99. https://doi.org/:10.1126science/275.5306.1593.

ScienceDirect. "Opiate Receptors." In *Biological Research on Addiction*, 2013. Accessed February 14, 2023. https://www.sciencedirect.com/topics/pharmacology-toxicology-and-pharmaceutical-science/opiate-receptor#:~:text=Opioid%2520receptors%2520are%2520found%2520at,%252C%2520thalamus%252C%2520and%2520the%2520cortex.

Suárez, Karol. "Cartel Violence in Mexico Forces People to Flee Their Homes, Leaving Ghost Towns Behind." *Courier Journal.* Updated November 12, 2021. https://www.courier-journal.com/story/news/investigations/2021/10/21/mexican-drug-cartel-violence-forced-migration-el-mench-michoacan/6009954001/.

Substance Abuse and Mental Health Services Administration. "Medicaid Coverage of Medication-Assisted Treatment for Alcohol and Opioid Use Disorders and of Medication for the Reversal of Opioid Overdose." HHS Publication No. SMA-18, 2018.

Thurer, Shari L. *The Myths of Motherhood: How Culture Reinvents the Good Mother.* Penguin Books, 1995.

United Nations Office on Drug and Crimes. "The History of Heroin." 1953.
https://www.unodc.org/unodc/en/data-and-analysis/bulletin/bulletin_
1953-01-01_2_page004.html.

Valentino, Rita J., and Nora D. Volkow. "Untangling the Complexity of
Opioid Receptor Function." *Neuropsychopharmacology* 43 (2018): 2514–20.
https://doi.org/10.1038/s41386-018-0225-3.

Vice News. "The Rise of Mexican Black Tar Heroin." YouTube, May 2, 2016.
https://www.youtube.com/watch?v=d_PQ407GkOs.

Ward, Beth. "The Depression-Era Glassware That Came in Boxes of
Oatmeal." *Astro Obscura*, April 6, 2018. https://www.atlasobscura.com/
articles/depression-era-glassware-colorful.

Wells, Janet. "A'Roma Roasters." *Bohemian*, August 26, 1999. https://
bohemian.com/aroma-roasters-1/.

Winborn, Mark, ed. *Shared Realities: Participation Mystique and Beyond.*
King Fisher Press, 2014.

Wren, Christopher S. "Holding an Uneasy Line in the Long War on Heroin;
Methadone Emerged in City Now Debating Its Use." *New York Times*,
October 3, 1998. https://www.nytimes.com/1998/10/03/nyregion/
holding-uneasy-line-long-war-heroin-methadone-emerged-city
-now-debating-its-use.html.

Zerell, U., B. Ahrens, and P. Gerz. "Documentation of a Heroin Manufacturing Process in Afghanistan." Federal Criminal Police Office, Wies-
baden, Germany, n.d. https://www.unodc.org/pdf/research/Bulletin07/
bulletin_on_narcotics_2007_Zerell.pdf.

Zerwick, Chloe. *A Short History of Glass.* Corning Museum of Glass, 1980.

Acknowledgments

My deepest gratitude to everyone who helped bring this book into the world, from its amoebic inception as rough pages of autofiction to my ambitious MFA thesis to the book you are holding right now.

I thank, first and foremost, my brilliant agent, Miriam Altshuler, for believing in my work from the very beginning, after hearing me read for five minutes at Bread Loaf. She took a chance on me before my manuscript was even complete, supporting me with patience, positivity, and warmth every step of the way.

I thank my editor, Chip Fleischer, for his enthusiasm and expertise, and for helping make this book the very best it could be, and the entire team at Steerforth — David Goldberg, Cate Fricke, Devin Wilkie, Helga Schmidt, and Zandra Rose — for their kindness, ardor, and tireless work making my book known.

A very, very special thank-you to Justin Hocking, my thesis adviser at Portland State University, but also my friend, mentor, cheerleader, inspiration, and guide. His help has been second to none, and I cannot thank him enough for all that he's done.

I also want to thank the rest of the entire MFA cohort, across strands, who provided feedback, inspiration, and camaraderie; and my professors who made me a better writer and continued to support my work long after graduation. Thank you Leni Zumas, Paul Collins, Michael McGregor, and especially Michele Glazer, who taught me, essentially, how to read. She introduced me to poetry that changed my life, broke my brain. She believed in my work with a tough-love, no-bullshit attitude for which I am forever grateful.

I thank the Rona Jaffe Foundation and their president, Beth McCabe, for their extreme generosity and support of not only my own work but also women far and wide. Without their largesse, this book would not exist.

I thank Susan Moore and everybody at Portland's Literary Arts for all they do for our state, our city, our community – enriching it with culture, encouraging writers and readers of all ages and backgrounds, promoting literacy, and always centering on diversity. The fellowship I received from them enabled me to finish my book and gave me the validation I needed during a difficult time.

I thank the late Mimi Miller, a founding member of the Community of Writers and benefactor of the George Pascoe Miller Scholarship, and the entire Miller family for their generous support and their ongoing recognition of native Californian writers.

A huge thank-you to the Regional Arts and Culture Council (RACC) for their advocacy of the arts and their massive contributions through their grants programs, of which I was a recipient. And a special thanks to the Independent Publishing Resource Center (IPRC) for making publishing and printing accessible to the community and for hosting numerous events that support writers and artists in the Portland area.

Thank you to the Bread Loaf Writers' Conference, to Mitch Jackson for hearing my voice, and to Bobby Fieseler for the walk to the creek, where we talked about moms and secrets and *Giovanni's Room*, which I finished that night on my Kindle, atop my tiny dorm bed, a party going on below, a drunk girl singing on the lawn. Thank you to the Sewanee Writers' Conference, to Elena Passarello and Alex Marzano-Lesnevich, the dream team! An extended thanks to Alex for being such a solid supporter of my work every step of the way, helping wherever they could. Thank you to Tin House, my first conference ever, and to Melissa Febos for her straight talk and inimitable genius. Thank you to

Brett Hall Jones and the Community of Writers — the most magical and supportive writers' conference I've ever attended.

A big cuddly hug to the Sou'wester Lodge in Seaside, Washington, my favorite place on earth, where I wrote the vast majority of this book. And to Common Ground Wellness Cooperative, where I heal, reflect, and regroup while listening to wind chimes from the soaking pool.

Thank you to my writer besties, my early readers, my accountability partners: the ones I sit in coffee shops with, laptop-to-laptop, and the ones I meet weekly on FaceTime to put down words with. These are also the people I want in my life forever, whom I consider family: Emily Flouton, Rosalie Chandler, Joshua James Amberson. And thank you to Tom Mickelson, who has championed me since my writing was hot crap, pushing me out of my comfort zone and helping me see the world anew.

I have loads of appreciation for all the writer and writer-adjacent friends I've met over the years or known all my life, who've selflessly helped me in numerous ways, both big and small: Deb Akers, Alex Behr, Kate Jayroe, Kit Haggard, Kim Coleman Foote, Chelsea Bieker, Dave Jarecki, Adam Strong, Ken Pallack, Alexander Lumans, JB Brennock, Lilly Dancyger, Dani Burlison, Wendy Noonan, and the entire 2023 CoW nonfiction cohort. They've all shown me what literary citizenship and community are.

Thank you to my beloved friends who show up for me, root for me, sing nü metal karaoke with me.

Thank you to Trader Joe's for not only providing me the flexibility and brain space required to write a book (or two or three) but also a family. I've grown up in their hibiscus-print shirts: from the irresponsible, freshly recovered crew member twenty years ago to the mate I am today. I thank them for all the opportunities they've given me and the life lessons and wisdom they've equipped me with.

...nk you to Jerilynn Wagner. The impact she made on my ...idn't fade over the years — it takes on new meaning upon every examination. Her forgiveness and magnanimity are holy.

Thank you to my huge, loving family. To my brothers and sisters and both of my dads. To the four grandparents I miss every day. To my nieces and nephews who give me hope for the future. To Aunt Diane for her endless affection, encouragement, and hilarious text messages.

Thank you to my darling Pat: my rock, my home, my steady forever love. And to our sweet boy Bucky, who purrs on my feet as I type this.

And most important, thank you to Mom. I found myself inside of her and herself inside of me. (I love you.)